Africa: Problems in the Transition to Socialism

Africa: Problems in the Transition to Socialism

Edited by Barry Munslow

Zed Books Ltd.
London and New Jersey

Africa: Problems in the Transition to Socialism was first published by Zed Books Ltd., 57 Caledonian Road, London N1 9BU, UK, and 171 First Avenue, Atlantic Highlands, New Jersey 07716, USA, in 1986.

Copyright © Barry Munslow, 1986.

Cover designed by Andrew Corbett.

Printed and bound in Great Britain by Biddles Ltd, Guildford and King's Lynn

British Library Cataloguing in Publication Data

Africa : problems in the transition to socialism.
1. Socialism — Africa
I. Munslow, Barry
335'.0096   HX439

ISBN 0-86232-427-0
ISBN 0-86232-428-9 Pbk

Contents

This book is dedicated to all those trying to build socialism in Africa.

List of Contributors

M.R. Bhagavan is at present working as a research and consultant economist, based at the International Institute for Energy, Resources and the Human Environment (The Beijer Institute), in Stockholm, Sweden. He is also a Research Officer in the Swedish Agency for Research Cooperation with Developing Countries (SAREC). Trained in physics, mathematics and economics, he has taught and researched in the universities of Munich, Manchester, London, Dar es Salaam and Zambia; has worked as a consultant to several bilateral and multilateral aid agencies – among them SIDA, UNCTAD and the EEC; and lectured as a visiting professor in several universities in Western Europe and India. His current research interests and recent publications are in the fields of the political economy of industrialisation, technological development and energy, in East and Southern Africa and India.

Robin Cohen is Professor of Sociology and Director of the Centre for Research in Ethnic Relations at the University of Warwick. He is the author of *Labour and Politics in Nigeria* (1974 & 1982) and *The New Helots: Migrants in the International Division of Labour* (1986), and is a member of the editorial working group of the *Review Of African Political Economy*.

Basil Davidson is a writer and historian. He is particularly well-known for his writings on the history and development of African civilisation in the medieval and pre-19th century periods, but he has also written extensively on the liberation movements of recent and contemporary times, notably those of the Portuguese colonies. His contact with the latter began in the 1950s, and subsequently he observed the struggle at first hand in Guinea-Bissau, Mozambique and Angola. In 1984 he wrote and presented an 8-part TV series, *Africa*, on the history and cultures of the continent, which has been shown in many parts of the world. His numerous visits to the Republic of Cape Verde began in 1974, shortly before its independence.

Bertil Egero works for the Swedish International Development Authority (SIDA) in Stockholm. Formerly he worked in both Tanzania and Mozambique and has produced a number of publications on development strategy and on population studies. He is currently working on a book on Mozambique to be published by the Scandinavian Institute of African Studies.

Barry Munslow is a Lecturer in the Department of Political Theory and Institutions, and Convenor of the Centre of African Studies at the University of Liverpool. He taught at the Eduardo Mondlane University in Mozambique in the late 1970s and has returned frequently to southern Africa since then. He is the author/editor of a number of books including, *Mozambique: the revolution and its origins* (1983), *Samora Machel: An African Revolutionary: Selected Speeches and Writings* (1985), *Proletarianisation in the Third World* (with Henry Finch, 1984), and is a member of the editorial working group of the *Review of African Political Economy*.

Bie Nio Ong is a researcher whose main interests are the sociology of health and illness, and women's roles in both First and Third World social policy and development issues. She is committed to combining academic research with political practice and therefore carries out her research in a participatory way. She is currently based in the Department of Sociology at the University of Liverpool.

Ben Turok is a senior lecturer at the Open University (UK). He is the author of *Strategic Problems of South African Liberation* and has edited two volumes – *Revolutionary Thought in the 20th Century* and *Development in Zambia*. Because of his opposition to apartheid in South Africa, he was one of the 156 people charged with High Treason in 1956. In 1962 he was imprisoned on new charges, this time for three years. On his release, he became first editor of *Sechaba*, the official journal of the African National Congress. He is a member of the editorial committee in London of the *Journal of African Marxists* and Director of the Institute for African Alternatives.

Preface

The heady optimism concerning the prospects for the new round of experiments in socialist development that followed the collapse of the old Portuguese colonial empire in the mid-1970s has, a decade later, given way to a rethinking of the problems in the face of the current grim struggle for survival. This book is a contribution to the reassessment that is taking place. But with the massive upsurge of popular resistance in South Africa new possibilities appear on the horizon. For, majority rule in South Africa would eliminate the major current impediment to those states in Central and Southern Africa with socialist aspirations. They are currently in the forefront of the international struggle against apartheid and bear the heavy cost, as their development efforts are wrecked by Pretoria's destabilisation policies.

This book is the outcome of a project, initiated in 1982 when we at the *Review of African Economy* were organising our biennial conference at the University of Leeds on the theme of the Transition to Socialism in Africa. Debates at that time and subsequently have been most useful. Some of the ideas developed in the introductory essay were advanced in papers given to the annual conference of the Political Studies Association; comments received were most helpful and encouraging.

Special thanks are due to my family and my parents for their continual support. In addition I would like to express my appreciation for the intellectual encouragement of Basil Davidson, William Tordoff, Phil O'Keefe and Lionel Cliffe.

The book was typed by Cathy Yorker and Pamela Ingham; their contribution is much appreciated.

To all the above and many others who remain unnamed, I wish to register my thanks, and state that none are responsible for the views expressed within these pages.

The editor and publishers acknowledge with thanks the Third World Foundation for Social and Economic Studies for their kind permission to republish the article by Ben Turok which first appeared in *Third World Affairs 1986*.

Barry Munslow
University of Liverpool

Introduction

by Barry Munslow

A generation has passed since African heads of state first proclaimed their commitment to lead their countries along the socialist path of development. This commitment coincided with the very beginning of the wave of independence sweeping the continent and, since that time, at the level of self-ascription at least, it has been echoed by many other African leaders. What has characterised all the experiences thus far is the gap between rhetoric and reality. Nowhere has socialism been constructed in terms that Marx would have understood. This, in spite of the fact that early African socialism eventually gave way to an open commitment to Marxist–Leninist theory both as the guiding principle for ruling parties and as the ideology of the state. The intention of this book is to make a retrospective appraisal of some of those countries which have most recently attempted such a transformation and upon which the latest aspirations of socialists, inside and outside Africa, have been focused.

It is easy to understand why the most recent failures have swelled the chorus of those who claim that socialism in Africa is nothing but delusion, doomed from its inception by the absence of the necessary material conditions upon which to build. Not the least of these missing elements is the absence of a strong, combative, self-conscious working class which could lead the revolutionary takeover and construct socialism on a strong technological base, a socialism with such high levels of production and productivity that the power of the world capitalist economy would be incapable of bringing it to heel. The colonial legacy of Africa's role in the global division of labour ensured that such economic and social structural conditions could not exist for some considerable time – probably until well into the 21st century.

Nevertheless, Africa's predicament and the limitations of capitalist development under conditions of dependency and neocolonialism drove Africa's leaders and political movements to attempt to find another way forward, based upon the conditions in which they found themselves. Ben Turok's contribution to this volume surveys the remarkable extent to which Marxist ideas have spread within the continent in the face of great adversity and opposition, and shows that considerable scope for further development clearly exists. Attempts have been made in various African countries, with

1

greater or lesser success, to utilise the theoretical tools available to analyse their own reality and embark upon the difficult task of transforming their societies. As Robin Cohen's contribution makes clear, Marxist ideas have not remained simply a foreign import, but have been studied and applied to the realities of the African situation. The record of these attempts is valuable for the lessons that may be drawn for the future. There have been dynamic innovations, successes in certain spheres and disasters in others. Of the successes, social welfare systems and widespread popular participation in self-determining organisation for change stand out. To these must be added the very survival of some states in the face of appalling destabilisation activities. This survival has been at considerable cost, not least that of retarding the timescale of transition.

On the negative side are the catalogues of economic failures, particularly in the vital agricultural sector, where too much was attempted too soon with too few resources. Living at the margins, on the periphery of the global economy, room for manoeuvre is extremely limited and mistakes are costly, sometimes even fatal.

But whatever the limitations, and these are manifold, there is still room for political initiative and transformatory action. In this respect we would part company with those who predict a structurally determined failure, whilst at the same time recognising many of the very real constraints that such authors rightly point out.[1] Political acumen and leadership, we maintain, does have an important role to play within the narrow margins of choice laid down by economic, environmental, social structural and geopolitical considerations. Such is the evidence from experiences outside the continent — Central America springs immediately to mind — as well as those within.

Before proceeding further, an important problem of definition needs to be addressed: what is meant by a 'transition to socialism'? Such a question has exercised the minds of many, and not all the conclusions warrant the sometimes tortuous nature of the debate. The long term goals of socialism are the abolition of private ownership of the means of production and of the extraction of surplus value by the bourgeoisie and the creation of a classless society where the power of the state is no longer required to enforce class rule. In the words of Gordon White, this involves:

> nationalisation of industry, socialisation of agriculture, abolition or limitation of markets, and the establishment of a comprehensive planning structure and a politico–ideological system bent on the transition to an ultimate communist society.[2]

But as the same author points out, a distinction has to be drawn between the final product and the progress of 'actually existing socialisms' in their transition towards these goals. Such a yardstick of progress may then be used to separate the wheat from the chaff amongst those states whose self-proclaimed adherence to some form of socialism bears little or no resemblance to their 'actually existing' situation and policies.

Such an evaluation is made infinitely more complicated because it is those societies that attempted the 'great leap' to socialism and the early attainment of these goals, that have fallen the hardest. Over-hasty efforts by revolutionary movements to use their so-called control of the state to nationalise industry, socialise agriculture, abolish markets and plan the economy have produced economic collapse and severe structural disequilibrium in the national economy, characterised by the breakdown of the linkage between town and countryside, industry and agriculture, the working class and the peasantry. Such linkages that do remain are usually through channels established in parallel black-market structures. In lieu of planning the economy, myths and dreams are created – in inverse proportion to the decline of the national productive base. Herein is posed the dilemma: to go the route directly prescribed by the classic definition of socialism, or to chart the necessary compromises with the major global powers, class forces, the market, incentives and non-socialist relations of production. These compromises ensure survival at a minimum (and hopefully beyond this), the production of a surplus to invest in a transitional effort and an understanding that existing states of consciousness, particularly amongst the peasantry, may be far from ready for more far-reaching transformations. Thereby, the ultimate result could entail a greater degree of democratic participation rather than the inevitable vanguard party directionalism which can, albeit unwittingly, fall into dictatorship.

One is dealing with an evaluation of process; and in the context of Africa, perhaps more than elsewhere, with one of *creating the conditions for a transition to socialism*. This has been characterised as the Popular Democratic phase of the revolution in the case of Mozambique, and the People's Democratic Revolution in the case of Angola. In both the intention is that the necessary conditions have first to be created before socialism can be built. Certainly these conditions would include, according to classical Marxist orthodoxy, a strong and more stable working class to avoid the current party substitutionism. One now finds attempts to build a vanguard party – Lenin's addition to the Marxist lexicon – without a vanguard class, with all the attendant problems, especially when the initial base of the party's power lay in the countryside rather than the town. Even after several years in power, the party's links with workers may remain fragile. This absence of a strong working class is symptomatic of the wider lack of developed forces of production, and reflects the complex interaction of capitalist and precapitalist modes of production in the social formations of Africa. For some, this lack inevitably limits the extent to which new socialist relationships of production can be created; consequently it raises the question of the potentially progressive role of other class forces, notably within the petty bourgeoisie and the peasantry, and later we shall explore the debate that has taken place on this issue.

Another important criterion in creating the conditions for socialist transition is the need for high levels of popular participation by the labouring classes (workers and peasants) in a self-transformatory exercise (for, as we later consider, the notion of a *single* vanguard class is hardly appropriate for Africa). This is a central element in the concept of 'people's power', which has been an important formulation developed by revolutionary movements in Africa to capture the participatory character of their revolutions. But, as we argue, the particular route by which socialist governments come to power has an important impact upon the extent of popular participation, at least initially. Even with those governments whose rise to power promised popular participation, however, there have been profound limitations. Continuing economic crisis can soon erode participatory politics. Such crisis results from external constraints and interventions, a weak internal base and policy failures.

One of the greatest weaknesses of the socialist effort to date in Africa is the failure to take sufficiently seriously the oppression of women. Women's struggles have been continually subordinated to national political struggles. Bie Nio Ong's chapter draws on both Marxist and feminist theories in an attempt to redefine the key conceptual issues concerning women's role in production and reproduction. She argues strongly for the need to reappraise women's productive labour, for, in the predominantly rural economies of Africa they play a pivotal role. Women's participation in political processes is contingent upon changing both the social relations of production and gender relations. The continued subordination of women's organisations to the ruling party, which is illustrated through the experiences of Zimbabwe, Angola and Mozambique, hampers such necessary transformations.

This book is divided into two parts. The first provides overviews of the development of Marxist thought and socialist movements in Africa and the problems encountered. The second part examines concrete cases; here no claim is made to comprehensiveness. The case studies are not representative of the different broad categories of African experience outlined in introductory sections; quite the reverse. They all tackle the various experiences of former Portuguese colonial possessions whose ruling parties won power following a protracted period of armed struggle. The prestige that these movements attracted, both in Africa and internationally, has led to the great interest in, and importance attached to their experiences. Unfortunately, language barriers and difficulties in carrying out research in these countries has meant that too little is still known about them. The three case studies (covering four countries) will go some way towards remedying this. The initial high hopes for these states (which were seen as being in the forefront of socialist prospects for Africa) have been severely shaken, given the serious setbacks these countries have undergone. The case studies help us to understand why these setbacks have occurred and lead us to a better appreciation of the difficulties they face.

Factors determining socialist development in Africa

In this introductory essay, we explore six factors which affect the development of socialism in Africa. Whilst not pretending that these are sufficiently developed to provide a clear typology of socialist experiences in Africa (if such an endeavour was meaningfully possible currently) it will at least highlight some of the major influences accounting for similarities and differences in the various national experiences. It is hoped that this discussion will contribute to building a framework of analysis of comparative African socialist experiences.

The six variables proposed are:

1. The route to power.
2. The socio-economic context, notably the internal class structure and the nature of the peripheral social formation's integration into both the regional and the global economic system.
3. The nature of the party's development strategy.
4. The extent of internal and external opposition.
5. Ideology and the party.
6. The nature of inherited state apparatuses and problems of their transformation.

In the following section we begin by identifying the routes to power and evaluate their success or failure in creating the political conditions for the socialist project in Africa.

Routes to power and forms of socialist experiment

In examining the experiences in Africa to date one hypothesis that emerges is the importance of the routes to power as a determinant of the post-takeover experience. Broadly four routes may be distinguished. The first of these is a peaceful transition to socialism associated with the first wave of independence. These represent the earliest attempts to confront the pitfalls of neocolonialism. The governments of Kwame Nkrumah in Ghana, Modibo Keita in Mali and Sékou Touré in Guinea paved the way. However, the first two experiments were rapidly brought to an abrupt end with military coups. There was also the rather idiosyncratic experience of Congo-Brazzaville, which appears to have tried to make up for with ideological expression what it lacked in practical political and economic practice.[3] Indeed, as Samuel Decalo has commented, 'Having declared for the Marxist option as early as 1963, Congo has been saddled ever since with the task of assuring potential investors that *in reality* nothing has changed'.[4] Detractors have labelled the regime 'champagne Marxism', not least as a comment on its corruption and continuing close ties with France.

As disenchantment with the palpable deficiencies of the early experiments set in, hopes were again raised with Tanzania, following the important Arusha declaration of 1967. This called for self-reliance and greater democratic participation to build towards an eventual socialism. There ensued an unprecedented intellectual flowering of discussion and theorising on socialism in

Tanzania, centred in the University of Dar es Salaam. Again, this was followed by bitter denunciations by those whose hopes had been raised, as it turned out, to unrealistic heights. Not least in the case of Tanzania, one sees the effects of the enormous barriers imposed upon the transitional effort by the global capitalist economy, which entered a severe depression in the 1970s, with deteriorating terms of trade, a massive increase in fuel import bills and declining markets for raw material products. As we argue later, such constraints were to 'tame' all regimes, whatever their route to power.

The unifying trait of this first wave of socialism was the peaceful nature of the transition to the adoption of a socialist strategy. When the Convention Peoples Party in Ghana and the Tanganyika African National Union in Tanzania came to power, they were reformist and had not mobilised the people politically for engagement in a socialist effort. Evidence would appear to indicate that greater popular commitment to transformation is achieved precisely by linking of the nationalist struggle with the wider socialist liberation struggle. With those states undergoing a peaceful route, the two forms of struggle were separated in time; the imperatives of a genuine leadership and cadre commitment to a programme of revolutionary change, later forged by those movements which engaged in illegal, 'life or death', armed national liberation struggles, was absent. This imposed a limitation not only on the commitment of the leadership, but on the level of mass commitment which a mobilisational programme could have realised.

A number of common characteristics of this group of states can be drawn out. The first is that the rhetoric of socialism was rarely translated into practice; however, this obviously differed in degree from case to case and should not undervalue the seriousness of intent or the importance of the gains made. Secondly, the emphasis was on African socialism rather than on scientific socialism. The former differs from the latter which we have already defined, by negating the relevance and centrality of class conflict. It emphasises a 'traditional' African egalitarianism and aims to achieve greater equality and participation by creating socialist values in society. Thirdly, and linked to this, there was the relative absence of Marxist theory, a meaningful vanguard party and effective mass mobilisation and organisation to encourage widespread participation. Instead, one finds the emergence of single-person rule and a growth in power of a bureaucratic petty bourgeoisie. Ironically, early influential studies in political science sought to differentiate the newly independent states into a pragmatic pluralist pattern and a revolutionary centralising trend, with the latter characterised as being strongly ideological with high participation and centralisation.[5] The accuracy of such a characterisation was soon called into question, however.[6] Indeed, Henry Bienen has argued that in none of the countries where a 'revolutionary centralising' regime has been said to exist, has it really existed in practice.[7]

A second major route to power for socialist regimes has been the radical military coup, such as that which occurred in Somalia in 1969, Benin and Madagascar in 1972, and Burkina Faso in 1983. (These have also occurred in North Africa, notably in Libya and Egypt, but this volume confines its scope to sub-Saharan Africa.) Again these marked an attempt to confront the pitfalls of neocolonialism and provide interesting case studies in their own right. But they faced the problem, as a result of their route to power, of creating a revolutionary party from scratch. In addition, the process of winning power did not include mass mobilisation and participation. However, these regimes did carry out major efforts to organise popular revolutionary structures to incorporate and mobilise the population in the aftermath of the takeover.[8] But with the absence of party cadres this task was not easy. In these revolutions from the top, as it is the military which initiates the process, there may also exist the tendency to revert to coercion rather than mobilisation to achieve their goals. In some cases there exists a tendency to impose military authoritarian rule. Markakis categorises the Ethiopian case as 'garrison socialism', seeing the overthrow of the Emperor as a military coup rather than a social revolution as other authors have argued.[9] Markakis sees the Ethiopian experience as characterised by a military state asserting its domination over all class forces, and insisting upon a highly centralised state opposed to powerful regional demands.

The importance of Markakis' analysis makes it difficult to conveniently place Ethiopia in a separate third category of social revolutions, with Ethiopia's of a particular kind. But Halliday and Molyneux argue persuasively that Ethiopia merits inclusion in the list of social revolutions of the twentieth century, for 'Whatever the final pattern of political rule in the post-revolutionary order, or the ultimate territorial boundaries of the republican state, a revolutionary change of political, social and economic structure has come about through a process in which mass movements played an important part.'[10] Yet they acknowledge that it displays many differences from other social revolutions and they use the formulation 'revolution from above' to identify the specificity of the Ethiopian case. The central thesis of this concept is that 'profound transformations of social and political structure can occur in a particular country, meriting the term "revolutionary" yet initiated and controlled not by a mass movement but by a sector of the pre-existing state apparatus.'[11] They argue that such a concept distinguishes this particular historical phenomenon as being different from a *coup d'état*, which involves a simple transfer of power between state personnel, and mass revolutions or 'revolutions from below'. Yet there is no doubt that, like radical military coups, with the initiative in the hands of the military, authoritarian practices may occur and the same problems in building a party may ensue, as evidenced by the incredible delays and difficulties in establishing a ruling party in Ethiopia. Addis Hiwet adds his voice to this debate by arguing that the subsequent repression and suppression of nationalities within Ethiopia are explainable, but not necessarily justifiable, within the context of a 'revolution'.[12] Perhaps the best way to summarize the situation is to recognise that Ethiopia is Africa's only post-independence example of a social revolution but that the military caused a distortion of the process. For whilst there was a consolidation of the anti-feudal dimensions of the revolution there was also repression of its popular autonomous dimensions. Hence whilst recognising that a third path exists of social revolution distinct from protracted guerrilla war, the Ethiopian experience does not provide a clear and unproblematic example of socialist transition.

The fourth route to power is that of protracted people's war and is associated with the second wave of independence in Africa; the first wave, from 1957 to 1968, was generally a peaceful decolonisation process. This second wave began in the mid-1970s with the collapse of the Portuguese empire. It included Zimbabwe, which became independent in 1980, and will eventually include Namibia, where the struggle led by SWAPO (South West African People's Organisation) is proceeding against the South African colonising power. The reason for the time lag between the first and the second waves is to be found in the particular nature of sub-metropolitan and settler colonialism. In essence the decolonisation exercise of the first wave was possible because a neocolonising option was open to the occupying powers. This was not so readily the case either with Portugal or with settler ruled Zimbabwe. Portugal's surplus extraction from her colonial territories depended upon the privileged economic access that direct political rule ensured. Maintaining this economic advantage when political rule ended, especially given increased open economic competition from the advanced industrialised countries, was never on the agenda for the economically weakest European colonial power.

We have argued elsewhere that Portugal is best characterised as a sub-metropolitan colonial power.[13] The Portuguese economy was dependent upon the advanced industrialised countries as an exporter of raw materials and labour in the same way that its colonies were dependent upon Portugal. This is evidenced by the high levels of foreign (i.e. non-Portuguese) capital present, particularly in Angola and Mozambique, its two largest territorial possessions in Africa which accounted for 95 percent of the land area that Portugal controlled. (The other territories were the tiny island states of Cape Verde, São Tomé and Principe and the West African enclave of Guinea-Bissau.) In Rhodesia, settler economic domination was directly dependent upon control of the state; hence the similar reluctance to engage in a genuine decolonisation exercise. With the independence of Zimbabwe settler economic influence inevitably declined, although not immediately because of the prudent development strategy pursued by the government; more will be said on this point later.

Nationalist parties were not legally permitted to organise in the Portuguese colonies. The dominant African nationalist parties in Zimbabwe, the Zimbabwe African Peoples Union (ZAPU) and the Zimbabwe African National Union (ZANU), were proscribed in the early 1960s. The option of a negotiated peaceful transition to independence was closed as a result, and the nationalist parties turned to armed struggle: in Angola in 1961, Guinea-Bissau in 1963, Mozambique in 1964 and Rhodesia in 1966. In all cases there was much faltering as the first hesitant steps were taken and experiments occurred with various, different forms of armed struggle. Mass insurrection in

Angola precipitated violent and bloody massacre by the settlers; a combined South African African National Congress/Zimbabwe African People's Union offensive into the Wankie game park in Rhodesia highlighted the errors of large unit operations without prior politicisation and mobilisation of the population. Debates over the question of strategy precipitated splits and defections from the leadership of Frelimo between 1962 and 1964. All the movements, without exception, though to varying degrees, found that the process of undertaking an armed nationalist struggle provoked new forms of debate and a periodic rethinking of approach. What proved most successful was the creative application to the African context of the Asian model of people's war developed by Mao in China and General Giap in Vietnam.

The key priority in this model was political mobilisation amongst the people and within the ranks of the army.[14] All-important was the careful period of political mobilisation prior to the initiation of the armed struggle. This flew in the face of the currently vogue model developed out of the Cuban experience which was elevated to the status of a general theory of the *foco*, notably by an outside observer, Regis Debray, with devastatingly disastrous results wherever it was applied.[15] It was subsequently (and rightfully) subjected to a barrage of criticism,[16] notably because of Debray's mistaken belief in the primacy of military action over political preparation. Indeed, Debray himself later wrote: 'Experience has belied the hypothesis I put forward... The rural guerrilla focos have *not* managed to surround themselves with the solid politico-military basis that would have enabled them to extend their sphere of activity'[17] Whilst not subscribing to the *foco* theory *per se*, Frantz Fanon is on record as advising both the Popular Movement for the Liberation of Angola (MPLA) and the African Party for the Independence of Guinea and Cape Verde (PAIGC), to begin their struggle 'without delay' as the peasants would rally to the irresistible force of insurrection.[18] Fanon used his influence to provide Algerian support to Holden Roberto's Union of the Peoples of Angola (the UPA, later renamed the National Front for the Liberation of Angola, FNLA), which adopted this strategy with predictable failure ensuing. Amilcar Cabral of the PAIGC proceeded with his careful period of political preparation before activating the military confrontation; the PAIGC's subsequent success provides the historical judgement on the effectiveness of his approach. Further confirmation was provided by the success of ZANU over ZAPU in the Rhodesian struggle, where ZANU's greater commitment to the strategy of protracted people's war was an important reason for its electoral victory in 1980.[19] ZANU learned the lesson of its earlier mistakes when it had involved itself in more conventional warfare. Herbert Chitepo, the external leader of ZANU, led the policy review and announced in 1973: 'We have since tried to correct this tragic error by politicising and mobilising the people before mounting attacks against the enemy.'[20]

Mobilisation is a key concept within the theory of people's war. Lars Rudebeck has analysed it as a complex process combining both social and political mobilisation in an intricate and interlocking pattern.[21] The social mobilisation he defines as *intransitive*, an awareness of the structural conditions of society; the political part is the *transitive* aspect of mobilisation, involving the political organisation and participation of the people. Mobilisation is necessary to gain support, but as Basil Davidson has argued, mass support is not in itself sufficient, but must be turned into mass participation.[22]

The potential strengths of this route to power for the post-takeover transition are several. In some countries, it created bases of power separate from the colonial or settler state that involved genuine popular participation. This was a learning process for those concerned and allowed for a building of self-confidence amongst the people, a process which was crucially important given the legacy of racist ideology and the colonial attempt to breed a feeling of impotence, incapacity and passivity amongst the subject population. Democratic methods have to be learnt and the war provided the impetus to this process. Secondly, this route created the possibility of forming a cadre party with a degree of experience and determination necessary to chart a pathway towards socialist transition. Thirdly it led these movements to turn increasingly to Marxist theory as a guide to understanding imperialism, the nature of class power and the state, above all, because the most successful exponents of protracted armed struggle, Mao and Giap, had shown the indispensability of Marxist analysis for their own experiences of struggle. Yet this ideological orientation did not mean political subservience to either the Soviet bloc or China. Instead it produced an indigenous application of Marxist theory by the leadership of the national liberation struggles to the realities of their own countries, though with varying degrees of thoroughness and conviction. To varying extents the protracted people's wars produced liberated and semi-liberated areas where alternative development strategies evolved that influenced post-independence thinking. These included structures of *poder popular*, a degree of women's emancipation (though far short of what was required), mass education, systems of preventative health care, important cultural transformations, a greater integration between leaders and the population and experimentation with new forms of production relations. All were tentative, in particular the latter, but were important for the learning process and acted as signposts for the future. Above all they act as the most advanced forms of socialist practice, with genuine democratic participation, that Africa has experienced.

An important recent development is the growth of protracted people's war as a form of struggle against neocolonial regimes. Notable here is the experience of the Sudan Peoples Liberation Movement/Sudan Peoples Liberation Army led by John Garang and in neighbouring Uganda the National Resistance Movement/National Resistance Army of Yoweri Museveni.

In sum, our argument has been that the route to power adopted has exerted a powerful influence over the prospects for socialist transition in the respective groupings of countries. Of the four routes, the protracted people's war has in certain ways proved to be the most propitious in creating some of the conditions for undertaking socialist transition: strong bases of support outside of the state apparatus, mass participation, preparing cadres for the formation of a vanguard party and the adaptation of Marxist theory to an indigenous reality before taking control of the state apparatus. That having been said, this 'head start' in the politics of socialist transition is a rapidly depletable resource, whose effects can be negated over the medium term by other factors that we will now consider.

But before that, it has to be said that these conclusions are drawn from reflections on experiences to date; we do not know the future potential of, say, the radical military coup. One can also foresee in South Africa, particularly in the widespread popular resistance starting from September 1984, conditions maturing towards a social revolution. It remains to be seen how rapidly organisational levels can catch up with the currently far higher levels of mass mobilisation.

From the discussion of the routes to power we turn to examine the socio-economic conditions within which the struggle to build socialism takes place.

The socio-economic context

Far from socialist transformations taking place under the impetus of an international proletarian upsurge in the advanced capitalist economies, as the bulk of Marx's writings suggested, revolutions have occurred in the main on the periphery of the global capitalist system. They have been inextricably tied to anti-imperialist nationalist movements and have relied upon mobilising the peasantry. This, in a nutshell, accounts for the difficult socio-economic context of socialist transitions, particularly in Africa, where the proletariat remains small, weak and divided with a poorly developed class consciousness and the bulk of the population are scattered peasant household producers. The forces of production are not developed, illiteracy rates are high and the level of skills is correspondingly low.

The African peasantry is in a different situation from the peasantry in, for example, Asia or Central America, where a highly exploitative landlord system of surplus extraction significantly destroyed their subsistence base. This may have some implications for the potential degree of radicalisation of the African peasantry. Pursuing the comparative frame of reference somewhat further, colonialism in Africa produced extreme levels of dependence and therefore a peculiarly high vulnerability to world recession, most recently in 1975–76 and from 1979 into the 1980s. This also contrasts markedly with the situation in China or even India, where the economies were far less integrated into global capitalism and their vulnerability to cycles of recession were therefore reduced, irrespective of whether a capitalist or a socialist path was being pursued.

We begin this section by surveying part of the debate that has taken place over class formation in Africa and its revolutionary potential. However, there is a need to analyse this theoretical debate within the specific national historical contexts for it to be made both meaningful and relevant. The case studies included in this volume discuss these issues concretely in their analysis of African states embarking on a socialist trajectory. In the second part of this section, we discuss the external economic constraints imposed by global capitalism.

Class formation and revolution

Class formation is conditioned by colonial rule and by the peculiar form of uneven and combined capitalist development on the global periphery. Under imperialism, processes of development and underdevelopment occur simultaneously. These factors result 'in the coexistence of multiple modes of production within the same social formation, and of multiple class relations based upon these different modes.'[23] In Africa, processes of proletarianisation and peasantisation were set in train, along with the growth of a petty bourgoisie and commercial and bureaucratic bourgeoisies. In eastern and southern sub-Saharan Africa a considerable white settler presence was established; this has contributed to the emergence of national liberation struggles, but has also acted as a brake and disruptive force on socialist construction. There is an apparent paradox here in that the socialist project can be inhibited, on the one hand, by a continuous settler presence, and, on the other, by its too precipitate departure, which leads to a collapse of production in the economy.

Much debate has centred around the question of classes in Africa. At its most primitive, an early school, exemplified in the work of Peter Lloyd, has argued that class concepts cannot be employed at all in Africa, and has propagated instead theories of elite and social stratification.[24] Several devastating critiques of this argument have been made and the importance of applying class analysis to the study of African societies is now a firmly established approach.[25] In the African context we are dealing with *classes in formation*, with complex trends and directions being the rule in contrast to the established social structures of western developed capitalist societies. Necessarily, therefore, many of the theoretical conclusions are tentative and will be subject to later refinement or even refutation. Secondly, there are obvious dangers in applying a class reductionist analysis. In Africa, not even the nations—let alone the classes—have become consolidated. It would, therefore, be hard to disagree with William Tordoff's general comment that 'class identifications have not yet emerged sufficiently to structure political conflict in most of sub-Saharan Africa'.[26] Amongst those writers employing a class analysis, a vigorous debate has developed concerning the revolutionary potential of the various classes, and it is to this that we must now turn our attention. A word of caution must first be sounded, however.

Many of the theorists of the development of underdevelopment school either ignored or gave perfunctory attention to classes. The peasantry, who make up a majority of the world's population, have a particular importance here. In the past, the peasantry has all too frequently been portrayed as being both passive and traditionalist. Gerrit Huizer, amongst others, has argued against this conventional thesis of peasant resistance to change, saying: 'It appears that peasants can be mobilised quite well if the purpose of the mobilisation is to change the existing status quo for a system under which the peasants can reasonably expect effective improvements.'[27] One of the major academic theoreticians of the peasantry, Eric Wolf, has written that 'Peasants often harbour a deep sense of injustice, but this sense of injustice must be given shape and expression in organisation before it can become active on the political scene. . .'[28]

Frantz Fanon goes much further than the others in arguing that the peasantry alone is a revolutionary class.[29] Not only did he see the peasantry as a spontaneously revolutionary class, he derided and dismissed the revolutionary potential of the Third World proletariat. This dismissal of the proletariat has been criticised by Vietnamese author Nguyen Nghe, who says that Fanon's analysis foundered on his inability to distinguish between genuinely proletarian elements such as dockers and miners and petty bourgeois groups such as taxi-drivers and clerks.[30] For most Marxists, the basis of the popular support for a revolution is a worker–peasant alliance. Fanon's observations on classes and class alliances have rightly been criticised for being shallow and misleading, but as one critic has observed, it was not so much what he said about classes but rather the fact that he focused on them which was really important.[31] Peter Worsely has pointed to the shortcomings in Fanon's analysis of the lumpenproletariat. Unlike Cabral, Fanon failed to differentiate between the groupings existing within this 'class'.[32] Fanon sees the lumpenproletariat as an ancillary class to the peasantry in the context of the African revolution, whereas most Marxist analysis regards the lumpenproletariat as being an unreliable ally. Basil Davidson, with Cabral, has argued that the peasantry does not represent the main revolutionary force that is in fact the revolutionary movement, but the peasantry provides the *base*, the main physical force, 'whose winning to the cause of change is essential to any success'.[33] This position is broadly the same as Wolf's, previously mentioned, and we tend to agree with it.

But peasants, as Saul and Woods suggest, must not be treated as a unified group.[34] The formation of a peasantry, and differences within the peasantry, must be seen as resulting from the interaction between the international economic system and the traditional socio-economic one. Colonialism brought African people into the cash economy through the sale of their labour and of their crops. Four variables, according to Saul and Woods, have defined the nature of participation by traditional agriculturalists (which they distinguish from the peasantry, which is formed under colonialism). The first of these is the presence of centres of labour demand, such as mines and plantations; next is a suitable environment for the production and marketing of crops; third is the presence of an immigrant group of settler farmers, and fourth is the presence of an educated elite able to take over political power from the colonial regime. Whilst presenting a far from exhaustive list, Saul and Woods have usefully pointed to the importance of an analysis of the political economy and the effect of capitalist penetration upon existing social formations. This is significant for a definition of the peasantry. For Saul and Woods, peasants are 'those whose ultimate security and subsistence lies in their having certain rights in land and in the labour of family members on the land, but who are involved, through rights and obligations, in a wider economic system which includes the participation of non-peasants'.[35] Teodor Shanin's definition strikes at the heart of the relationship between the peasantry and the world:

> The peasantry consists of small agricultural producers who, with the help of simple equipment and the labour of their families, produce mainly for their own consumption and for the fulfilment of obligations to the holders of political and economic power.[36]

In the case of lusophone (Portuguese speaking) Africa, it was the political power of the Portuguese colonial state which the peasants had to face. For all our earlier criticisms of Lloyd, he did highlight an important point in a later work: that in tribal societies where landlordism is not an issue, the peasant farmer tends to see the state as the agent of exploitation.[37] But there is a big difference between identifying the state as the agent of exploitation — forced labour and forced cash crop cultivation were universally implemented by district administrators in Portuguese Africa almost to the end of the colonial period — and taking concerted action against that state. To what extent, as Fanon would argue, there was a natural peasant spontaneity or whether the revolutionary force provided by the nationalist movement (as Cabral and Davidson argue) was decisive, as we tend to believe, has been the subject of much debate and will continue to be so. Our own research, based upon the evidence available, suggests that leadership and organisation provided by the nationalist movement produced a qualitative leap in the form of resistance which peasant spontaneity alone could never have achieved.

John Saul, in an article on the Mozambique revolution, concluded that peasant spontaneity had been very important.[38] But he also noted those factors qualifying the revolutionary potential of the peasantry, not least of which was the unevenness and recent nature of capitalist penetration into the African continent. This left standing 'pre-capitalist social networks and cultural preoccupations — particularly a range of variations on kinship relations and upon the theme of ethnic identification — which mesh closely with the survival of the subsistence agricultural core of the system'.[39] Peasant spontaneity was present for Saul, but required an outside impetus which (like Cabral) he saw coming from the petty bourgeoisie and 'semi-proletarianised urban hangers-on' who initially formed the nationalist movement.[40] We will return to this question again after examining the debate on the working class.

Proletarianisation is not a clearly defined and unambiguous phenomenon in the Third World.[41] The process has differed markedly from that in the West. There has been much dispute over who actually constitutes the working class in Africa. V.L. Allen has gone as far as suggesting that in the African context, peasants, the lumpenproletariat, migrant workers and permanent workers *all* belong to the working class.[42] Whilst correctly indicating that certain similarities exist in their economic situation, his approach is intellectually unduly mystifying and conceptually befogging. The classical definition of the proletariat is that it is completely divorced from ownership of the means of production. But in much of Africa, retention of a limited ownership of the means of production in the peasant base and the migratory system itself prevent a complete proletarianisation from occurring. The important distinction needs to be made, therefore, between a migrant and a permanent proletariat.

There has remained a certain unease amongst writers not only concerning the definition of the proletariat but also over its role in African revolutions.[43] Some authors have maintained the Marxist orthodoxy that it is only the working class that can carry the mantle of socialist revolution in Africa.[44] This is a determinist approach which, like the theories of peasant spontaneity, neglects the importance of revolutionary leadership and organisation and the constraints under which the class operates. As with the peasantry, opposite positions are held by different authors on the revolutionary potential of the African proletariat. Fanon has argued that in the African context the working class forms a 'labour aristocracy' whose interests are congruent with neocolonial elites rather than with the peasantry.[45] But this thesis has by now been widely discredited, and even some of its original advocates have reversed their positions.[46] At the opposite extreme we have the theory that no socialist revolution is possible in Africa because of the absence of a sufficiently developed proletariat.[47]

In relation to the proletariat and the peasantry in the African context, we prefer to adopt Robin Cohen's overall view that 'class and class consciousness have a partial manifestation which may be activated in certain conditions and in certain measure. The research problem is to identify what these conditions are and what social forces act to induce class conflict'.[48] As Laclau and Mouffe have argued, the case for historical necessity, with the gradual unfolding of a succession of modes of production, has been confounded by real world events; revolutions therefore are never inevitable.[49]

Shanin has successfully argued that recent history has brought into question any belief in a single, natural, and sole revolutionary class. Rather, it is the ability of revolutionary elites to build coalitions of classes and groups that is important. He concludes:

> at the risk of sounding tautological, the only irreplaceable and absolutely necessary element in socialist revolution, in the light of past experience, are the socialists who execute it: their commitment, their ability to see reality, and their capacity to build up powerful mass alliances, using every crack in the social system of domination and exploitation.[50]

In an important contribution, John Saul has identified the conditions and circumstances within which such a leadership can emerge. In the African context, he sees this emanating from the petty bourgeoisie, given the relatively indeterminate nature of that class in formation coupled with the 'relative autonomy' of the post-colonial state. For socialist transformation to ensue, the subordinate classes of workers and peasants must become the 'paramount actors'; an 'active role for the subordinate classes is likely to grow out of a complex dialectic established between themselves and the petite bourgeoisie', but this will provoke a fierce struggle inside the ranks of that class.[51] He goes on to indicate that such an outcome is most likely under the circumstances of protracted guerrilla war, which would certainly support some of the conclusions reached in the previous section concerning the routes to power. Our discussion to date leads us to conclude that in place of gross generalisations concerning the central importance of the peasantry or the proletariat as *the* revolutionary class in the African context, attention could more profitably be focused on the complex political, social, cultural and economic conjunctures and historical processes of particular societies.

International constraints

The prospects for the transitional effort are closely proscribed by a particular social formation's integration into both the regional and global systems. Under colonial capitalism, African states were ascribed the role of raw material exporters in the international division of labour. This made their economies dependent and highly vulnerable, particularly to the effects of periodic long wave recessions. This pattern of reliance upon raw material exports and imports of manufactured goods, technology and skilled personnel remained in the post-independence period, making it difficult to reorientate the economies towards self-sustaining economic growth. In turn, this inheritance determined particular configurations of class formation and imposed strong limitations on these states' economic options. The limitations of neo-colonialism under a capitalist development strategy, with its attendant inequalities, spurred the quest for alternatives.

The economic constraints on building socialism are clearly apparent when we look at the industrial sector where the already weak base has been yet further undermined by the effects of the world recession. In 1980, sub-Saharan Africa accounted for only one percent of world manufacturing value-added.[52] Under the impact of the world recession, industrial output in Mozambique fell 13.64 percent in 1982 alone,[53] whilst Tanzania's industrial exports fell 40 percent in 1981 and even further the following year.[54] Tanzanian industry was working at 70 percent capacity in 1978 but this has now fallen to around 25 percent. Only Zimbabwe appeared capable of limiting the effects of the recession with industrial production growing 25 percent in the first two years of independence, declining 8 percent between 1981 and 1984, with estimates for 1985 of a growth rate of 6 percent.[55] We cannot do justice in a short essay such as this to the profound impact of the current world recession, but there is a growing valuable literature on the subject.[56] We can note, however, that one of the results of the collapse of industrial production has been the reduction in the size of the working class, as shown in our case study of Angola.

African states opting for socialist development are trapped on the periphery of the global capitalist system and have to survive within it. A recent study of Somalia's period of socialist development argues that it would be wrong 'to conclude that "scientific socialism" led Somalia out of economic poverty, or changed Somalia's role in the world division labour. Somalia remains a poor country that exports animals to Arabia and bananas to Europe'.[57] However, the authors also conclude that in the period of the socialist economic programme (1969–74) it was demonstrated that collective action *can* yield productive results. The need to survive within the global capitalist system exists because the socialist bloc economic grouping COMECON is both unable and unwilling to permit the full integration of those African states opting for socialism. Whilst membership of COMECON has been requested by both Angola and Mozambique, for example, no positive response has been received. This is in part a function of the Soviet Union's position as a global military superpower but not yet as an economic superpower. This reality is implicitly recognised in writings from the Soviet Union. Soviet theories, first of the 'non-capitalist road of development' and later of 'states of socialist orientation', recognise the fact that most Third World socialist countries will remain for some time within the global capitalist economy. Naturally they stress that increasing economic co-operation with the socialist bloc is vital and beneficial. But the reality is that the socialist countries accounted for only 7 to 8 percent of the foreign trade of Third World countries by the mid-1970s.[58] As the Angolan case study in this volume shows, Angola's trade relations more than a decade after independence remain dominated by the West. (It is no less true however, that most Marxist states in Africa have depended heavily upon the provision of military supplies from the socialist countries to defend themselves. Without this it is hard to see how they could have survived.)

The economic constraints limiting the possibilities for socialist development are mapped out in the country studies. Many of these limitations are relevant to other African states attempting similar transitions. Zimbabwe, however, stands out as a relative success story, in that its economy is the only one not to have suffered the same degree of collapse. How are we to account for this and what lessons, if any, may be applicable to other countries?

The first point to make is that Zimbabwe has a much stronger and more balanced economy than other African states which have embarked upon a socialist trajectory. This is a function of the fact that the settlers grasped the political reins of power from the colonial authorities in the 1920s and used their control of the state to build up the economy and their own class base by introducing protective legislation. The imposition of United Nations sanctions following the Unilateral Declaration of Independence by the Smith regime led to a decade and a half of import-substitution industrialisation. At the same time, the connivance of the Republic of South Africa enabled those sanctions to be circumvented in those key areas which could have caused economic collapse. As in Nicaragua,[59] the new government's policy has been to avoid a rapid and comprehensive extension of state ownership. It aims to combine different types of ownership and regulate markets rather than to replace them. Extensive efforts have been made to provide the necessary conditions to encourage a rapid growth in peasant-marketed production. More generally, the emphasis has been on avoiding undermining existing successful production, even though this production is capitalist in form. This has obviously placed greater constraints on the speed of transition to socialism. Certainly in the key agricultural sector, the land reform process has been considerably slowed down.[60] White commercial farmers do make an important contribution to production, but the evidence suggests that they are failing to use to full effect at least half of the country's prime agricultural land that they occupy in the Mashonaland region.[61] This creates the potential, therefore, for continuing land reform measures, but the models employed for resettlement will need revision if better land-use and hence higher productivity is to ensue. But as we indicate in the following section, Zimbabwe's case is exceptional; the norm for those states undertaking a socialist development effort is one of severe structural disequilibrium.

Development strategies

The models of socialist development adopted by huge resource-rich countries such as the Soviet Union and China have proved incapable of being implemented in the current African context. Heavy industrialisation with an emphasis on large scale, high technology production, has proved everywhere in the continent to be a disaster, particularly in the vital agricultural sector. Especially in regard to agriculture, the new states have neither the political nor the technical capacity to undertake far-reaching programmes of agrarian reform and administer huge unwieldy state farms. Whilst in the long term heavy industrialisation may be necessary because socialism cannot be built by redistributing scarcity and poverty, the question of timing is all important. We will begin by examining some of the problems faced in agriculture, given the existing received wisdom concerning the Marxist project, before going on to explore a much more promising development trajectory for the Peripheral Socialist Economies (PSE). Our focus on agriculture is called for by the current crisis of food production faced by many states in Africa, particularly by those opting for a socialist development trajectory.

One can understand the attraction of large scale mechanised production to socialist governments. It appears to offer the prospect of high productivity, quality controlled production, centrally planned, with the mobilisation of a surplus for development purposes no longer at the mercy of peasant proclivities or local power holders.[62] It could facilitate the commercialisation of crops, offer an important socio-political benefit of building up the working class and, more generally, provide a 'do-it-yourself' panacea for the state over the vexing production question. One can also understand the appeal of such an approach to a 'commandist' tendency within state apparatuses inherited from the colonial era. The legacy is frequently an authoritarian and hierarchical bureaucratic state structure. Large state farms appear at first sight more amenable to the dictates of the 'plan'. They offer neater solutions than can be envisaged by a policy directed at transforming methods of rural production amongst hundreds of thousands of dispersed peasant family producers.

The measurement of outputs and inputs is therefore that much easier; the compilation of tables and charts is facilitated for office-bound and capital city-based administrators. There is also the prestige factor attached to advanced petrochemically-based agricultural technology, the visible sign of entering the 'modern' world on a par with the advanced industrialised economies. Centralised agricultural production provides a solution, in sum, which best suits the interest of the central bureaucracy, not least because it involves the continual expansion of its power and importance. To the parties which espouse Marxism-Leninism, it is the development strategy orthodoxy that is a mark of their political persuasion. This orthodoxy is also the advice that such parties and governments receive from the socialist bloc experts who are brought in to compensate for the desperate lack of indigenous cadres.

The state farm policy has frequently come unstuck because a rigorous costing exercise was not employed at an early stage to show that returns did not merit the high level of investment. One estimate of the projected cost of energy inputs into Ethiopian agriculture suggests that by 1990 the earnings from export sales will not even be sufficient to cover the petroleum input costs to drive the farm machinery.[63] Dunman highlights the danger with regard to the experience of state farms in the Soviet Union:

> it soon transpired that, being under the direct control of the government, they acquired an importance out of proportion to the area they occupied in providing the surplus for the market which the economy so urgently needed. They were in a privileged position for investment; and because their work had an element of experiment in it, the profit criterion for their performance was not stressed.[64]

Although state farms have had some successes in the socialist bloc, these have been in the second generation following the takeover, when the state's capacities were already built up.

In addition, state farms are especially vulnerable in the context of the overt political, military and economic attack to which a number of states opting for socialism have been subjected. In particular, those in Southern Africa have faced massive destabilisation orchestrated by the apartheid regime in South Africa. This campaign has involved the arming and support of rebel groups in addition to direct military intervention. State farms provide a highly vulnerable target, as proved by the attacks of Ian Smith's Rhodesian settler army on the state farm complex in Gaza province of Mozambique in 1978-79.[65] This vulnerability has another dimension as well: the diversion of so many resources into the state farms when the peasantry is in crisis can be utilised by rebel gangs to spread discontent amongst the peasants. Again, the case of Mozambique is illustrative. The crisis in the south of the country in part reflects the loss of migrant labour remittances (principally from the mines of South Africa) for a population which had come to rely on these for at least four generations.[66] The state had wrongly assumed that the peasantry earned a subsistence living; in fact it relied on wage labour to guarantee its reproduction. The inevitable structural — and political — crisis that resulted from the loss of off-farm income was worsened by war and drought.

Certainly there is no simple or generalisable solution to the problem of agrarian transformation. Countries such as Mozambique and Angola have amongst the hardest of tasks. They suffer the multiple yoke of recent decolonisation, an extended period of war before independence and continuing fighting since. When to these burdens are added those shared with many other states in Africa, notably world recession and drought, then the extremely serious situation that both countries face can well be appreciated.

State farms both in Angola and in Mozambique have experienced a labour shortage. In Angola, the supply of migrant labour from the central part of the country to the northern coffee plantations was severed because of the war. Both countries have significant unemployment and underemployment and one would imagine that the supply of labour would be ample. However, state farms were growing cash crops and paying a wage. In a situation of extreme scarcity of food and consumer items, the possession of currency was not of any use and therefore provided no incentive for labour recruitment.[67]

Many specific and detailed reasons can be drawn up for the lack of success when the state becomes the direct producer, but the overriding reason is the weakness and extremely limited capacity of the state machine, specifically of its human and material resources. Two external considerations are likely to reduce the state's capacity to intervene even further. The first of these is the chronic balance of payments problems resulting from the high price of petroleum imports, declining terms of trade, past failures in agriculture, and as a consequence, but also compounding the problem, rising indebtedness. These constraints make improbable in the short run any widespread renewal of large scale importation of agricultural machinery for massive state run projects. A second and related constraint is the increased dependence of African countries on the International Monetary Fund. The 'conditionality' of IMF loans includes, amongst other things, pressure to reduce the numbers of state personnel. Exogenous factors, then, coupled with necessary, if at times belated, reflection on the track record to date indicate that perhaps the role of the state as direct producer will be less commonly found in the future. This inevitably raises the issue of what role the state should then perform.

Fitzgerald has developed a useful model for analysing Peripheral Socialist Economies (PSE) based upon his extensive experience of Nicaragua.[68] He draws upon the work of Kaleki in dividing the PSE into two output sectors. Department I refers to the producer goods sector, which in a PSE is principally concerned with the production of primary product exports. Department II is subdivided, with IIa producing basic needs wage goods (food and basic services); the most important of these, food, is provided by the rural peasant sector. Department IIb, the urban manufacturing sector, produces consumer goods for urban consumption in addition to consumer goods for the peasant sector. The crucial relationship internally concerns the exchange between the food produced in IIa to feed the workforce in Departments I and IIb, and thereby stimulate their production, and the incentive to market food surpluses by the provision of the consumer goods for the peasant sector.

Given the competing demand for scarce resources of labour and capital between the three sectors, it is the government's role to decide on the allocation of these two resources. Its decisions depend upon its overall development strategy. The government lacks the ability to directly control production in the peasant sector although it can determine the internal terms of trade. Although the state can control to some extent production in the export sector it is still constrained by the prices of its exports which are determined by the world market. The greatest opportunity for the state to exert its influence, therefore, lies in sector IIb, urban manufacturing, which is the only one in which both output and price can be planned.

Looking first at labour allocation, the key trade-off lies between IIa and I, both of which tend to be labour intensive. Department I, consisting in the main of mining and commercial agriculture, tends to rely in the African PSE context on migrant and seasonal labour, which is drawn from the peasant sector IIa, creating the nub of the labour competition. In the absence of capital to purchase new technology, increasing production relies on increasing the labour supply; depending upon how this labour is allocated, it implies either greater food production or greater export earnings with a corresponding fall in the other sector. Removing labour from IIa carries the danger of seriously weakening the peasant base, whose food production is required for all the other departments.

The capital trade-off is generally made between the two sectors where mechanization is most readily undertaken, departments I (primary exports) and IIb (manufacturing). An expansion of the latter at the expense of the former can reduce future investment by restricting foreign exchange earnings, whilst the reverse reduces the provision of IIb goods to IIa and therefore reduces the levels of marketed food production.

Planning decisions need to be based upon the complex interactions occurring between the departments over the allocation of limited resources. Such decisions will determine the pattern of economic development and the living standards of the population. This strikes at the core of the economic basis of the worker-peasant alliance for the transitional project and if mishandled, can increase the country's vulnerability to destabilisation. The distribution of basic needs goods is determined by wage relations, with the wage as both a unit of exchange and an incentive for production. For the wage to be effective, however, it must provide access to goods, and for workers in departments I and IIb this means primarily access to the marketed surplus of IIa. For the peasant producers in IIa, real income is determined not only by the price they receive for their products but by the cost and availability of the goods they demand in exchange. The 'internal terms of trade' in the model refers to the demand and supply of IIa and IIb goods. Hence manipulation of the internal terms of trade is the means whereby the government increases the standard of living of the population and ensures its class base of support.

The source of investible surplus in the form of foreign exchange for growth and transition derives from department I production, as does the foreign exchange requirement for the other two departments. This means that the external terms of trade determine the potential investible surplus. Surplus can be generated by: normal profit, arising from reasonable charges for equipment used; excess profit, from the payment of wages below the normal rate (a practice which a socialist government would want to minimise); and differential rent, derived from the production of exports at costs of production less than the globally determined market price. Fitzgerald sees the latter as the key source of primitive accumulation.

The colonial economies of lusophone Africa largely derived their surplus from excess profit; forced labour laws and obligatory cash crop production provided the incentive for the articulation between departments. With independence such coercion stopped and such commercial links as did exist between town and countryside collapsed with the exodus of Portuguese shopkeepers. The components of the collapse in Angola are outlined in great detail in the chapter by Bhagavan and need not be repeated here. Both in Angola and in Mozambique the solution was sought in a state farm policy which failed, for the reasons noted earlier. Effectively the peasant sector, department IIa, was ignored, while little effective control was exercised by government over the internal terms of trade. Without the necessary price incentives and infrastructure, and because of an extreme scarcity of manufactured goods, the supply of food diminished to a trickle except on the burgeoning black market. The economies thereby lost both basic goods production and the potential for the peasantry to produce surplus for export.

Fortunately, earlier mistakes have now been recognised[69] and efforts are being made to restart the engine of the economy by providing basic needs goods to the peasantry as an incentive to produce a marketable surplus.[70] The problem, however, is that the long term effect of earlier policies has been to increase vulnerability to outside destabilisation; these activities continue at such a high level that implementing the new policies is proving extremely difficult. This leads us on to a discussion of internal and external opposition, but before that there is a final note to make.

A number of important issues are raised by this discussion, although unfortunately more work needs to be done before satisfactory answers can be provided. Of central importance are the implications for transforming social relations of production in the PSE and this is but little developed in the Fitzgerald model. Such considerations cannot be discussed in the abstract but must refer directly to the inherited situation in any particular PSE. The state has then to devise a strategic plan for the reorganisation of the labour process and the transformation of social relations of production. In department I, given our earlier emphasis on the limitations of the state's capacity to control and run the mining sector and large state farms, there is likely to be a continuing role for foreign ownership and therefore capitalist relations of production until such time that the panoply of skills and finance required to run these efficiently are available to the state. Clearly some small beginnings are necessary in this regard both for strategic and educational reasons. Whilst the stabilisation of a working class is important politically, given the two-way reliance of department I and IIa on seasonal and migrant labour, this has to be handled cautiously and within an appropriate time frame. However, the stabilisation of the work force is necessary to improve its technical skills and to lay the foundations for socialist production relations within the state enterprises.

In department IIa a package of measures are required to raise per capita food production. There are some lessons to be learnt here from Zimbabwe where incentive prices, credit, extension and improved and expanded marketing infrastructures have encouraged spectacular increases in peasant household marketed production. However, this comes with a price attached, namely an increase in social and spatial income differentials with peasant farmers in the more isolated marginal areas not receiving the benefits. Greater consideration has to be given to the development of various forms of co-operativisation, initially for the purchasing of inputs and marketing of surplus. More creativity is also required in the mutual harnessing of familial incentive to the co-operative endeavour.

External and internal opposition

External destabilisation has been extensive in Angola and Mozambique and present, though to a lesser extent, in Zimbabwe. This hostility has emanated from the white settler state of Rhodesia, until independence in 1980, and above all from South Africa, which remains the bastion of opposition to the socialist project in central and southern Africa. Direct military intervention, as with the occupation of southern Angola by the South African Defence Force, has accompanied the arming, training, financing and furnishing of logistical support for internal opposition forces — notably UNITA (National Union for the Total Independence of Angola), the MNR (National Resistance Movement) in Mozambique, and the so-called 'dissidents' in Zimbabwe. Such activities have been devastatingly effective in destroying development initiatives in Angola and Mozambique by forcing resources and cadres into military defence. The results cast serious doubts on the viability of the socialist project until such time as black majority rule is achieved in South Africa. The struggle for socialism in Southern Africa in no small measure has been transformed into a struggle for survival.

23

Although South Africa has been the most overt centre of external opposition, other cases exist to the north. The United States Central Intelligence Agency's activities include: involvement in Ghana from the overthrow of Nkrumah in 1966 to recent attempts against the Rawlings regime; involvement in the Patrice Lumumba affair in the Congo in 1961; and an active role during the Angola war of 1975-76.[71] The United States, of course, has not been the only Western power involved in such efforts to thwart progressive change.

Historically, all attempts to build socialism have faced outside attack. In African states, the vulnerabilities are heightened, given the weak nature of their economies, the state's limited capacities and the understandable failure to consolidate a national identity out of the given colonial heritage. Ethnic, cultural and regional fissures leave great scope for those with the will and capacity to meddle. In the case of those central and southern African states linked to South Africa's regional sub-system, the vulnerability is further heightened.[72] Given the nature of the South African regime, there are few constraints upon its ability to carry out overt destabilisation. In President Machel's words, 'The Western countries witnessed our destruction passively, not concerning themselves with the violence used against our people.'[73] Western strategists obviously differ over the best means to neutralise socialist experiments. Some see 'engagement' rather than disengagement and overt opposition as the best means to achieve this end. Clearly much depends upon the global balance of forces at any particular conjuncture, but what is certain is that global considerations exert powerful constraints on the socialist project and cannot be wished away.

States with a white settler population can expect strong resistance to any attempt to build socialism. These settlers either act as a brake internally where a compromise has been reached with them, as in Zimbabwe following the Lancaster House agreement, or as a potent base for counter-revolution, as in the case of Angola and Mozambique, where they fled to South Africa and Portugal. A small section of the white settler community has subsequently played an important role in the destabilisation of both those countries. The core of the internal military wing is usually formed by harnessing the nationalist party losers, as in the case of UNITA in Angola, or by gathering a core from within the ranks of the colonial military forces, as in the formation of the MNR in Mozambique (which was created by the Rhodesian intelligence services before being handed over to the South Africans in 1980'.[74] If an internal opposition force does not already exist, it is clear that it will be created, for this is the best means to deflect international criticism from the state directing the operations. The usefulness of guerrilla tactics and warfare in counter-revolution has been proven. From the experience of states attempting a socialist project in central and southern Africa, it also appears that the less the economic leverage over the targeted country, the greater will be the level of military intervention.

Concerning the internal class struggle, again there is no substitute for the specific analysis of the concrete situation, as provided by the case studies in this volume. All highlight the dangers of the state bureaucracy and of 'aspirants to the bourgeoisie'. Failures in economic planning with the spectacular growth of parallel markets create opportunities for the emergence of an influential commercial bourgeoisie, all the more dangerous because its operations are covert. The development of the on-going internal class struggles (which will be further discussed in the following section) is in part dependent upon, and related to, external class struggles. It is hard to disagree with James Petras, therefore, when he writes that, 'Political forms and external relations in the period of transition are dictated by the needs of survival and consolidation under conditions of intense internal and external pressure by inter-locked classes.'[75] Perhaps there are some lessons to be learnt here from Central America, where remarkable class, religious and other coalitions have been put together in Nicaragua and in El Salvador, to give but two examples.

Ideology and the party

Revolutionary parties in Africa which have taken state power have found themselves absorbed in managing the state apparatus to the neglect of maintaining a sufficient separation of the party from the state. This has taken the form of the top leadership being overwhelmed by tasks of state management, frequently with few leaders having sole responsibility for party affairs. This was acknowledged to have been the case in Mozambique, where in the first five years of independence not a single member of the top leadership had exclusive responsibility for party work separate from state office.[76] The founding conference of the PAICV (African Party for the Independence of Cape Verde) following the coup in Guinea–Bissau of 1980, admitted a similar neglect as a reason for the coup and drew this as a lesson for itself. The case studies in this volume by Bertil Egero and Basil Davidson are highly revealing of the problem of party leadership, particularly as regards maintaining political mobilisation and organisation amongst the population and building socialist democratic structures. Basil Davidson draws interesting contrasts between Cape Verde where this was successfully managed and Guinea–Bissau where it was not.

The relative strength of the revolutionary organisations ideologically, organisationally and numerically has an important, indeed vital, impact on the prospects for transition and on the direction of state policy. The Ottaways have suggested that a distinction can usefully be drawn between what they term 'Afrocommunist' states and the earlier experiences of 'African Socialism'.[77] This distinction is particularly revealing of the ideological, organisational and policy differences between the two groups of parties. The authors suggest, broadly speaking, five distinguishing features. First, they say, Afrocommunist states differ in their ideological perspective from the earlier African Socialist states. The most notable feature of this ideological distinction is that they clearly adopt Marxist-Leninist principles in opposition to a philosophical base of African Socialism which was a belief in a simple classless communal organisation said to already exist in African societies. The early African Socialist states believed that the class cleavages clearly identified in industrialised societies were absent on the African continent. Overall, the ideology of African Socialism was somewhat of a ragbag of ideas and was far less worked out in terms of its principles and coherence than Marxism–Leninism.

The second difference is that related to foreign policy. Associated with the earlier African Socialist experiments was a belief in two essential principles. The first of these was Pan-Africanism, and the second was non-alignment. Non-alignment was defined as being a distinguishing position adopted in the international arena, putting African states neither in the Eastern communist bloc nor in the Western capitalist bloc. There is a profound difference between this and the foreign policies of Afrocommunist states in that, first of all, Pan-Africanism has broadly been dropped as a plank of the ideological platform. Secondly, non-alignment is seen far more in terms of a common set of interests between socialist countries and the Third World societies in their opposition to neocolonialism, imperialism and generally the development of capitalism on a world scale.

The third difference that the Ottaways identify is that the Afrocommunist states have 'a vision not only of the final goal, but also of the dynamics of the process of change, hence the pace of reform was much swifter, more systematic and marked by fewer contradictions than was the case in the African Socialist countries'.[78] The fourth distinguishing feature is the continuity of ideas and institutions within these states; this has served to make African Marxist-Leninist governments much less personalised and dependent on a single individual leader. In a sense this would offer a distinction with, say, 'Nkrumahism' in Ghana, where the ideology is associated very much with the particular political contribution made by an individual leader.

The fifth and final characteristic is that the Marxist–Leninist states are distinguished by their attitude to the state and its role. They openly accept statism. The authors draw the distinction between this acceptance of the need for the state to control and direct the economy in the Afrocommunist states and a *de facto* statism which might have emerged in many of the African Socialist policies (which their original philosophy belied). They note the exception, however, of the Algerian experience. This, they suggest, signifies that the real relevance of Marxism–Leninism to the African countries may reside in the fact that it offers a package of techniques and a solution to the problems of organising a society for radical change. In a sense, then, they see the Algerian leadership adopting methods and techniques but certainly not the ideology of the Marxist–Leninist states of Eastern Europe.

Which countries then, would fit into the African Socialist category of the Ottaways? The Ottaways include: Tanzania under Julius Nyerere, Ghana under Nkrumah, Zambia under Kaunda, Guinea under Sekou Touré. These they distinguish from the Afrocommunist states of Ethiopia, Mozambique and Angola. Other states are included in the two different categories but these are the main ones. They do not draw, as the foregoing discussion might suggest, an absolute distinction between Afrocommunist and African Socialist states, as they envisage transitional societies. They see a definite link between the African Socialists of the 1960s and the Afrocommunists of the 1970s, marking a kind of halfway point towards orthodox Marxism–Leninism. These transitional societies, so designated, were reacting to the problems they were encountering in their efforts to implement socialism in their countries; in particular, these include an understanding that certain sectors of their societies would oppose their African socialist project, notably aspiring entrepreneurs, traders and businessmen, and the bureaucratic class emerging within the state apparatus.

The second feature of these transitional societies is that they began to see the limitation of the mass party on which the earlier African Socialist societies based their political mobilisation. The idea of the mass parties was that they would incorporate all segments of society within it; hence in the case of Nkrumah's Ghana, at one point the party's membership included two million out of a total population of four and a half million. A third feature of these transitional societies was the beginnings of a realisation that some of those states which had adopted African Socialism as their mantle were doing very little to reform their own country along socialist lines. Indeed, many, and in particular we may point out Senghor's position in Senegal, were developing along model neocolonialist or incipient capitalist lines. The Ottaways consider that the two most articulate representatives of transitional societies were Touré and Nkrumah, though several others like Ben Bella of Algeria and Modibo Keita fall into the same general category. They are transitional in that their countries, under their leadership, moved slowly from the classic exposition of African Socialist ideas to increasing disenchantment and then to an acceptance of a variety of features of Marxist–Leninist states, notably the need for a vanguard party, the acceptance of class differences within their societies, and the need for class struggle to take place internally. Touré, however, presided over an increasingly repressive dictatorship and there is evidence that he backed away from Marxism in the final years of his rule. In contrast, Nkrumah's ideas moved much more in the direction of Marxism after his overthrow by military *coup d'etat* in 1966. After that time, he entered into a vigorous polemic with the concept and ideas of African socialism, writing:

> Such a conception of socialism makes a fetish of the communal African society. But an idyllic African classless society (in which there were no rich and poor) enjoying a drugged serenity is certainly a facile simplification; there is no historical or even anthropological evidence for any such society. I am afraid the realities of African society are somewhat more sordid.[79]

If we turn to look at the basic principles of Afrocommunism as annunciated by the Ottaways, then we see first of all a clear rejection by the political leaders that there is an African, Asian or even Latin American socialism distinct from Marxism–Leninism as a whole. President Samora Machel of Mozambique has made this point with particular clarity: 'The great thing about Marxism is that, it being a science, it can adapt to all conditions. There is no African Marxism, Asian Marxism, European Marxism. There is only one Marxism.'[80] The leadership of the MPLA in Angola has also defined its position in a similar vein. Lucio Lara in an interview given to the *African Communist* has said:

> Clearly for the MPLA there has always been only one expression of socialism, known precisely as scientific socialism. Experience has shown that all that rhetoric [about African socialism] has not led to concrete steps showing a true socialist option. . . . These 'socialisms' are basically disguises for one or other form of colonial exploitation.[81]

The second major feature of the Afrocommunist societies is that they put to the fore class conflict as the moving force of social change. Their literature refers to the classes in their societies, notably the working class, peasantry, national bourgeoisie, and petty bourgeoisie, and they see the post-takeover period as being one of intensified class struggle. In particular, in these societies where no advanced capitalism existed, the national bourgeoisie is extremely weak or virtually absent. There is, however, a strong petty bourgeoisie, comprised of civil servants, small businessmen, intellectuals, university graduates, middle ranking military officers, traders, etc. This class has always proved analytically problematic because of its catch-all character. Marxist theory sees the petty bourgeoisie as a vacillating class with sections which can be won to the revolutionary project, whilst others will necessarily oppose it. The Afrocommunist states all see the importance of basing the revolution on the proletariat; the problem, of course, is that the proletariat is very weak. The vitally important transitional stage is seen as a period in which the working class can be strengthened and grow in power, so progressively neutralising the reactionary petty bourgeois elements. The movements see this intermediary phase as a people's democratic, or national democratic, revolution, in which revolutionary intellectuals, workers and peasants will be moulded together by the party. A problem that these Afrocommunist states have is that the proletariat played a very small role in the coming to power of these movements, all of which were essentially the result of peasant based revolutions. A further characteristic of the Afrocommunist states is that they see a small vanguard party based in the working class as a necessity, and Marxism–Leninism as the ideology of the revolutionary process. They do not accept the mass party associated with the African Socialist states.

Finally, the Ottaways try to ascertain the origins of Afrocommunism; here they note the important influence of the communist parties and metropolitan centres of the respective colonial rulers. Hence, the French, Italian and Portuguese communist parties are said to have had an important influence on the revolutionary movements in the colonies.

Whilst these two authors have gone some way towards describing the similarities of certain African Marxist states in relation to both African Socialism and the northern communist states, there are dangers in carrying this notion too far. In terms of their ideological development, Crawford Young has spoken of a 'triumph of eclecticism [which] means that the new wave of Afro-Marxist regimes is not homogeneous in ideological interpretation or policy practice. . .'[82] By 'eclecticism', Young is referring both to the breakdown of the communist monolith and to the influence of a variety of currents of thought in the radical anti-imperialist Third World milieu, all of which have influenced the ideology of the African Marxist states. We would add, as being even more important, African revolutionaries' own interplay of theory and practice and stubborn determination to devise their own paths, not only in relation to the Soviet and other northern Marxist experiences but equally in relation to that of their sister movements. Anyone who has spent time in discussion with the political leaders of these movements will vouchsafe this fact. By making their own revolutions in their own circumstances, they have had to develop Marxist theory to suit their own needs. No revolutionary movement anywhere has succeeded by borrowing an exact formula from another revolution. Such an operation is doomed to failure as those who have tried have discovered to their cost, and to the cost of those who followed them.

David and Marina Ottaway use the term Afrocommunism for the parallels they see with the Eurocommunist movement. They argue: 'We have chosen the term "Afrocommunism" deliberately for its analogy to the foreign policy component of Eurocommunism, because we think there is a very valid parallel.'[83] They go on to say that in the industrialised nations of Western Europe there has been a rethinking of how a communist state might come into existence, what policies it should pursue internally, and how it should relate to the Soviet Union. One of the most important aspects of Eurocommunism is its commitment to maintain national autonomy from the Soviet Union and a rejection of the Brezhnev doctrine of Limited Sovereignty. In this sense, then, it is a determination to maintain national autonomy and sovereignty in relation to the Soviet Union, that is the shared characteristic of Eurocommunism and of Afrocommunism. The Ottaways rightly stress that there is a strong determination by the Afrocommunist states to maintain their own national independence but also to further their economic growth. Hence, the authors write,

> The Marxist-Leninist leaders are convinced that the socialist countries provide the best model for establishing control over their economies. But they realise there can be no economic growth without capital investment, modern technology, and the hard currency needed to buy it, all of which they have found to be more available from the West than the Soviet bloc. In other words, in order to obtain their goals, the African Marxist–Leninist countries need both the East and the West.[84]

We agree with some of the Ottaways' analysis, notably the importance they give to the indigenous development of a Marxist theory and to the experience gained by these movements in a national liberation struggle, their rejection of the notion of client or satellite status in relation to the Soviet Union and China, and their distinction between the Marxist-Leninist states and the earlier African Socialist experiences. However, there are certain problems with their concept of Afrocommunism. The first is that Eurocommunism is based on a notion of cultural similarity within Western Europe. Does this same situation apply in the African context? Is it possible to see a basic cultural similarity between Mozambique and Ethiopia, to give but one example? I think the answer must be in the negative. Their social structures are different, and the way the movements came to power are no less different. Hence it is potentially highly problematic to try to draw an analogy of common culture. They hold some views in common: the notion that there has to be a dynamic development effort to pull the countries out of their poverty and that there has to be the creation of a vanguard party. Even so, only now have Ethiopia's military rulers finally got around to forming such a party. Secondly, Eurocommunism represents a break-away from a Stalinist approach which preceded the new Eurocommunist policies adopted by the parties in Western Europe. The Afrocommunist states never adopted the Stalinist model, and therefore have not had to reformulate their movements and programmes in the same way. However, one common element is that the communist parties of Western Europe underwent a major change during the Second World War: because they were fighting a popular guerrilla war of resistance, they were forced to democratise their movements. Some parallels exist here with the national liberation struggles of the Third World and the imperative towards popular participation, as Davidson has so admirably demonstrated.[85] Whilst seeing the value of the Ottaways' analysis in helping us to explore the differences between the parties and their various socialist projects for Africa, the concept of Afrocommunist to describe the Marxist–Leninist variant would appear to be inappropriate. The straightjacket is too constricting, given that we are dealing with parties applying Marxist theory to their own experiences.[86] The formulation 'Marxist states in Africa' would appear to be more accurate.

Marxist–Leninist parties which grew out of national liberation fronts have all experienced great difficulties. During the national liberation struggles, the bulk of the supporters were drawn from the rural areas. Once power was taken, the urban population – working class, petty bourgeoisie and lumpen-proletariat – entered in greater numbers. In certain cases, many experienced cadres were killed in the fighting to overthrow colonial rule and new cadres, many without wartime experience, had to be created. The relative strength ideologically, organisationally and numerically of the party is clearly a vital consideration. And keeping the party separate from the state and at the same time closely linked with the population is equally crucial. Our case studies in the second part of the book explore these issues in detail.

What the foregoing discussion has revealed is the importance of ideology and the party in shaping the path of socialist transition. African Socialism offers no viable alternative for such a transition. The Marxist states in Africa have to face enormous difficulties in building their parties. In some cases, notably Ethiopia, the process has been painfully slow. In others significant progress has been made. By the time of Frelimo's Fourth Congress in 1983, the party had a membership of 110,000 representing about 2 percent of the adult population. However, rigid and doctrinaire application of Marxist ideology will do a disservice to the party and the country in the complex circumstances of Africa.

Transforming inherited state apparatuses

In his address to the nation on independence day, President Samora Machel pinpointed the problem that revolutionary movements face with their inherited colonial state apparatuses. He said:

> The state is not an eternal and immutable structure. The state is not the bureaucratic machinery of civil servants, nor something abstract or a mere technical apparatus. The state is always the organised form through which a class takes power in order to fulfil its interests. The colonial state, an instrument of domination and exploitation by a foreign bourgeoisie, and imperialism which has already been partially destroyed by the struggle, must be replaced by a People's State, forged through an alliance of workers and peasants. . . a state which wipes out exploitation and releases the creative initiative of the masses and the productive forces.[87]

Engineering just such a transformation from colonial to 'People's' state, however, has proved to be enormously difficult. For whilst new political structures to encourage mass participation have been created, their effectiveness has been hampered by illiteracy, lack of experience of democratic organisation (not least among the cadres appointed to guide the process), and more generally, a legacy of authoritarian and racist colonial rule. In most states, the flight of those with the technical and managerial skills left a vacuum; those who have filled the positions vacant have been drawn from the urban petty bourgeoisie.

In his chapter on Mozambique, Bertil Egero examines these problems. Not the least of these are party/state relations which involve a *de facto* alliance between a revolutionary leadership and a non-revolutionary, or in some cases counter-revolutionary, social stratum within the state apparatus. Egero notes that the factors which once brought about broad participation in the days of the armed liberation struggle have now changed. *Poder Popular* recognises the need to mobilise popular support for a strategy of transformation which is not yet part of the ideology of peasants and workers. Given a poorly organised working class and a disorganised peasantry, these classes cannot objectively assume state power. Hence the party is initially the controlling force in alliance with the bureaucratic and petty bourgeoisie. Because of its weak class base, the revolution faces dangers of elitism and bureaucratisation. The popular assemblies are unable as yet to provide a safeguard of democratic representation against these. The chapter on

Mozambique reveals the practical problems of trying to build alternative structures of power.

In this situation, education is paramount in developing the material and ideological conditions for a transformation of state structures and the creation of a genuine worker-peasant state. This is obviously a lengthy process. In the meantime there appears no alternative other than to rely on an urban petty bourgeoisie to run the state apparatuses. The party leadership, the bulk of which is occupied in running the top state structures, recognises the limitations of the structures of popular power in controlling the state apparatuses and tends to centralise decision making in its own hands. This inevitably leads to delays in executing tasks and creates the longer term danger of making centralisation a virtue rather than a necessity. External military threats and the need for tight security exacerbate this tendency. For instance, Angola's unhappy experience leading up to the Nito Alves coup attempt of 1977 has left a legacy of mistrust. The problems with the base level Action Committees at that time, which were open to manipulation, led to an overreaction on the part of the leadership and a return to tighter centralised control. Whatever the circumstances of the individual case, the fact remains that there will always be perfectly 'justifiable' reasons to maintain tight centralised control rather than risk the inevitable twists, turns and possible reverses that extending popular control of the state inevitably sets in train.

The central theme in Basil Davidson's chapter is the relationship between mass participation and 'substitution' by the party. He shows how and why the latter supplanted the former after 1977 in Guinea-Bissau, while the opposite has been the case in Cape Verde. The comparative analysis of these two countries is an important one and is more widely instructive.

Greater attention has been given in the literature to analysing the transitional economy than to analysing the transitional state in the African context. This sets an important topic for future research agendas. The debate on the post-colonial state and its relative autonomy appears to have ground to a halt in the 1980s and the question of its relevance to those African societies pursuing a socialist project remains largely unanswered. Given the structurally underdeveloped nature of the class base of the new state and of the class consciousness of the formerly subordinated classes, what concretely is implied for the extent to which the state can be truly captured and transformed in its structures and practices?

Analysing the problems of transforming the state apparatuses of a particular country requires an understanding of that state's colonial inheritance and of the specific class forces and their dynamic. The capacity to transform the state is constrained by these factors and by the nature of the country's political economy and its position within the international division of labour. With today's acute economic crisis, the state is increasingly constrained by the International Monetary Fund and the World Bank. Lionel Cliffe's comment on Zimbabwe shows how these external and internal forces combine to create the enormous problems that many states opting for socialism face:

> Diplomatic pressure, conditions for receiving aid, the very form of aided projects, the style of work of technical-assistance personnel and the insistence by international companies on a hospitable climate for investment will all be crucial pressures, merging with those from the state structures, the civil service and those black burueaucrats and politicians who will be content with mere reform.[88]

The possibility of building new democratic structures and effective worker–peasant power will also depend upon the route to power. For as we indicated earlier, which route is taken will determine the degree of opportunity for mass participation and the creation of popular organisational structures. Unfortunately, it has often been the case that the vitality of popular organisation during the struggle for power has waned with independence under the relentless pressures of economic decline and destabilisation. These combined pressures appear to lead towards a greater level of centralisation of power, not least as a security measure. The dangers of such a tendency are all too apparent.

Conclusion

If this introductory essay and the contributions to this volume appear at times to be overly sombre in tone, they are not intended to cast doubt on the need to find a way forward for the socialist project in Africa. The neo-colonial alternative provides no solution. But neither, it must be said, do some of the proposed 'socialist' paths devised and implemented in Africa to date. Textbook formulas derived from classical definitions of socialism or existing socialist bloc models do little to help chart a strategy of survival, growth and long term transition under Africa's existing unpropitious conditions. Given the existing balance of class forces, the high degree of internal and external opposition, the vulnerability to global market forces and superpower rivalry, the legacy for the future of the particular route to power of the revolutionary nationalist leadership, the weakness of the post-colonial state's capacity and the necessarily experimental nature of development strategies, the way forward will need to be innovative and thereby heretical, based on the concrete analysis of the concrete situation. Whatever progress is made will depend in turn on the nature of the global, regional and national contexts at any given conjuncture.

Even when the route for power seemed to create the most favourable conditions for democratic and participatory socialism there were still severe limitations. As Basil Davidson writes of Guinea-Bissau in his contribution to this volume, 'effective movement towards economic transformation in the liberated zones could not be a realistic project: there was no time and fighting was fierce'. Such a comment is more widely applicable. He goes on to reflect:

Other forms of participation, often remarkably advanced, had won the liberation war and cleared the way for further progress; but now it would be the weight of economic influence as between sectors and as between classes, sub-classes or privileged groups that would be decisive in shaping the future.

In an important new book, John Saul has explored the problems of the leadership-mass action dialectic in the post-independence period in Mozambique. He notes that genuine popular control is fragile and that in the context of a vanguard-party system, the risks of authoritarianism are many. He takes care to point out that the experience of Frelimo is less one of deliberately stifling popular initiative than of failing to stimulate it and effectively empower the people sufficiently. One passage in particular captures the very different problems and circumstances of post and pre-independence periods:

> Put simply, the politics of national liberation appear in retrospect to have been far more straightforward than those in the current phase. There were contradictions then, as we have seen, but the goals were nonetheless clearer, the means more straightforward, the scale smaller, and the pace of the expansion of that scale more comfortably under Frelimo control. After independence the scale became infinitely vaster, the stratum of middle-level cadres too thin on the ground and too ill-trained, the challenges – not least South Africa's on-going war – literally overwhelming in their scope and variety . . . Not surprisingly, even the most solid senior leaders have been reduced under such circumstances to fire-fighting a seemingly endless series of emergencies rather than finding time to concentrate on the slow, patient, ongoing political work which would serve to consolidate a firmer political basis for the revolution.[89]

This introductory chapter has tried to map out some of the broad determinants of socialism in Africa. Whilst not being exhaustive it has tried to capture some of the key forces at work. It has emphasised a rather limited number of countries because of their role at the forefront of socialist experiments in the continent and because little is known about them still. The volume as a whole is intended to contribute to debates on the socialist project in Africa, and, more generally, to inform a wider audience.

Notes

1. For this discussion see B. Munslow, 'Is Socialism Possible on the Periphery?' *Monthly Review*, Vol. 35, No. 1, 1983.

2. G. White, 'Revolutionary Socialist Development in the Third World: An Overview' in G. White, R. Murray and C. White (eds) *Revolutionary Socialist Development in the Third World* (Wheatsheaf Books, Brighton, 1983) p. 1.

3. For information on the political perceptions of the leadership of the Congolese Worker Party see the interviews contained in E. Cleaver, *Revolution in the Congo* (Stage 1, London, 1971).

4. S. Decalo, 'Ideological Rhetoric and Scientific Socialism in Benin and Congo Brazzaville' in C.G. Rosberg and T.M. Callaghy (eds), *Socialism in Sub-Saharan Africa. A new Assessment* (Institute of International Studies, University of California, Berkeley, 1979) p. 248 (emphasis in the original).

5. J.S. Coleman and C.G. Rosberg Jr. (eds), *Political Parties and National Integration in Tropical Africa* (University of California Press, Berkeley, 1964) p. 5.

6. H. Bienen, 'The Ruling Party in the African One-Party State: TANU in Tanzania', *Journal of Commonwealth Political Studies*, Vol. V, No. 3, November 1967.

7. H. Bienen, 'Political Parties and Political Machines in Africa', in M.F. Lofchie (ed), *The State of the Nations* (University of California Press, Berkeley, 1971).

8. On the more recent of these attempts in Burkina Faso see V. Brittain, 'Introduction to Sankara and Burkina Faso', *Review Of African Political Economy*, No. 32, April 1985.

9. See J. Markakis, 'The Military State and Ethiopia's Path to Socialism', *Review Of African Political Economy*, No. 21, 1981.

10. F. Halliday and M. Molyneux, *The Ethiopian Revolution* (Verso, London, 1981) p. 12.

11. Ibid, p. 26.

12. A Hiwet, 'Analysing the Ethiopian Revolution', *Review Of African Political Economy*, No. 30, 1984. In the case of Ethiopia we have well-established revolutionary movements fighting against the government. See B. Davidson, L. Cliffe and B.H. Selassie (eds), *Behind the War in Eritrea* (Spokesman, Nottingham, 1980); D. Pool, 'Revolutionary Crisis and Revolutionary Vanguard: The Eritrean People's Liberation Front', *Review Of African Political Economy*, No. 19, 1980; J. Gebre-Medhin, 'Nationalism, Peasant Politics and the Emergence of a Vanguard Front in Eritrea', *Review Of African Political Economy*, No. 30, 1984; S. Holland and J. Firebrace, *Never Kneel Down: Drought, Development and Liberation in Eritrea* (Spokesman, Nottingham, 1985).

13. B. Munslow, *Mozambique: The Revolution and its Origins* (Longman, London, 1983) chapter 2.

14. See for example General Giap, *People's War, People's Army* (Frederick A. Praeger, New York, 1962), p. 55.

15. R. Debray, *Revolution in the Revolution* (Penguin, Harmondsworth, 1968) and *Strategy for Revolution* (Pelican, Harmondsworth, 1973).

16. See for example L.M. Vega, *Guerrillas in Latin America. The Techniques of the Counter – State* (Pall Mall Press, London, 1969); L. Huberman and P. Sweezy (eds), *Regis Debray & the Latin American Revolution* (Monthly Review Press, New York, 1968). Some questioned the accuracy of his interpretation of the Cuban experience; see R. Gott, *Guerrilla Movements in Latin America* (Nelson, London 1970) p. 9.

17. R. Debray, *A Critique of Arms*, Vol. 1 (Penguin, Harmondsworth, 1977) p. 100.

18. B. Davidson, 'On Revolutionary Nationalism: The Legacy of Cabral', *Latin American Perspectives*, Issue 41, Vol. 11, No. 2, 1984, p. 26.

19. L. Cliffe, J. Mpofu and B. Munslow, 'Nationalist Politics in Zimbabwe: The 1980 Elections and Beyond', *Review Of African Political Economy*, No. 18, 1980.

20. Quoted in D. Martin and P. Johnson, *The Struggle for Zimbabwe* (Faber and Faber, London, 1981) p. 13.

21. L. Rudebeck, *Guinea–Bissau: A Study of Political Mobilisation* (Scandinavian Institute of African Studies, Uppsala, 1974) p. 244.

22. B. Davidson, J. Slovo and A. R. Wilkinson, *Southern Africa: The New Politics of Revolution* (Pelican, Harmondsworth, 1976) p. 42.

23. D.L. Cohen and J. Daniel (eds), *Political Economy of Africa* (Longman, London, 1981) p. 75.

24. See for example P.C. Lloyd, *Africa in Social Change* (Penguin, Harmondsworth, 1969).

25. The *Review Of African Political Economy* has played a particularly important role in promoting this approach. But see also D.L. Cohen 'Class and the analysis of African Politics: Problems & Prospects' in D.L. Cohen and J. Daniel, op. cit. For a discussion of the complexities of the use of this term 'class' in Africa, see also the interesting essay by J. Copans, 'The Marxist Conception of Class: Political and theoretical Elaboration in the African and Africanist Context', *Review of African Political Economy*, No. 32, April 1985.

26. W. Tordoff, *Government and Politics in Africa* (Macmillan, London, 1984) p. 95.

27. G. Huizer, *Peasant Rebellion in Latin America* (Penguin, Harmondsworth, 1973) p. 2.

28. E.R. Wolf, *Peasant Wars of the Twentieth Century* (Faber and Faber, London, 1971) p. xvi.

29. F. Fanon, *The Wretched of the Earth* (Penguin, Harmondsworth, 1974) p. 47.

30. See D. Caute, *Frantz Fanon* (Fontana, London, 1970) p. 72.

31. Pan Af, *Frantz Fanon* (Pan Af, London, 1975) p. 104.

32. P. Worsley, 'Fanon and the Role of the Lumpenproletariat' in R. Miliband and J. Saville (eds), *The Socialist Register 1972* (Merlin Press, London, 1972).

33. B. Davidson, 'The African Prospect' in R. Miliband and J. Saville (eds), *The Socialist Register 1970* (Merlin Press, London, 1970) p. 41; A. Cabral, *Unity and Struggle* (Heinemann, London, 1980).

34. J.S. Saul and R. Woods, 'African Peasantries' in T. Shanin (ed), *Peasants and Peasant Societies* (Penguin, Harmondsworth, 1971) p. 104.

35. Ibid., p. 105.

36. Ibid., p. 240.

37. P.C. Lloyd, *Classes, Crises and Coups* (MacGibbon and Kee, 1971) p. 99.

38. J.S. Saul, 'African Peasants and Revolutions' in *Review Of African Political Economy*, No. 1, 1974.

39. Ibid., p. 49.

40. Ibid., p. 51.

41. For a discussion of the problems see B. Munslow and H. Finch (eds), *Proletarianisation in the Third World. Studies in the Creation of a Labour Force Under Dependent Capitalism* (Croom Helm, London, 1984) chapter 1.

42. V.L. Allen, 'The Meaning of the Working Class in Africa' in *Journal of Modern African Studies*, Vol. 10, No. 2, 1972.

43. See R. Sandbrook and R. Cohen (eds), *The Development of an African*

Working Class (Longman, London, 1975).

44. See for example A. Callinicos, *South Africa After Zimbabwe* (Pluto Press, London, 1981).

45. F. Fanon, op.cit.

46. See for example P. Waterman 'The "Labour Aristocracy" in Africa: Introduction to an Unfinished Controversy' in D.L. Cohen and J. Daniel (eds), op. cit. The earlier advocacy of the labour aristocracy thesis in G. Arrighi and J. Saul, *Essays on the Political Economy of Africa* (Monthly Review Press, New York, 1973) has been subsequently qualified in a 'reconsideration' by one of the authors, see J. Saul, *The State and Revolution in Eastern Africa* (Heinemann, London, 1979) chapter 12.

47. J. Mendes, *La Revolution en Afrique*, Paris, 1971.

48. R. Cohen, 'Classes in Africa: Analytical Problems and Perspectives', *The Socialist Register 1972* (Merlin Press, London, 1972) p. 252.

49. E. Laclau and C. Mouffe, *Hegemony and Socialist Strategy* (Verso Editions, London, 1985).

50. T. Shanin, 'Class, State, and Revolution: Substitutes and Realities' in H. Alavi and T. Shanin (eds), *Introduction To The Sociology Of 'Developing Societies'* (Macmillan, London, 1982) p. 328.

51. J. Saul, *The State and Revolution in Eastern Africa*, p. 9.

52. UNIDO, *World Industry in 1980* (UN Biennial Industrial Development Survey, New York, 1981) p. 31.

53. UNIDO, *County Report in Mozambique, March 1984* (UNIDO, 1984).

54. *Lloyds Bank Economic Group Report on Tanzania*, 1984.

55. *Financial Times*, 21 August 1985.

56. See P. Lawrence (ed), *World Recession and the Food Crisis in Africa*, (James Currey in association with the *Review Of African Political Economy*, London 1986); and J. Carlson (ed), *Recession in Africa* (Scandinavian Institute of African Studies, Uppsala, 1983).

57. D.L. Laitin and S.S. Samatar, 'Somalia and the World Economy', *Review Of African Political Economy*, No. 30, September 1984, p. 67.

58. V. Solodovnikov and V. Bogoslovosky, *Non-Capitalist Development: An Historical Outline* (Progress Publishers, Moscow, 1975) p. 202.

59. For the Nicaraguan case see for example G. White and K.Young (eds), *Nicaragua after the Revolution: problems and prospects* (IDS Discussion Paper, Brighton, January 1985).

60. See B. Munslow, 'Prospects for the Socialist Transition of Agriculture in Zimbabwe', *World Development*, Vol. 13, No. 1, 1985.

61. D. Weiner, S. Moyo, B. Munslow and P. O'Keefe, 'Land Use and Agricultural Productivity in Zimbabwe', *Journal of Modern African Studies*, Vol. 23, No. 2, 1985.

62. For an extensive discussion of these issues see L. Cliffe and B. Munslow, 'The Politics of Agrarian Transformation in Africa: The State, Bureaucracy and Participation', a paper given to the Annual Conference of the Political Studies Association, University of Manchester, April 1985 and forthcoming in a volume prepared by the United Nations Food and Agricultural Organisation on agrarian transformation in the centrally planned economies of Africa.

63. P. O'Keefe, L. Kristofferson and G.T. Goodman, 'Issues in Ethiopian Energy Policy', in V. Baum (ed), *Energy and Development* (Oxford University Press, 1985).

64. J. Dunman, *Agriculture: Capitalist and Socialist* (Lawrence & Wishart, London, 1985) p. 118.

65. On this point in particular and the more general problem of agrarian transformation in Mozambique see B. Munslow, 'State intervention in agriculture: The Mozambican experience', *Journal of Modern African Studies*, Vol. 2, No. 2, 1984.

66. R. First, *Black Gold: The Mozambican Miner, Proletarian and Peasant* (Harvester Press, Brighton, 1983).

67. Centro de Estudos Africanos, *O trabalhador sazonal na transformação duma economia de plantações* (Universidade Eduardo Mondlane, Maputo, 1981).

68. The elements of the model are drawn from two sources E.V.K. Fitzgerald, 'The Problem of Balance in the Peripheral Socialist Economy: A Conceptual Note', *World Development*, Vol. 13, No. 1. 1985; and by the same author 'Planned Accumulation and Income Distribution in the Small Peripheral Economy', in G. Irvin and X. Gorostiago (eds), *Towards An Alternative for Central America and the Caribean* (Institute for Social Studies, The Hague, 1983). I have also benefited extensively from the unpublished work of Oscar Marleyn and Christopher Pycroft on this model.

69. For a summary of Frelimo's new strategy following its important Fourth Congress held in 1983, see B. Munslow and P. O'Keefe 'Rethinking the revolution in Mozambique', *Race and Class*, Vol. XXVI, No. 2, Autumn 1984.

70. It is ironic that such a solution was suggested many decades ago by the Russian communist anarchist P. Kropotkin, who wrote 'Bring to us your produce, and take from our stores and shops all the manufactured articles you please', cited in *The Conquest of Bread* (Penguin, Harmondsworth, 1972) p. 10.

71. For general details of CIA activities concerning destabilisation, see E. Ray, W. Schaap, K. Van Meter and L. Wolf (eds), *Dirty Work 2: The CIA in Africa* (Zed Press, London, 1980). For a specific account of the activities in Angola there is the detailed testimony of the CIA's head of the task force, J. Stockwell, *In Search of Enemies* (Futura Publications, London, 1979).

72. For a discussion of these problems see B. Munslow. 'Disengagement from a Regional Sub-System: Problems and Prospects', *Journal of Area Studies* No. 4, Autumn 1981.

73. Mozambique Information Office, *News Review* (London), No. 37, 1984.

74. See P. Fauvet, 'Roots of Counter-Revolution: The Mozambique National Resistance', *Review of African Political Economy*, No. 29, July 1984; J. Hanlon, *Mozambique: The Revolution Under Fire* (Zed Press, London, 1984) chapter 21.

75. J.F. Petras 'Class and Politics in the Periphery and the Transition to Socialism' in *Union of Radical Political Economists*, Vol. 8, No. 2, Summer 1976, p. 21.

76. B. Munslow, *Mozambique: The Revolution and its Origins*, p. 171.

77. D. and M. Ottaway, *Afrocommunism* (Africana Publishing Co., London, 1981).

78. Ibid., p. 202.

79. K. Nkrumah, *Revolutionary Path* (International Publishers, New York, 1973) p. 440, quoted in Ibid., p. 19.

80. Quoted in Ibid., p. 25.

81. Quoted in Ibid., p. 25.

82. C. Young, *Ideology and Development in Africa* (Yale University Press, London, 1982) p. 27.

83. D. and M. Ottaway, *Afrocommunism*, p. 210.

84. Ibid.

85. B. Davidson, *Special Operations Europe: Scenes from the Anti-Nazi War* (Gollancz, London, 1980).

86. To illustrate this point see B. Munslow (ed), *Samora Machel: An African Revolutionary: Selected Speeches and Writings* (Zed Press, London, 1985) in particular chapter 6.

87. *Mozambique Revolution*, 25 June 1975.

88. L. Cliffe, 'Zimbabwe's Political Inheritance', C. Stoneman (ed), *Zimbabwe's Inheritance* (Macmillan Press, London, 1981) p. 34.

89. J. Saul (ed), *A Difficult Road: The Transition to Socialism in Mozambique* (Monthly Review Press, New York, 1985) p. 101.

2: Marxism in Africa: The Grounding of a Tradition

by Robin Cohen

It is necessary to strictly delimit the scope of this chapter, as the title can be more widely understood than I intend. I am interested principally in how a body of thought, European in origin and initially referring largely to European experiences, came to be applied to the circumstances of the African continent. Second, I have concentrated nearly exclusively on Marxist (or Marxist-inspired) theory and pay little attention to the numerous and diverse attempts at creating a socialist practice—in the liberation struggles more generally, and in specific states such as Guinea–Bissau, Nkrumah's Ghana, Tanzania, Mozambique, Algeria, and others. This makes the present exercise somewhat artificial in that it violates one of the precepts of Marxism, namely the connection between practice and theory. Nonetheless, given my focus, I have to assume the realm of reality, not describe it. Third, while I accept that non-African Marxists writing about Africa have always had an influential role in defining a continental Marxist tradition, I argue that this has ineluctably given way to systematic reformulations by indigenous intellectuals and revolutionaries and those from the African diaspora. In this chapter, I describe the beginnings of this process of indigenisation, but I do not pretend to be comprehensive. The breadth and variety of contemporary Marxist theory written by Africans is now too great to be documented here.

For those who would assert a universal science of historical materialism, the rough distinction that I make between 'external' and 'internal' African Marxism is of no relevance, or indeed may be thought to have racist implications. My defence is two-fold. First, 'external' Marxist writing about Africa does not refer to the race of the writer, but to a recognisably metropolitan-centred view of the world. Characteristically, African colonies, as with colonies in general, were seen as places where European powers competed for raw materials and dumped cheap manufactured goods. Theories of imperialism focused on *European* rivalries and *European* expansion. Thus Lenin and Luxemburg (both drawing on Hobson) were interested in European mining capital in South Africa, but the voices of African miners are heard not at all. With the exception of South Africa, the continent remained as obscure to them as to their non-Marxist contemporaries. Second, the issue of the 'externality' of Marxist theory in relation to Africa is one which preoccupies left-wing African scholars themselves. Let me refer, for example, to Usman's central contribution to a Centenary Conference on 'Marx in Africa' convened at Zaria in 1983. He poses the question in this way:

> What has this man, who is not an African, and is not from the African diaspora, who knew so little about the Africa of his days, got to do with the analysis of its contemporary politics one hundred years after his death. . . This issue may appear superfluous to participants at such a conference, but it cannot be responsibly avoided, in a conference like this, at this particular moment in African historical development.[1]

As Usman argues elsewhere in his paper, a common charge directed against Marxist scholars in Africa is that they espouse an 'outdated foreign ideology'. The micro-grain of truth in such a caricature provides a potent rallying cry for anti-progressive elements. I seek to confront such views by showing how what clearly *was* an alien tradition, gradually became grounded in African traditions and realities. This process of internalisation was led, I suggest, by four major theorists, two from the African diaspora in the Caribbean and two from the continent itself. In the first phase, Padmore and Nkrumah effected a shift from general anti-imperialist and anti-colonial sentiments to a search for a revolutionary African state. In the second phase, Fanon and Cabral effected a transition from the belief in the potency of a revolutionary state to the need for a revolutionary class alliance. Though all four of these figures are frequently objects of separate commentary and analysis, I hope to show, through a re-examination of their central texts, both how their work grounds a continuous tradition of indigenising Marxism and how the theory changes as the wholly natural and legitimate process of contextualisation occurs.

From anti-imperialism to a revolutionary state: Padmore and Nkrumah

In the pre-1939 period, one of the major currents in radical continental thought was the anti-colonial and anti-imperial struggle. This, of course, resonated theoretically with Lenin's preoccupation with imperialism as the means whereby capitalism prolonged its historical role on the world stage. At a more instrumental level, the success of anti-colonial movements was deemed vital to the continued survival of the Soviet Union, at that point the sole national embodiment and assumed guarantor of 'socialism'. The Communist International (the 'Comintern') thus spent much of the 1920s debating the character and relative strengths of anti-colonial movements.[2] It also made a number of attempts, both at the analytical and practical level, to weld nationalist sentiments to socialist ends. Bodies like the Red International of Labour Unions encouraged the formation of the International Trade Union Committee for Negro Workers (ITUC–NW), which had strong African representation. The Comintern itself eagerly sought delegates from the colonised world, while, within the USSR, specialist training and research units were created to service the needs of 'the toilers of the East'—an expression that was extended to cover the whole colonised world.

It was within this matrix of anti-colonial and anti-imperial activity that the first fruits of a distinctive Marxism, applied to the African continent, appeared. One of the most important, but hitherto obscure figures of this pre-war period was Albert Nzula, the first black General Secretary of the Communist Party of South Africa (CPSA), who in 1932 collaborated with two Russian colleagues in producing a wide-ranging book on forced labour in Africa.[3] It was the period too when the debate about the wisdom of supporting a black national republic prior to a class struggle in South Africa, tore the CPSA apart. The ramifications of this debate still continue to bedevil the South African left.[4] Finally, it was the period in which two black Trinidadians—Malcolm Nurse (who was to become George Padmore) and C.L.R. James—appeared like blazing comets announcing their support of the international communist and Pan-Africanist movements.

Padmore, the first figure whose work I shall examine, oscillated between the two rival poles of attraction for revolutionary black intellectuals, communism and Pan-Africanism. His initial and basic political sentiments in the early part of his life were reflected in his book, *The Life and Struggles of Negro Toilers*, first published in 1932.[5] It revealed his fierce loyalty to the Comintern and reflected his central role in establishing and running the ITUC–NW. In a pamphlet describing the work of the ITUC–NW, Padmore bitterly denounced black reformists and 'misleaders' like W.E.B. Du Bois, Garvey, Kadalie (the leader of the South African Industrial and Commercial Union) and A. Phillip Randolph, the black leader of the Pullman Workers Union in the US.[6] Seventeen years later, after Padmore's involvement with the famous Manchester Pan-African Congress, a sinner had been changed to a saint. He dedicated his book *Africa: Britain's Third Empire* to Du Bois, no longer a 'misleader', but the 'Father of Pan-Africanism, Scholar and Uncompromising Fighter for Human Rights'.[7]

Another seven years later and his break with communism was apparently complete. His *Pan-Africanism or Communism?* (1956) was a carefully drafted, yet, in a sense, inexplicit, *mea culpa*.[8] Communists and the Comintern had taken 'erroneous' positions: yet it remained unsaid that Padmore was far from an outsider to such errors. He had helped to formulate and implement some parts of the Comintern's policy. What was now explicit was a total reversal of his position on other black leaders. A. Phillip Randolph was 'the most distinguished Afro-American Socialist'; W.E.B. Du Bois was 'a man of tremendous moral courage and integrity'; Kadalie was 'the uncrowned king of the black masses . . . the whites feared him as they feared Dingaan, the last of the Zulu warrior kings'. As for Garvey, who had previously been the main black target of Comintern abuse, he fought 'the Communists with their own weapons of half-truth, villification and thuggery . . . he was the first black leader to force them to keep their hands off Negro organisations'.[9] Absolutely central to his change of heart on black leadership was Padmore's insistent argument that communists were trying to subvert black organisations for instrumental ends. He proclaimed that blacks were keenly aware that the communists' interest in them

> is dictated by the ever changing tactics of Soviet foreign policy, rather than by altruistic motives. Their politically-minded intellectuals know that the oppressed Negro workers and peasants are regarded by the Communists as "revolutionary expendables" in the global struggle of Communism against Western capitalism. They know that Africans and peoples of African descent are courted primarily to tag on to the white proletariat and thus to swell the "revolutionary" ranks against the imperialist enemies of the "Soviet Fatherland".[10]

Such attacks, and the bitterness of Padmore's sense of betrayal, led to a widespread assumption that he totally abandoned his past convictions in favour of an undifferentiated appeal to race and nation. This, however, is a misrepresentation. His anger was directed at the contemporary institutions and parties which purported to represent his early socialist convictions rather than at socialism *per se*. In like manner, one can profess to be a Christian, yet despise the church. He retained an affection for the led, if not the leaders, of the communist movements and he continued to insist on the need for a non-dogmatic Marxism.

These retentions and redefinitions are apparent in several places in *Pan-Africanism or Communism*? For example, he endorses Paul Robson's view that there was a lack of racial discrimination in the Soviet Union by recounting the story of a Moscow performance of *Uncle Tom's Cabin* where 'the entire audience was in tears'. Blacks, he argued were displayed sympathetically in Russian literature (Pushkin was, he reminds us, of African descent) and were accepted at 'all levels of Russian society'.[11] Not only did he seek to rescue the Russian people from their leaders, but he sought to rescue a creative Marxism from the rigidities of orthodox communists:

> Even Lenin taught that Marxism is not a dogma to be mechanically applied, but a guide to action, according to local circumstance and the political development of a people. Had Lenin and Mao Tse-Tung been doctrinaire Marxists, they could never have led successful revolutions. Dogmatism is the disease of parvenu-communists. "There are people who think that Marxism is a kind of magic truth with which one can cure any disease," declares Mao Tse-Tung. "We should tell them that dogmas are more useless than cow-dung. Dung can be used as fertilizer".[12]

This reference to Mao's innovative adaptation of Marxism is paralleled by equal praise for Tito in reworking Marxism to 'serve the particular interests of his country'.[13] The notion of adaptation to a particular local circumstance is the key to understanding Padmore's comparison between Marxism on the one hand and Pan-Africanism and Garveyism on the other. Like Marxism, they too originated outside the countries where they were first applied. As Marxism needed its Titos and Mao Tse-Tungs, so Pan-Africanism needed its Drs. Azikiwe and Nkrumah.[14] Such leaders, Padmore thought, would both be able to capture the hearts of the black masses and deflect the orthodox communists from exploiting the anti-colonial movement for its own ends. However, in a passage crucial for its recognition of the insufficiency of race awareness, he argues that socialist principles have to supplement nationalist appeals: 'The only force capable of containing Communism in Asia and Africa is dynamic nationalism based upon a socialist programme of industrialization and co-operative methods of agricultural production'.[15]

In effect, Padmore sought to build a theoretical bridge to his socialist convictions through the medium of African nationalism. The capstone and practical means to this end was government, as 'only responsibility can develop the latent potentialities of a subject people, as events in the Gold Coast have shown'.[16] The personification of this transition was of course Nkrumah himself who, with Padmore had serviced the 1945 Pan-Africanist Congress. The Declaration drafted by Nkrumah that concluded the Congress provides a clear statement linking anti-imperialist sentiment to the demands for self-government:

> The object of imperialist powers is to exploit. By granting the right to the colonial peoples to govern themselves they are defeating that objective. Therefore the struggle for political power by colonial and subject peoples is the first step towards, and the necessary pre-requisite to, complete social, economic and political emancipation.[17]

The Declaration ended with a self-conscious echo of the *Communist Manifesto* that bordered on parody: 'Colonial & Subject Peoples of the World — Unite'. The deference to orthodoxy was even more apparent in the rather unlikely salute concluding Nkrumah's 1947 pamphlet *Towards Colonial Freedom*: 'Peoples of the Colonies Unite: the Working Men of All Countries are Behind You'.[18] His broad analysis of imperialism again is conformist. Nkrumah affirms that the 'most searching and penetrating analysis of economic imperialism has been given by Marx and Lenin' and goes on to summarise Lenin's *Imperialism: The Highest Stage of Capitalism*.[19]

However, the difference between an 'external' analysis, such as Lenin's and an 'internal' analysis of imperialism, such as Nkrumah's, soon becomes evident. Nkrumah turns his fiercest blast against the face of imperialism he knew best — missionaries, anthropologists, traders, concessionaires and administrators. The main thrust of the pamphlet is to challenge the ideological pretensions and political practice of the imperialist powers, despite a reverential nod in the direction of Marx and Lenin. It is against the doctrine of 'trusteeship' or 'partnership' (the British variant) and against the doctrine of 'assimilation' (the French and Portuguese variant) that his polemic is most effective. These, and other schemes, were all camouflages. African countries in the sway of the British would never be given white dominion status, nor were current proposals for constitutional reform anything but 'show gestures'. 'Independence would not come through delegation, gifts, charity, paternalism, grants, concessions, proclamations, charters or reformism, but only through a complete change of the colonial system'.[20]

Again, the solution appeared obvious. It was the same one at which Padmore had arrived: self-government was the *sine qua non* to change Africa's destiny. .Nkrumah's famous quasi-biblical dictum, 'Seek ye first the political kingdom and all else shall be added', succinctly captured this outlook. Yet the major question marks over the success of this strategy, the issue of which units were to be politically captured and in what sequence, remained undertheorised and inexplicit. As early as 1947, Nkrumah had argued that Liberia's political and economic predicament showed that one state alone could not 'throw off the foreign yoke'. *West* African unity was essential.[21] As the vagaries and misfortunes of the drive to Pan-African unity unfolded, Nkrumah was to shift his position many times. His most uncompromising view appeared in *Africa Must Unite*, a book dedicated to Padmore, where he argued for a political Union of African States, in which economic planning, a military and defence strategy and foreign policy would all be decided at a continental level.[22] But behind this clarion call there was some uncertainty and loose theorising. Nkrumah flounders around various 'examples' of unified states—the USA, the USSR, Australia, Canada, Switzerland and Venezuela—without any clear analysis of the conditions under which unification occurred or the differences between these countries and the Africa of the 1960s.[23] He is uncertain as to how to handle the case of South Africa (apparently considering it outside of Africa), and is hostile to the 'very idea' of regional federations, considering this to be 'fraught with many dangers', 'a form of balkanisation on a grand scale' and likely only to lead to 'the development of regional loyalties'.[24]

Yet despite the political rhetoric of his frequent assertion that Ghana's freedom would be meaningless without African unity, it was clear that by agreeing to accept territorial decolonisation on the model proposed by the British (and with modifications the French), Nkrumah effectively conceded the balkanisation of the continent. The partial and regional groupings defined at the Casablanca and Monrovia conferences of 1961, the Lagos conference in the next year and the paper unions that were effected with Mali and Guinea, were bound to be a disappointment. By accepting political independence in a territorial unit defined by the departing colonial power, Nkrumah had in practice, if not in theory, conceded the cause of African unity. By the same token, he had ignored his own admonition in *Neo-colonialism*, his academically most ambitious book, that opposition to neo-colonialism (which he saw as the stage after imperialism not predicted by Lenin) would fail unless unity was achieved:

> The foreign firms who exploit our resources long ago saw the strength to be gained by acting on a Pan-African scale. By means of interlocking directorships, cross-shareholdings and other devices, groups of apparently different companies have formed, in fact, an enormous capitalist monopoly. The only effective way to challenge this economic empire and to recover possession of our heritage, is for us also to act on a Pan-African basis, through a Union Government.[25]

Nkrumah's political theory was, in short, wholly compromised by his acceptance of office in a country which provided too small a stage for the realisation of his ideas. The result is that Nkrumah spent much of his time puffing up his own ego and the supposed symbolic and pioneering role of the Ghanaian state. In his autobiography, titled *Ghana*, the two tasks were totally conflated.[26] His collection of speeches, *I Speak of Freedom* (1961), is even more vainglorious in its reproduction of photographs with famous people and in the constant recitation of the impression he made on various dignitories, including the Queen, Harold MacMillan and others not previously known for their commitment to socialist ideas.[27]

The transformation of a modestly-sized and modestly-endowed west African state into the germ of a pan-continental revolution was accomplished by political declaration and public relations rather than analysis. The Ghanaian state was simply deemed to be revolutionary and the flag-bearer of African aspirations.[28] Yet within Ghana the working class and peasantry had not engaged in any sustained class struggle in support of the Convention Peoples' Party, or independently expressed affirmations of Pan-African or other forms of internationalism. What was perhaps equally damaging to Nkrumah's own self-delusions, were the delusions wrought by sympathetic outside observers who found in Ghana a projection of their own wishful thinking. Ghana-enthusiasts were to be followed by Tanzanophiles, supporters of Biafra, then adherents of socialist governments in Mozambique, Guinea–Bissau, Angola and even Somalia. In the Ghanaian case, a sense of disillusionment and betrayal followed, with the disillusioned either arguing that bureaucratic distortions and international constraints sabotaged sound revolutionary ideology, or that the CPP never in fact managed to mobilise a sufficiently large segment of the population or train a group of committed cadres.

In Biafra, the stress on 'authenticity' and popular mobilisation, as embodied in the Ahiara Declaration, struck sympathetic chords in the Western, particularly social democratic, left. But here again the claim to revolutionary purity was damaged by the inconsistent images that Biafra projected (the go-getting entrepreneurship, the appeal to religious solidarity, the flirtations with reactionary powers).

Tanzania provided the most influential model of all: a constant stream of debate stemmed from Nyerere's humanistic vision of the construction of socialism—a vision particularly appealing to left elements disillusioned with the Stalinist aspects of previous institutionalised 'socialisms'. The growth of a left-opposition within Tanzania has continued to provide an inspiration even where scepticism regarding the success of governmental measures has set in. In addition, the new states of Guinea–Bissau and Mozambique have now been elevated to the status of vanguardist states following the success of liberation movements in those two countries.

Centring revolutionary aspirations on the creation and development of a revolutionary state was (and where this belief is still held, is) in error for three major reasons. First, the relationship between nationalism (especially in weak, small African states) and socialism was undertheorised or not theorised at all. Second, there was no appreciation of the anti-statist logic in much socialist thinking. Because colonialism was superficially expressed through the colonial state, it was naively assumed that its capture would in itself be liberatory. Third, at the early stages of the indigenisation of a continental Marxist tradition, there was little appreciation of the contours of class differentiation and the nature of class struggle. The most prominent of Africa's progressive leaders—including Lumumba, Senghor, Mondlane, Nyerere, Sekou Touré and Nkrumah—sought at first to abolish the problem of social differentiation by denying the existence of classes in the 'traditional' African context and, by inference, in their own modern countries (though Nkrumah[29] was to change his position on this later).

Even where the intentions of the leadership are favourably judged, neither the practice nor the theory of Marxism, can be constructed 'from the top down'. A statist perspective needs to give way to the voices of the dispossessed and subordinate themselves. Again, an African and a writer of African descent produced a considerable advance in this respect, when adapting Marxism to the African continent.

From a revolutionary state to a revolutionary class alliance: Fanon and Cabral

Like much iconoclastic writing written with passion and in the heat of experience, Fanon's formulations on the revolutionary role of various subordinate classes do not stand up well to empirical and scholarly scrutiny. His three major works,[30] have been objects of a large critical literature, much of it challenging his view of the Algerian struggle and his more general propositions.[31] There is little point in reviewing the debates here as many of them are well-known. For the sake of brevity, I shall mention what I consider Fanon's major contributions to the indigenisation of African Marxist thinking and also boldly state my reservations with his class analysis.

Fanon's first and enduring contribution was to try to unshackle minds bent to the purposes of colonialism. The Algerian revolution provided him with symbolic and significant (though not necessarily representative) cases to show that resistance to 'imperialism of the mind' was possible. Perhaps the most telling and extended observation is his description of how the veil, symbolic of women's oppression in an Islamic society, was used as a form of resistance:

> Removed and reassumed again and again, the veil has been manipulated, transformed into a technique of camouflage, into a means of struggle. The virtually taboo character assumed by the veil in the colonial situation disappeared almost entirely in the course of the liberating struggle. Even Algerian women not actively integrated into the struggle form the habit of abandoning the veil.[32]

The decolonisation of the intellect and sentiment was also necessary to create a rupture with the European communist and socialist parties. His bitterness over the position of the French left is particularly visible when he describes their reaction to the news that ten French civilians were killed in Algeria:

> The entire French Left, in an unanimous outburst, cried out: We can no longer follow you! The propaganda became orchestrated, wormed its way into people's minds and dismantled convictions that were already crumbling. The concept of barbarism appeared and it was decided that France in Algeria was fighting barbarism. A large proportion of the intellectuals, almost the entire democratic Left, collapsed and laid down its conditions before the Algerian people: condemn the bombs and we shall continue to give you our friendly support.[33]

This passage is interesting, in that Fanon does not emphasise the specific material benefits derived by the metropolitan working class (and other classes) from colonianism: his major target is the pusillanimity of the metropolitan intellectuals and their immediate collapse ('their convictions already crumbling') into racism. While Fanon played a large role in demystifying the European left to African intellectuals, it would also be fair to add, I think, that he failed to develop a convincing internationalist position. While he was ready to denounce pseudo-solidarity, he did not define true solidarity (a task that still remains for contemporary African Marxists).

Fanon's other lasting contribution, in my view, was to correctly characterise the new ruling group as the class 'on the make'—the class which would use the fruits of independence to offset its historic disadvantage of not having amassed wealth before it acquired political power. Who cannot now agree with these words twenty-five years after Fanon first wrote them?

> In under-developed countries the bourgeois phase is impossibly arid. Certainly, there is a police dictatorship and a profiteering caste, but the construction of an elaborate bourgeois society seems to be condemned to failure. The ranks of decked-out profiteers whose grasping hands scrape up the bank notes from a poverty-stricken country will sooner or later be men of straw in the hands of the army, cleverly handled by foreign experts.[34]

In short, what Fanon achieved was to cut away the psychological prop, needed even by Nkrumah, to evoke the spirit of the European proletariat in support of Africa. The colonised peoples of Africa were on their own, not to be patronised by the European left and not to be beguiled by the promises of the new bourgeoisie.

So much for Fanon's positive contribution. Where Fanon was in error, to be blunt, was in his characterisation of the subordinate classes. This is a debate in which I have participated intermittently for over a decade and there are many nuances that would have to be added in a full account. But I would put the strongest rebuttal in this form. Fanon's peasantry was not sufficiently differentiated; it was by no means wholly revolutionary. He caricatured the working class and failed to see its political potential. He romanticised the urban lumpenproletariat and found a revolutionary trajectory where none existed. These are bold statements, but let me reinforce them by citing a supporting view by Nwafor. He also refers to the —

> erroneous formulation of Fanon on the role of social classes in the African revolution: his dismissal of the embryonic working class as a revolutionary force, based on the claim that the colonized proletariat is a "pampered", "comparatively privileged" social class. . . his treatment of the peasantry as a undifferentiated social whole, and the extraordinary view of the peasantry as "the only spontaneously revolutionary force" in colonial societies—as though, anyway, spontaneity were in itself a revolutionary virtue and not a weakness. . .in which furthermore, this undifferentiated whole not only is the only revolutionary force, but even more astonishingly, is "capable of directing the people's struggle"; his systematic attempt to cultivate and promote distrust and conflict instead of unity between the proletariat and the peasantry; the romantic and absurd celebration of the lumpenproletariat, which though it is seen as. . .the "hopeless dreg of humanity" will nevertheless emerge, outside of history and its class situation, as the "urban spearhead" of the revolution, etc.[35]

While developing this critique of Fanon, Nwafor favourably contrasts the work of Amilcar Cabral whom he sees as offering 'a rich and unerring guide' to the problems of forging a revolutionary alliance of all the exploited and oppressed'.[36] The word 'unerring' perhaps smacks of faith, not logic, but I would again broadly concur with Nwafor. Before turning to Cabral's class analysis, for which he is justly praised, it is worth mentioning just two of his other observations which represent an advance on prior African Marxist thinking.

First, on the issue of neocolonialism, Cabral refines Nkrumah's view, which tended to affirm a uniformity between the colonial powers, even though the power of American finance capital and the South African Oppenheimer empire lurked not far behind.[37] He concurs in the view that 'independence was given to the colonised countries by the colonial powers as a means of securing the indirect domination of colonised people' but is immediately constrained to add that Portugal could not accomplish this feat because it did not have the necessary economic infrastructure to do so. Portugal could be an imperialist agent, but not an imperialist power. As he put it in a marvellously succinct phrase, Portugal 'cannot decolonise because she cannot neocolonise'.[38] Though this might appear at first to be a minor variation on a common theme, Cabral is able to use this observation to understand why the armed struggle had to take the form it did. In most neocolonial or cognate dependency theories, there is no way of explaining why the struggle for socialism has to take the form of a national liberation struggle. By precisely understanding the nature of Portugal's own weakness, Cabral is able to show that there is a structural logic behind the armed struggle. Equally, he shows that it was not fortuitous that Britain's African colonies (with the notable exception of Kenya, where the presence of settlers upset the neocolonialist apple-cart) were constitutionally decolonised.

Cabral's second great strength is one that echoes Padmore's observations on Tito and Mao Tse-Tung: he theorises with relevance and modesty, but without excess reverence for received Marxist canons.

> Moving from the reality of one's own country towards the creation of an ideology for one's struggle doesn't imply that one has pretensions to be a Marx or a Lenin or any other great ideologist, but is simply a necessary part of the struggle. I confess that we didn't know these grand theorists terribly well when we began. We didn't know them half as well as we do now! We needed to know them in order to judge what measure we could borrow from their experience to help our situation – but not necessarily to apply the ideology blindly just because it is very good ideology.[39]

I felt it necessary to preface my remarks on Cabral's class analysis with his views on Portuguese colonialism and the construction of his own ideology precisely because there has been a tendency among some sections of the African left to assume too wide an applicability for Cabral's views on class. This does not, of course, mean that they apply only to Guinea–Bissau, but that due caution along the lines indicated by Cabral himself, needs to be exercised when transposing the context.[40] Cabral's views are also informed by very practical considerations – which groups have proved amenable to the ideological messages of the national liberation struggle? Thus:

> In Guinea the peasants are subjected to a kind of exploitation equivalent to slavery; but even if you try to explain to them that they are being exploited and robbed, it is difficult to convince them by means of an unexperienced explanation of a technico-economic kind that they are the most exploited people; whereas it is easier to convince the workers and the people employed in the towns who earn, say, ten escudes a day for a job in which a European earns between 30 and 50 that they are being subjected to massive exploitation and injustice, because they can see.[41]

Although Cabral was to find in the peasantry a ballast of cultural resistance which could be turned to the purposes of national liberation, there is no doubt that the balance of his analysis of the peasantry contradicts Fanon's belief in the 'revolutionary spontaneity' of the countryside. Equally, far from seeing the working class as part of the 'bourgeois fraction of colonised peoples' (Fanon) the working class is seen by him as an essential part of the revolution, particularly in the post-colonial phase. However, he again makes the hard-headed point that, in Guinea at least, the working class was too small to play the role of a dominant class, both because it could not bring the physical might to bear on the colonial state apparatus, and because it could not provide a major source of revolutionary class leadership.[42] This view was consistent with the fact that Guinea, even by comparison with other West African states, was underdeveloped in respect of commercial and industrial employment.

As to the lumpenproletariat, he moves to a position much closer to that of Fanon, but only by subordinating Fanon's (and Marx's) category within a wider notion of 'déclassés'. For Cabral, the lumpenproletariat proper (beggars, prostitutes, the permanently unemployed and so on) conforms to the classical account provided in the *Communist Manifesto*. They easily became the 'bribed fools of reactionary intrigue' (as Marx and Engels put it) and in Guinea were normally penetrated by the notorious secret police, the PIDE. In this respect, Cabral's view on the lumpenproletariat appears to be in contrast to Fanon's argument that the lumpenproletariat could act as 'the armed spearhead of a revolution based in the countryside'. But this is only superficially the case as the lumpenproletariat is for Cabral only one section of the déclassés. He writes:

> The other group is not really made up of déclassé peoples, but we have not found the exact term for it; it is a group to which I have paid a lot of attention and it has proved to be extremely important in the national liberation struggle. It is mostly made up of young people who are connected to petty bourgeois or workers' families, who have recently arrived from the rural areas and generally do not work; they also have close relations with the rural areas as well as with the towns (and even with the Europeans).[43]

The clue to unlocking this ambiguous group lies in seeing it as culturally (or if you like ideologically) ambivalent — part country and part town, African but Europeanised. Even though this group came from at least two (and perhaps more) classes, it shared this cultural ambiguity with that section of the petty bourgeoisie that threw in its lot with the nationalist struggle. We can immediately recognise the empathy Cabral feels for this group in his own autobiographical aside. 'To take my own case as a member of the petty bourgeois group which launched the struggle in Guinea, I was an agronomist working under a European who everybody knew was one of the biggest idiots in Guinea; I could have taught him his job with my eyes shut but he was the boss: this is something which counts a lot, this is the confrontation which really matters. This is of major importance when considering where the initial idea of the struggle came from'.[44]

In constructing his revolutionary class alliance, Cabral was careful to distinguish between the nationalist phase — where of necessity the progressive elements of the petty bourgeoisie had to predominate, and the post-colonial phase where, in his famous phrase, it has to 'commit class suicide' and give way to the hegemony of the working class. In nearly every African country where petty bourgeois elements have seized control of the nationalist movement, even where they have enunciated a radical programme (as in Tanzania), they have clung on to the post-colonial state for dear life. Cabral's murder gave us a clear enough signal that such a tendency would predominate. The 'second independence', the debouching of the anti-colonial struggle into the struggle for socialism, is a long time coming!

Conclusion

I have not sought to develop any startling new theoretical propositions in this chapter. Rather, by re-examining the views of four major political theorists, I have tried to show how a distinctive Marxism, relevant to the African continent, became established from the 1930s onward. Moreover, as the limits of earlier formulations became clear, ordered and successive thematic logics developed. Early general attacks on imperialism gave way to detailed anti-colonial programmes which often were structured around the specific political and ideological practices of the different colonial powers. In the case of Portugal, Cabral was able to show how the distinctive character of the metropolis impelled the logic of a particular form of struggle. The object of the anti-colonial struggle was too often seen simply as the capture of the colonial state rather than the activation of a revolution from below. The seizure of political power, and the stalling of further popular initiatives (as Cabral and Fanon concurred) was in fact the particular object of struggle by the pro-nationalist section of the petty bourgeoisie or (where it was better developed) the bourgeoisie proper. On the question of when such a class could be displaced or superseded and which elements were likely to be involved, there is disagreement between Fanon and Cabral.

I have not myself been slow to indicate my disagreement with or acceptance of the views of all four theorists with whom I have dealt. But this chapter is primarily not intended as a critique, but a more positive demonstration that Africa has long developed a distinctive Marxist tradition of its own. It is politically important to show that this is the case as there are always detractors ready to make assertions to the contrary. In a recent study of *The New Communist Third World* it is claimed that:

> A separate African Road to Socialism is more often talked about than, say, the Polish (or indeed the Vietnamese) Road. But in practice Polish Communist policies or wishes are specific and definite, spring in fairly clear ways from local circumstances and traditions, and form a permanent though developing body of more or less coherent doctrine. But none of this can be claimed for any form of Afro-Marxism. Africans. . .are simply not educated enough, nor have they a long and impressive enough tradition to found a viable native form of Marxism, or indeed any other all embracing ideology.[45]

This can obviously be dismissed as insulting or racist rubbish, unamenable to the evidence I have presented of the long grounding of a Marxist tradition on and in Africa. But such crude revivals of the cold war, with Africans playing the role of passive dupes to the machinations of the Kremlin, need refutation for another purpose and another audience. As Usman argues, Marxist ideas are frequently dismissed before they are heard, on the grounds of their impotency or their supposed alien quality.

> In many countries today to be associated with Marx's name, alone, can bring instant and brutal punishment, often in the form of torture or

execution, by official or unofficial armies or death squads. . . In countries like Nigeria where today the current development of the political struggles does not allow for the open repression of anyone associated with Marx's idea, these ideas are distorted, devalued, or just confused, ridiculed and mystified by those who live from the exploitation of man by man, and their intellectual clients. The commonest way these ideas are devalued, and denied, is to dismiss them as not being African.[46]

What I hope I have shown is that Marxist ideas applied to the African continent have a history, tradition and internal logic. Their emergence in Africa is consistent with a universal tendency in Marxism to move away from the narrow orthodoxies of received Marxism, towards versions firmly anchored in local circumstances. Contemporary leftist theorists in Africa have a rich tradition on which to draw.

Notes

1. Y.B. Usman, 'Karl Marx and the Analyses of the Politics of Contemporary Africa', a paper given to the *Centenary Conference on Marx and Africa* (Ahmadu Bello University, Zaria, 14–18 March 1983) pp. 1, 4.

2. See J. Degras (ed), *The Communist International 1919–1943. Documents Vol. II* (Frank Cass, London, 1971). This is not to say that this was the only preoccupation. Within three African countries— Egypt, Sudan and South Africa—early communist parties were formed, each with their distinctive preoccupations. In the French colonies, extensions of the French communist and socialist parties were also established in the pre-war period. As they tended to be dominated by metropolitan organisations or concerns, I've considered them to be 'external' to Africa. The same is largely true of the specialist groups of Soviet Africanists that were formed in the 1920s and 1930s, though there is a major figure of this period, Endre Sik, whose work has recently attracted some sympathetic and critical attention by Marxist scholars (E. Sik, *Establishing Marxist Study of the Socio-Economic Problems of Black Africa*, mimeographic extracts of a paper delivered to NIANKP, Moscow, 13 April 1929; H. Bernstein, 'Marxism and African History–Endre Sik and his Critics', *Kenya Historical Review*, Vol. V, No. 1, 1977; C. Darch and G. Littlejohn, *Endre Sik and the Development of African Studies in the USSR: a Study Agenda for 1919*, mimeograph paper, Centre of African Studies, Maputo, Mozambique, n.d.). I've also ignored the cultural revivals begun in association with *Présence Africaine*, which though external in one sense, did provide a useful meeting ground for colonised blacks from the Caribbean and Africa.

3. A. Nzula et al, *Forced Labour in Colonial Africa* (Zed Press, London, 1979).

4. No Sizwe (pseudonym), *One Azania, One Nation: the National Question in South Africa* (Zed Press, London, 1979).

5. G. Padmore, *The Life and Struggles of Negro Toilers* (Sun Dance Press, New York, 1979).

6. ——— *What is the ITUC – NW?* (a pamphlet issued by the organisation, 1932).

7. —————— *Africa: Britain's Third Empire* (Dennis Dobson, London, 1949).

8. —————— *Pan-Africanism or Communism: the Coming Struggle for Africa* (Dennis Dobson, London, 1956).

9. Ibid., pp. 107, 304, 305, 349.

10. Ibid., pp. 289–90.

11. Ibid., p. 314.

12. Ibid., p. 345.

13. Ibid., p. 345.

14. Ibid., p. 319.

15. Ibid., p. 339.

16. Ibid., p. 339.

17. K. Nkrumah, *Towards Colonial Freedom* (Heinemann, London, 1962) pp. 44–5 (first published, 1947).

18. Ibid., p. 43.

19. Ibid., pp. 11, 13.

20. Ibid., pp. xvi, xviii.

21. Ibid., p. 33.

22. K. Nkrumah, *Africa Must Unite* (Mercury Books, London 1965) pp. 216–22.

23. Ibid., pp. 205–15.

24. Ibid., pp. 214, 219.

25. K. Nkrumah, *Neo-colonialism: the Last Stage of Imperialism* (Nelson, London, 1965) p. 259.

26. —————— *Ghana (Autobiography)* (Heinemann, London, 1957).

27. —————— *I Speak of Freedom* (Heinemann, London, 1961).

28. See for example K. Nkrumah (1961) op. cit., pp. 232–44.

29. K. Nkrumah, *Class Struggle in Africa* (Panaf Books, London, 1970).

30. F. Fanon, *Studies in a Dying Colonialism* (Monthly Review Press, New York, 1965); *The Wretched of the Earth* (Penguin, Harmondsworth, 1967a); *Towards the African Revolution* (Monthly Review Press, New York 1967).

31. See for example B.M. Perinbam, 'Fanon and the Revolutionary Peasantry: the Algerian Case', *Journal of Modern African Studies*, Vol. 11, No. 3, 1973; and N. Nghe, 'Frantz Fanon et les problèmes de l'indépendence', *'La pensée*, 107, 1963.

32. F. Fanon (1965), op. cit., p. 61.

33. —————— (1967), op. cit., p. 79.

34. Ibid., (1967a), p. 140.

35. A. Nwafor, "Imperialism and Revolution in Africa", *Monthly Review*, April 1975, p. 27.

36. Ibid.

37. K. Nkrumah, *Neo-colonialism*, op. cit.

38. A. Cabral, *Our People Are Our Mountains* (Committee for Freedom in Mozambique, Angola and Guinea, London, 1972) p. 14.

39. Ibid., p. 21.

40. McCulloch draws the interesting conclusion that Cabral's work 'is far more relevant to the task of forging a general theory of class conflict in Africa', precisely because it is, 'at least formally confined to an exposition of the characteristics of Guinean Society'. By contrast, Fanon's work, by

starting from more general principles, is less widely applicable. (J. McCulloch, *In the Twilight of Revolution: the Political Theory of Amilcar Cabral* (Routledge and Kegan Paul, London, 1983) pp. 62–63.

41. A. Cabral, 'Brief Analysis of the Social Structure of Guinea–Bissau' in P. Gutkind and P. Waterman (eds), *African Social Studies: a Reader* (Monthly Review Press, New York, 1977) p. 230.

42. J. McCulloch, op. cit., pp. 72–73.

43. A Cabral (1977), op. cit., p. 288.

44. Ibid., p. 121.

45. P. Wiles (ed), *The New Communist Third World* (Croom Helm, London, 1982) pp. 20–21, cited in B. Munslow, *Afrocommunism*? (Working Paper No. 4, Dept. of Political Theory and Institutions, University of Liverpool, 1984).

46. Y.B. Usman, op. cit., pp. 3–4.

3: The Left in Africa Today

by Ben Turok

The African continent is experiencing more instability and dislocation than at any time since the end of colonial rule. Most countries are undergoing severe political crises with governments becoming increasingly discredited as they fail to deliver the promises they made at independence. The goodwill accorded them in the early years when the African masses took pride in their apparent independence has now gone. Instead, there is a growing acceptance that neocolonialism, the successor to the colonial system, is largely moribund. An extraordinary torpor fills the air. The forces of production have received no major impetus; the ruling classes are mainly parasitic on foreign capital. State capital and private indigenous national capital lack the drive to launch autocentric development.

Notwithstanding the moribund character of the neocolonial system and the poverty of the majority of the people, there are few instances of substantial organised opposition. There are no large political parties representing labour; even the trade unions often lack organic links with the bulk of the working class. Significant peasant associations are the exception, while other forms of popular organisation are equally scarce. In the multi-party states the established parties contend for office without offering real alternative policies. In the one-party neocolonial states, radical opposition forces are largely coerced into silence. Only the military seem to loom as a constant threat to the regimes, though their capacity to exercise physical power is not matched by their ability to put forward alternative political programmes.

In this scenario, what scope is there for Marxism, the natural alternative to neocolonial capitalism? On the face of it, not much. Indeed, one scholar scoffed at 'neo-Marxist scholarship', which searches in vain for political radicalism in sub-Saharan Africa.[1]

Others take a different view. In possibly the most thorough study of emergent communism in Africa, the Ottaways noted that seven of Africa's 50 independent countries were under the rule of self-proclaimed Marxist-Leninist leadership while another nine embraced some brand of socialism. (Since their count, Zimbabwe and Burkina Faso have joined the ranks.) They concluded that the 'probability of the spread of Marxism-Leninism to other black African countries also seemed extremely high'. Belief in a rather orthodox Marxism-Leninism seemed to be growing steadily and 'the opportunities have multiplied for the Afro-Marxists to come to power'.[2]

The Ottaways believe that in some countries at least, Marxist–Leninists are not 'just mouthing rhetoric' but are seriously attempting to build a communist economic and political order. Furthermore, they maintain that these developments are rooted in internal processes and are not the consequence of external Soviet or Cuban pressures as Western sources often suggest. Indeed, they argue that the Soviet Union is actually rather sceptical about these tendencies, referring to 'socialist-oriented states' and 'pre-socialist reforms' when African leaders make much larger claims about their efforts.

These perceptions are echoed in another major study which found that a new Marxist dynamic was underway. Objective conditions favour its development: 'radical forces, even if small in number, have a substantial chance to assume control of the reins of local authority here and there'.[3] The study also found that the impetus for this shift to the left lies in internal, not external, developments. The Soviet Union would not wish to dispute such findings— except that it would insist that Soviet material aid to Mozambique, Angola and the African National Congress of South Africa has proved its genuine support for countries and movements with whom the Soviets have some affinity.

Observers who are far from sympathetic to communism therefore agree that Marxism–Leninism will make considerable headway in the coming period. It is also now widely acknowledged that Marxism–Leninism has taken root in Africa and is being applied creatively.[4] This chapter sets out to explore the current political basis for such an expansion. This is a difficult task, however. There are no systematic sources and few considered assessments on which to draw; even the proponents of Marxism have not brought together the necessary data. What follows, therefore, is necessarily a preliminary survey of the situation. However, the material presented below does point to a substantial Marxist presence in Africa, with considerable potential for mutual encouragement and cross-fertilisation over the whole continent. A Pan-African Marxist movement is not in prospect but the scope for its development clearly exists.

The bearers of Marxist ideology

Apart from a few countries such as South Africa and the Sudan, where Marxism has had a long history, its presence in the rest of Africa is for the most part quite recent. The Pan-African movement made some moves towards Marxism during its early period but there was no fusion with it. For instance, the Fifth Pan-African Congress, held in Manchester in 1945, adopted Marxist socialism as its philosophy, and several important leaders such as Nkrumah paid extended visits to the Soviet Union. But moves of this kind were aborted by two developments.[5]

First, Britain adopted a policy of co-optation of African leaders following the advice of Sir Andrew Cohen: 'successful cooperation with nationalism is our greatest bulwark against communism in Africa'.[6]

Secondly, anti-communism found strong supporters within the Pan-African movement itself. George Padmore's book, *Pan Africanism or Communism: The Coming Struggle for Africa*, succeeded in forcing the removal of Marxist conceptions of class struggle from Pan-Africanism and replacing it with nationalism. It is not clear now why Nkrumah and other radicals allowed this to happen, but it may be that the urge to build an alliance with reformists like Senghor and Houphuet–Boigny (who were important figures in anti-colonial movements) was a factor. Subsequently, within Ghana itself, British demands that independence be ceded to 'responsible' people encouraged the watering down of Nkrumah's ideological stance. After independence he adopted a mystified form of socialism which he called 'Consciencism', which more charitable critics ascribe to a need to placate his class opponents in Ghana. Given Nkrumah's prominence in the Pan-African movement, others followed his lead with only W.E.B. Du Bois, the grand old man of Pan-Africanism, moving to the left over the years and joining the US Communist Party towards the end of his life.

A class explanation for the abandonment of Marxism in the post-independence period was given in an outstanding essay written by Walter Rodney for the Sixth Pan-African Congress in Dar es Salaam in June 1974. Rodney, a Guyanese historian who steadily gained in stature as an outstanding Marxist until his assassination, argued that independence was the turning point for Africa. Whereas during the anti-colonial struggle the petty bourgeoisie, as the leading class, had played a progressive role, it now betrayed the nationalist cause. The petty bourgeoisie accepted a subordinate role to imperialism and neutralised or eliminated Marxist and other left wing elements. Rodney argued that in turning on the socialists, these leaders became an obstacle to the African revolution. Their Pan-Africanism became enshrined in the formal institutions of the Organisation of African Unity (OAU), which became an institution for resolving petty squabbles between reactionary regimes. Meanwhile, attempts to establish Pan-Africanism as the focus for movements which espoused class politics made no headway.[7]

The barring of Marxism from the official arena did not, however, eliminate it from the continent. Instead, the evident political barrenness of its surrogate, African Socialism, and the floundering of most independent regimes, created a need for an alternative. The basis for a critique of post-independence society was laid by Frantz Fanon whose trenchant exposure of colonial indoctrination touched a raw nerve. He unveiled the true role of the indigenous bourgeoisie as an unproductive, parasitic class confined to the role of intermediary between the indigenous people and imperialism. Its political parties in the post independence period were engaged in a fraudulent game of deceiving and demobilising the people.[8]

One of those influenced by Fanon was Amilcar Cabral, who became one of the foremost critics of neocolonialism and the inspiration for the revolution in Guinea–Bissau. Cabral's first concerns were that revolution should not end in the mere 'raising of a flag' and that it should establish socialism. Without ever acknowledging himself as a Marxist, Cabral has never-theless been one of the most important bearers of Marxism in Africa and beyond. Apart from the power of his analysis of the process of revolutionary struggle, Cabral also brought the prism of class analysis to bear on colonialism and neocolonialism, in a way which put his theories well in advance of those of his contemporaries.

While he was in office, Nkrumah's ideological work was confounded by the desire for originality for its own sake. His writing after his removal from office gained in clarity and commitment. His books were widely read across the continent, reinforcing interest in the basic propositions of Marxism-Leninism. His contemporary Sekou Touré's record was the reverse. Having made a great impact with his early published work on the struggle for democracy and socialism in Guinea, he retreated into obscurantism in later years.

Few other political figures were significant bearers of Marxist thought until Mozambique and Angola were liberated and their respective parties adopted Marxism–Leninism. During the struggle, however, publications like *Mozambique Revolution*, which had a fairly wide circulation, were written in what were basically Marxist concepts.[9]

Arguably an important element in hampering the development of Marxist thought in Africa was the reluctance to confront the dominant political pronouncements of people like Nyerere and Kaunda. It was certainly impossible for Cabral, Neto and others, who clearly differentiated between social democracy and scientific socialism, to set up an alternative theory for diplomatic reasons. It therefore fell to intellectuals in the universities and research institutes, who were not under the same constraints, to do so. Even here, however, the critique of 'official socialism' took an indirect form, mainly through the fundamentalist analysis of underdevelopment, imperialism and the like.

One leading figure has been Samir Amin, Africa's foremost political economist, whose books are essential reading in every university. His work on dependency, stalled development, and imperialism has advanced Marxist theory considerably, notwithstanding certain idiosyncratic views on 'Soviet imperialism' and 'imperialist' Western Marxists.[10]

Amin's position was vigorously attacked by Wadada Nabudere on the grounds that he and other centre-periphery theorists had departed from Lenin's conception of imperialism and finance capital. The crucial element was the production relationship between the imperialist bourgeoisie and the working class across national boundaries, not market problems of unequal exchange. Amin, said his critics, held a conception of exploitation which failed to differentiate adequately between classes in the centre and which militated against the creation of a broad alliance of classes in the colonies and neocolonies against imperialism. The indigenous bourgeoisie could yet be patriotic since imperialism constrained its growth.[11] As we shall see, these issues have persistently haunted Marxist thought and frustrated the develop-ment of a consistent strategy in many countries.

Another important intervention has been Issa Shivji's path-breaking analysis of class formation and class struggle in Tanzania.[12] He argued that the ruling social group was irreversibly petty bourgeois and reactionary. His position was attacked by John Saul who held that there was a progressive wing within the ruling petty bourgeoisie which was attempting to move, albeit unsuccessfully, to socialism.[13] The debate has echoed across the continent as judgements are made about the character of the classes in power in post-colonial states. In a powerful analysis, Nzongola-Ntalaja has argued that the petty bourgeoisie of colonial times becomes the state bourgeoisie of neocolonialism, continuing to perform the role of intermediary between imperialism and the people. It cannot, therefore, be progressive.[14] A similar position had been debated in relation to Kenya, turning around whether the bourgeoisie was an 'auxiliary class' to foreign capital, or a class capable of a certain degree of autonomous growth.[15]

Rather more explicitly political writings, in the sense of an overt attempt to pose strategic alternatives, have been scarce in African universities, an exception being Claude Ake's *Revolutionary Pressures in Africa*.

Babu's recent *African Socialism or Socialist Africa*? has been widely read. An important vehicle for radical authors is the *Review Of African Political Economy* which has established an international reputation as the most scholarly journal in African studies. The *Journal of African Marxists* is more explicitly committed to a Marxist perspective. It gives preference to work by African authors, and aims to stimulate Marxist study groups rather than serve as a purely academic vehicle. The journal has functioning national committees in various countries and has become a significant focus for Marxist discussion and organisation on the continent.

In the absence of open political debate in most neocolonies, the work of academics may be the only vehicle for serious discussion. Although this work is often individualistic and idiosyncratic it may reach beyond the campus, sometimes carrying radical ideas to a wider public. Marxist student groups exist on most campuses, becoming the nucleus for embryonic Marxist organisations in the case of Ghana, Zaire, Liberia and the Gambia. It is common for political tensions generated on campus to spill over into wider society, at times triggering off important battles. There has been a clear link between student politics and army action in the Sudan, Ghana and Kenya.

But there is, nevertheless, a vast gap between the work of intellectuals and student politics, and the political life of Marxist parties in Africa. These parties are numerous, active across the continent, and publish a considerable body of literature. Yet they are rarely mentioned in the official press or even in academic literature.

For instance, the *African Communist*, organ of the South African Communist Party (the oldest on the continent, being founded in 1921) is a source of useful documentary material and comment. The Sudanese Party also publishes a *Sudan Bulletin* which does not however have as wide a circulation.

The *African Communist* lists the following communist and workers parties ·in Africa: the Communist Party of Tunisia, the Party of Independence and

Labour of Senegal (previously known as the Party of African Independence, PAI), the Party of Liberation and Socialism of Morocco, the Communist Party of Lesotho, the Communist Party of Reunion, the Congolese Party of Labour, the South African Communist Party and the Communist Party of the Sudan.[16]

There are many other parties as well which are either communist or Marxist–Leninist: the Egyptian Communist Party (which publishes *Al-Intisser*), the Workers Party of Ethiopia (WPE), the Socialist Workers and Farmers Party of Nigeria, the Peoples Revolutionary Party of Benin, the Liberation Movement of São Tomé and Principe, the Democratic Party of Guinea, the Party of Unity and National Progress of Burundi, the Vanguard of the Malagasy Revolution, the Progressive Peoples Front of the Seychelles, the Party of the Socialist Vanguard in Algeria (which replaced the Algerian Communist Party), the African Independence Party of Cape Verde (PAICV), the African Independence Party of Guinea and Cape Verde (PAIGC), Frelimo, MPLA Workers Party, and a movement of socialist orientation, the Polisario Front in the Western Sahara.

Membership figures for these Marxist parties are scarce. One source claimed that there were 60,000 members of 'Moscow-aligned' communist parties in 1971, with the largest being in Senegal, Nigeria and Madagascar.[17]

Several Western studies have found that there is a noticeable tendency for Africa's communist parties to hold views which are somewhat distinct from current Soviet positions. This is not to suggest that there are serious disagreements. Some of the points of divergence can be indicated briefly.

Soviet theorists tend to stress that the achievement of independence was a major victory for progressive forces everywhere. Independence meant that Africa was no longer a reserve area of imperialism, but potentially a part of the world anti-imperialist camp. Leaders are referred to as 'revolutionary democrats' who pursue a progressive direction even though they have no substantial working class base. Some are said to become scientific socialists in due course. This positive view also applies to state interventions, such as nationalisation, which are seen as first steps in solving national problems of development. It is said to open the way to a non-capitalist development leading to socialism, a transition which is feasible because the bourgeoisie is weak and capitalism is not well entrenched. All but the most flagrantly compradorist fractions of the bourgeoisie are treated relatively positively and great emphasis is placed on their natural desire for genuine political and economic independence from imperialism. An alliance of forces which includes sections of the bourgeoisie is seen to be essential: 'The denigration of the national aspect of the revolution leads to ultra left and destructive policies'.[18]

Critics of these positions instead highlight the class differences which have been exacerbated after independence. In particular the bourgeoisie and petty bourgeoisie are castigated as having betrayed the independence struggle and used their new powers within the state to gather the fruits of political independence. Furthermore, despite independence, the bourgeoisie and the state have become increasingly compradorist, appendages of foreign capital. There is therefore no real basis for an alliance with the bourgeoisie, or sections of it, against imperialism. Even state nationalisations are merely a device to enhance foreign exploitation with a share of the benefits going to the indigenous bourgeoisie. Hence Marxists should stress class struggle rather than national unity against imperialism.

There are some Marxists, however, such as those in the Sudanese Communist Party, who deploy a more flexible analysis of the bourgeoisie and petty bourgeoisie and of the nature of possible alliances against imperialism and neocolonialism. As we shall see, this party also developed a sophisticated approach to alliances with elements of the military against the extreme reaction of the Numeiri regime.

Marxism and national liberation movements

Before independence, African Marxists grappled with the strategic and tactical problems posed by the nature of the class forces in the liberation movements in their countries. Aware that the working class was often not the leading force and that their own role was not primary in the broad coalitions, they nevertheless wanted to remain an independent force within the larger national liberation movement. This has been the classical position of Marxism–Leninism to ensure that socialist objectives are not lost sight of in the struggle for broad democratic goals. But there was also a fear of betrayal on the part of the petty bourgeois leadership which they felt might renege on the revolution which had to be both national, i.e. establishing a genuinely independent state, and democratic, i.e. releasing the political energies of the working people. This aspiration to an independent role has not been easily sustained, and there has been a wide range of experiences in the relationship between Marxists and the national liberation movements.

In Algeria, for example, communists came into conflict with the National Liberation Front (FLN) leadership which wanted the Communist Party to abandon its separate existence and join in the common struggle in a single organisation. The CP refused and faced a long clandestine struggle to establish its legitimacy. Even in 1977, the CP continued to declare its aim of a successful 'mass front and an authentic vanguard party'.[19]

Similarly, in Egypt, when the radical officers overthrew King Farouk in a coup on 23 July 1952, their action was accompanied by the jailing of trade unionists and communists.[20] Subsequently the Communist Party dissolved itself in order to facilitate the consolidation of the anti-feudal and anti-imperialist forces but this did not save them from repression. The party was revived in 1975 with the objective of renewing the struggle for a genuine national democratic revolution and subsequent advance to socialism.[21]

The Sudanese Communist Party has long maintained a stubbornly independent position despite the temptation to merge with the many broad political coalitions of popular struggle (similar to those which overthrew

Numeiri in 1985).[22] But sustaining its independence has meant that it has suffered severe repression when the tide was running against freedom, as it has frequently since independence in 1956.

The South African experience has been quite different. Close co-operation exists between the principal elements in the liberation struggle, the African National Congress (ANC) and the South African Communist Party (SACP). But this has not always been the case. The African National Congress, founded in 1912, was controlled by petty bourgeois nationalists in the first decades of its existence. At the same time a diverse group of white trade unionists and emigrés from Eastern Europe began to coalesce into a communist party which was formed in 1921. After a decade of misguided dedication to organising white workers, the party slowly reoriented itself to the black working class, and adjusted its policies to the need for national liberation of the oppressed black people. The ANC, in turn, slowly shed its anti-communism. Since that time, the SACP has kept its independent organisation and journal while struggling to develop and intensify its alliance with the ANC. This process is greatly assisted by the joint membership of communists in the two organisations, some at the highest levels. The effect of this collaboration is that the ANC has been influenced against narrow nationalism and chauvinism, while the SACP has avoided the trap of sectarianism.

The paths followed by Marxists–Leninists in Angola, Mozambique and Guinea–Bissau were different again. In each case there were committed Marxist–Leninists among the leadership from the beginning of the liberation struggles, for instance Agostinho Neto, who was President of the MPLA, and Marcelino Dos Santos, who became Vice President of Frelimo. As liberation drew nearer these Marxists wished to see the emergence of an explicitly Marxist organisation prior to independence but it was not possible. However, within seven months of independence, the MPLA declared its adherence to Marxism–Leninism and to the goal of a 'peoples democracy' with the workers as a 'leading force' in society. Likewise, Frelimo's Third Congress in February 1977 adopted Marxism–Leninism and transformed the liberation front into a 'vanguard party of the worker-peasant alliance'.[23] While the role of a few leaders was crucial to this development, it is also the case that the nature of the struggle had laid the basis for a move to the left. The long years of struggle had created socialist cadre and anti-capitalist policies. Machel has also revealed that there was a *de facto* vanguard within Frelimo made up of members of the army, whose role was seen increasingly to be essentially political.[24] This rather novel formulation clearly requires further study.

These movements broke with precedent in Africa. Leaders like Sekou Touré and Nkrumah had shown considerable political courage and undoubtedly understood scientific socialism. But they were reluctant to pursue socialism, perhaps for fear of endangering the coalition of forces which brought them to power.

In countries like Madagascar, Benin and the Congo there were no significant Marxist groups before independence. The creation of Marxist states has been as much due to the personal convictions of a few individuals at the top than anything else. The inconsistencies of these regimes, and their weakness, is unsurprising in view of the absence of developed class forces in support of a socialist programme.[25]

Marxist states in Africa

The emergence of Marxist states in Africa is therefore more a result of action from above than the expression of a mass proletarian movement led by a communist party as in Russia, China or Vietnam. That African Marxist states cannot easily implement socialist policies is not surprising; this cannot be done without the people having gone through a substantial experience of fighting capitalism and so gaining a positive attitude to socialism. It is probably accurate to say that the totality of socialism on the continent is small. Yet this is only half the picture.

There are now more than twelve states whose ruling parties espouse Marxism or some related form of scientific socialism as the official ideology. These are: Ethiopia, Benin, São Tomé and Principe, the Congo, Burkina Faso, Guinea, Burundi, Malagasy, Seychelles, Cape Verde, Mali, Guinea-Bissau, Mozambique, Angola, and Zimbabwe.

Many of these states are Marxist in name only, with little having been achieved in transforming the relations of production, mobilising working people, and creating the infrastructure of a socialist state. The difficulty of doing so is evident in a country like Ethiopia where a Marxist–Leninist party, the Workers Party of Ethiopia, was established only in 1984. In Mali the ruling socialist-oriented party of President Moussa Traore, the Democratic Union of the Mali People (UPDM), has been in continuing difficulty and is now faced with an opposition Marxist–Leninist party, the Party of Revolution and Democracy (PMRD).[26]

While these states proclaim their allegiance to Marxism–Leninism with great vigour, their degree of movement in a recognisably socialist direction is open to question. No doubt a major factor is the absence of a class conscious working class with the necessary experience of fighting a capitalist class in a class, as opposed to national, struggle. Another is the difficulty of breaking dependency relations with former colonial powers. Many of these countries are small, and their capacity for reorienting their economic relations is extremely limited. So rhetoric comes easy but fundamental restructuring is another matter.

Despite these limitations, the fact that so many regimes should opt for Marxist–Leninist ideology is itself significant. Some argue that it is a smoke-screen for petty bourgeois accumulation through the state. Yet why do these states chose Marxism–Leninism? Why the revolutionary ideology of Cuba and Vietnam, an ideology so dangerous to the survival of capitalism? Why not 'authenticity' or 'humanism' or 'Ujamaa' or 'Negritude'? The most plausible explanation seems to be that there is an imperative for these regimes to identify with an ideology which promises an alternative to neocolonialism and which properly resonates with the aspirations of their masses. Whether the leaders of these states have a genuine commitment to Marxism–Leninism or not (which can only be determined by their actions) there is some imperative for them to adopt revolutionary rather than reformist positions.

A puzzling new addition to Marxism–Leninism in Africa is Zimbabwe. Although the ruling party ZANU made great play of Marxism–Leninism during the war of liberation, it was often claimed by critics that this was somewhat artificial. Indeed, its early years in power have not been notable either for a dismantling of white economic power, or for a curbing of that tendency which has been the hallmark of African independence in most countries, the rapid evolution of an African petty bourgeoisie using political and administrative office for personal accumulation. One explanation is that, in its insecurity, the Mugabe regime finds it necessary to reintroduce the ideology of the war to keep the loyalty of the thousands of militants who fought the war in the name of Marxism–Leninism, rather than for African power or ethnic hegemony. Without their support, the regime would crumble. If this argument is correct, it would be yet another demonstration that Marxism–Leninism has established a following on the ground in Africa.

A Soviet source claims that 'socialist-oriented countries', a wider category than I have used which includes Tanzania, Zambia and others, covers 30 percent of the land surface and 25 percent of Africa's population.[27] If we add the number of parties and movements, the Marxist presence in Africa is considerable indeed, and the potential resources in both financial and personnel terms are massive. It is all the more remarkable, therefore, that none of the Marxist states has established a political centre for the advancement of Marxism on the continent. (Though Nkrumah did establish the Ideological Institute at Winneba in 1960.) This absence is obviously not due to a lack of resources. There is, clearly, no commitment to encouraging a Pan-African Marxist movement, or even to collaboration between Marxist governments, though the movements in the former Portuguese colonies did establish the organisation CONCP and the five lusophone states do meet from time to time. Each of the Marxist states have bilateral relations with the Soviet Union and with other socialist countries which are seen as 'natural allies'. Treaties of friendship have been signed by Angola, Mozambique, Ethiopia, Congo and others, though none has been admitted to COMECON. Mozambique was refused entry recently. It is understandable that Pan-Africanist ideology, which became entangled with anti-communism, should be replaced by 'proletarian internationalism', thereby including the socialist camp and the working class of the West, but it is not clear why regional co-operation for economic and political purposes has not occurred.

The only public evidence of such co-operation was a conference of communist and workers parties of Africa held in 1978, which adopted a 'Communist Call to Africa'.[28] Yet participation was clearly very limited and there has been no obvious campaign to pursue the issues raised. Indeed the only time representatives from Marxist states and communist parties seem to meet, at least publicly, is at some commemorative conference in Eastern Europe, such as the 1985 meeting marking the centenary of the Berlin Conference.

Curiously, reformist socialists have not been so tardy. They have created an Inter-African Socialist Organisation (IAS), headquartered in Tunis, with affiliations from Djibouti, the Gambia, Ghana, Mauritius, Morocco, Senegal, Somalia, Sudan and Tunisia.[29]

Marxists against neocolonial regimes

Nationalists often resisted the participation of Marxists—as individuals or groups—in the anti-colonial struggle. Yet the need for unity meant that ideological differences were overcome in the common cause of gaining independence. But since independence, Marxists have generally been isolated, as petty bourgeois and bourgeois elements put themselves at the head of the new regimes. The ideology of national development precluded any prioritisation of the claims of the working people while criticisms of bourgeois accumulation were denounced as being destructive.

At a seminar held in Cairo from 24 to 29 October 1966 entitled Africa: National and Social Revolution, several North African communists deplored the growing repression in their countries. Arguing that genuine independence had not been won and that imperialism was on the offensive and resorting to neocolonialism to thwart social revolution, some participants urged the intensification of struggle against the internal bourgeoisie which was seen to be blocking the path to genuine independence and socialism.[30]

A great deal of Marxist literature, however, particularly that from the socialist countries, seems reluctant to recognise that Africa has entered a new stage in its history: the period of neocolonialism. In contrast to colonialism, where the enemy was a foreign power, under neocolonialism, the immediate enemy lies within each country, in the shape of a comprador bourgeoisie generally in command of the state apparatus. Against the power of this bourgeoisie, African Marxists are a small force in an inhospitable arena. The natural base of Marxism is the working class. But this class is undeveloped, and therefore Marxists face great difficulty in establishing themselves. Furthermore, due to considerable confusion among theorists on the nature of neocolonialism, the problem of alliances has yet to be resolved.

The struggles of Marxists have met with drastic repression, the outstanding example being the Sudan. There, political independence under civilian rule in 1956 was followed by a coup and reactionary military rule. The Communist Party tried unsuccessfully to organise a general strike a few years later but it was not until 1964 that the universal disaffection and dislocation in the country brought back civilian rule. In 1965 there was a return to military rule, which was again overthrown by a progressive wing of the military, supported by the Communist Party and trade unions. Although a communist was included in the cabinet the Party was under constant pressure to dissolve itself in favour of a one-party system. Having seen the fate of the Egyptian communists, however, it demurred.[31]

On 12 February 1971 Numeiri, then President of the Revolutionary Command Council, accused the CP of treason and arrested 84 leading members. On 19 July 1971 there was a coup against Numeiri but two days later he returned to power and acted with great ruthlessness against the officers who led the coup and the communists. The position of the Party continued to be extremely tenuous thereafter, though its influence remained undiminished.

The strategy and tactics of the Sudanese Communist Party throws a great deal of light on the problems facing communists in other African states where the forces of the left are still undeveloped. On several occasions sections of the military have taken action against reaction without CP agreement. But where such actions have been supported by the masses, the CP has thrown in its own weight despite reservations about the prospects of success. In no other neocolony has a communist party achieved equal prominence or sustained a comparable struggle. Perhaps the nearest instance is the Cameroon where a long established Marxist movement, the Union of the People of Cameroon (UPC) waged a relentless struggle, both armed and political, against a violently repressive regime.

In Senegal, the left has been fragmented as in no other African country, with five parties claiming to be Marxist. Three of them originate from the PIA, which was founded in 1957. These are the LD–MPT, whose secretary-general is Abdoulaye Bathily and has no international affiliations, the PIT which is led by Dansokho and is recognised as the 'official' Marxist party by the Soviet Union, and the PIA which is led by Diop and is recognised by Rumania. The LCT and OST are small Trotskyist-inclined parties, while the PPS is a small non-Marxist socialist party. The AND–JEF/MRDN and UDP are thought to be Maoist in orientation.

In Nigeria, there has always been an abundance of socialist groups and journals. The largest and closest to Marxism–Leninisn was the Socialist Workers and Farmers Party which was formed in the early 1960s but ceased to exist in 1966. The Biafra War interrupted left politics and it was not until 1974 that a national Movement for Peoples Democracy was created. In 1976 an All-Nigerian Socialist Conference was held in Zaria but it failed to bring about the unity of the left. Ultimately, a group led by Ola Oni, a much respected national figure, became impatient with unity talks and formed the Socialist Party of Workers, Farmers and Youth. Two months later an alternative party came into being, the Socialist Working Peoples Party with a leadership drawn partly from trade union officials. This party has recently published a journal, *New Horizon* containing a section of material from *World Marxist Review*. Among other Nigerian left journals are *Theory and Practice*, *Vanguard*, *Socialist Journal*, *Social Forum* and *Nigerian Democratic Review*.

The general trend has been for Marxist-inspired groups, usually formed at universities, to come to prominence rather unexpectedly. A study of three

West African states found that such groups were important to the coups in Upper Volta and Dahomey and to a lesser extent in the Central African Republic. In Togo (1967), Congo Brazzaville (1963) and the Sudan (1963) such groups 'provided demonstrations, agitators and conspirators for the groups that seized power'.[32]

The combination of university-based Marxist groups consisting of staff and students with junior officers is a frequent occurrence and constitutes a strong element in political actions which are often successful, though generally only in the short term.

In the Gambia a combination of the Gambia Socialist Revolutionary Underground Party (GSRULP), said to have a Marxist orientation, elements of the police and army, and the students' organisation Movement for Justice in Africa (MOJA), held Banjul for three days in the coup of 30 July 1981, and were only dislodged from power by the Senegalese army. (An alternative version is that a move to oust the Prime Minister came from within the cabinet but as it gained an unexpected left momentum the Senegalese army intervened to stop the rebellion.)

In Kenya the university has been a centre of Marxist activity for many years – according to President Moi it is 'a breeding ground for subversion'. During 1982 there was continuing unrest on the campus, and the university was closed for an indefinite period. There were widespread reports that the students were involved in the Air Force coup of 1 August 1982 which posed the most serious threat yet to the Kenyan government. Hard evidence of collaboration between the students and the Air Force has not been produced but the state has argued that this was the case. Some students were allegedly killed in the shooting, while 60 were detained, some on very serious charges.[33]

The resurgence of the left in Ghana can be traced to the first Rawlings coup on 4 June 1979. Realizing that the opposition forces were too powerful, Rawlings resigned after a mere three months in a tactical retreat. Soon after, the June 4th Movement was formed with Rawlings as a founding member and later its chairman. Its organ, *The Workers' Banner*, launched on 26 October 1981, adopted a revolutionary line and sought to act as a political vanguard. In the second Rawlings coup on 31 December 1981, this movement was called upon to provide ideological support to the new government to help mobilise the People's Defence Committees and Workers' Defence Committees, Another movement had also come into being in 1980, the New Democratic Movement (NDM). It was formed by intellectuals who had previously existed in clandestine groups and circulated a publication, *Direction*. The NDM sought to develop a working class base and espoused policies which led to its being dubbed 'orthodox Marxist' as against the 'populist' June 4th Movement. However, in a matter of two years or so, both movements became alienated from the Rawlings regime on the grounds that it was retreating from a principled left position especially in its relations with the IMF.

Experience in Ghana and elsewhere indicates that a relatively small group of students and intellectuals cannot do more than generate a mood of resistance to a reactionary regime or support rebels in the army. They cannot fundamentally influence the direction a coup will take once the initial principal action has been taken. Indeed, in the case of a military coup, the radical character of the new government is likely to be soon dissipated as it begins to reflect its class interests, in most cases those of the bourgeoisie.[34] But this does not mean that student groups are insignificant. Indeed, there are cases where campus disturbances have sparked off wide actions.

Marxist students have acted in concert with workers as well as the military. In Zaire, a national student organisation, the General Union of Congolese Students (UGEC), in which a Marxist–Leninist wing was prominent, constituted the most stable and vocal legal opposition in Zaire in the 1960s. At its 1966 Congress it voted unanimously to make Zaire a socialist state and adopted scientific socialism as its ideology. Although the UGEC did not overtly go out to the workers, its protests and the arrests of its leaders made a considerable impact on the 'lumpenproletariat and the urban workers. It is thought that the massacre of Louvanium University students in 1969 was partly due to the fact that large numbers of Kinshasa workers had joined the protest'.[35]

There can be no doubt that the youth and student rebellions in Soweto and Langa in South Africa introduced a new willingness to sacrifice jobs, houses, and life itself in the mass upheavals in South Africa in the last decade. In a political vacuum, where opposition has been demolished or crushed, revolutionary-minded students may well have an impact way beyond their numbers and far outside their own class environment.

However, it would be a mistake to exaggerate the importance of student rebellions. Few have been able to sustain their actions for long. Yet other opposition groups have also experienced equal difficulties in establishing united action for long periods. Sustained and organised opposition is the exception. This may be partly due to 'the intricate mechanisms of neo-colonialism' which are a more elusive target than the colonial state.[36] The controversies in Marxist literature about the role of the petty bourgeoisie indicates that there is a real problem in identifying allies and targeting enemies. A far more persuasive reason in explaining the weakness of the opposition is the massive repression, especially of Marxist–Leninists, that has spread across the continent.

The situation in a country like Zambia is instructive. President Kaunda permits a considerable degree of press freedom and freedom of expression. He has facilitated the existence of a Marxist-oriented research bureau within the ruling party, UNIP, and he has allowed the teaching of scientific socialism in schools and defended it against attack by powerful church interests. Yet it cannot be said that Marxism–Leninism as a political tendency is free to flourish in Zambia, and that efforts to create a Marxist–Leninist organisation would not be crushed. Similarly, in Tanzania, in the heyday of Marxist agitation at the University of Dar es Salaam, President Nyerere made no bones about his strong opposition. Marxist–Leninists have learned that social democratic one-party states are not hospitable to revolutionary alternatives.

Perhaps the major strategic problem facing Marxist movements is the absence of solidarity across the continent. Walter Rodney revealed that African governments had agreed that dissident movements would not be allowed to operate from other territories. This rule has been largely observed but with the exceptions such as anti-Idi Amin groups in Tanzania, and perhaps a few others.

In anticipation of this coalition of governments against dissidents, the UPC urged, in May 1962, the creation of a Pan-African movement of radical organisations. The UPC opposed the proposal for a union of heads of state[37], fearing that such an organisation would isolate African revolutionary anti-imperialist and anti-neocolonialist forces and stifle the struggle for genuine independence and socialism. This proposed union of African heads of state became the OAU; there is no doubt that it has been a necessary organisation. But looking at the state of the left in Africa today, it is difficult to dismiss totally the UPC's call for a truly revolutionary Pan-African movement.

Notes

1. R. Jeffries, 'Political Radicalism In Africa: The Second Independence,' *African Affairs*, Vol. 77, No. 308, July 1978, p. 335.

2. D. and M. Ottaway, *Afrocommunism* (Africana Publishing Company, New York, 1980) pp. 1–2.

3. D.E. Albright, *Communism in Africa* (Indiana University Press, 1980) p. 232.

4. See the chapter by Robin Cohen in this volume.

5. K. Nkrumah, *Africa Must Unite* (Heinemann, London, 1963).

6. *Pan-Africanism: The Struggle Against Neocolonialism and Imperialism* (Afro-Caribbean Publications, Canada, 1975) p. 44.

7. *Sixth Pan African Congress: Resolutions and Selected Speeches* (Tanzania Publishing House, Dar es Salaam, 1976) p. 21–34.

8. F. Fanon, *The Wretched of the Earth* (Penguin, Harmondsworth, (1967).

9. Frelimo, *Mozambique Revolution* (Frelimo, Dar es Salaam).

10. S. Amin, *Class and Nation* (Heinemann, London, 1980).

11. D.W. Nabudere, *The Political Economy of Imperialism* (Zed Press, London, 1977) p. 235.

12. I.G. Shivji, *Class Struggles in Tanzania* (Tanzania Publishing House, Dar es Salaam, 1975).

13. J. Saul, The State in Post-Colonial Societies: Tanzania in J. Saul, *The State and Revolution in East Africa* (Heinemann, London, 1979).

14. Nzongola-Ntalaja, 'Class Struggle and National Liberation in Zaire' in B. Magubane and Nzongola-Ntalaja, *Proletarianization and Class Struggle in Africa* (Synthesis Publications, San Francisco, 1984).

15. C. Leys, *Underdevelopment in Kenya* (Heinemann, London, 1975) p. 271.

16. *The African Communist* (Inkululeko Publications, London, No. 54, 1973).

17. D. and M. Ottaway *Afrocommunism*, p. 30.

18. *African Communist*, No. 73, 1978. p. 126.

19. *African Communist*, No. 70, 1977, p. 126.

20. J. Woddis, *Armies and Politics* (Lawrence and Wishart, London, 1977) p. 72.

21. *African Communist*, No. 65, 1976.

22. F.B. Mahmoud, *The Sudanese Bourgeoisie: Vanguard of Development?* (Zed Press, London) p. 138.

23. D. and M. Ottaway, *Afrocommunism*, p. 76.

24. B. Munslow (ed), *Samora Machel: An African Revolutionary: Selected Speeches and Writings* (Zed Press, London, 1985).

25. K.N. Brutents, *National Liberation Revolutions Today* (Progress Publishers, Moscow, 1977).

26. *African Communist*, No. 90, 1982, p. 67.

27. G. Starushenko, *Why More Countries are Opting for Socialism in Africa and the World Today* (Novosti Publishing House, Moscow, 1982) p. 70.

28. *African Communist*, No. 75, 1978.

29. The full list of participants at the inaugural conference in Tunis, 26–28 February 1981, was: Chairman: President Bourguiba; Chairman of the Council: President Senghor; affiliates: Popular African League for Independence of Djibouti, Peoples Progressive Party of Gambia, Peoples National Party of Ghana, Mauritius Labour Party, Mauritania Social Democratic Party, Istiqlal of Morocco, Socialist Union of Popular Forces of Morocco, Socialist Party of Senegal, Revolutionary Socialist Party of Somalia, Socialist Union of Sudan, Destour Socialist Party of Tunisia. The official ideology was identified as 'democratic socialism'.

30. *African Communist*, No. 75, 1978.

31. J. Woddis, *Armies and Politics*, p. 104.

32. V.T. Le Vine, 'The Coups of Upper Volta, Dahomey, and the Central African Republic' in R. I. Rotberg and A.A. Mazrui (eds), *Protests and Power in Black Africa* (Oxford University Press, New York, 1970), p. 1070.

33. C. Legum, *Africa Contemporary Record* (Africana Publishing Company, 1982–3) pp. B--172.

34. J. Woddis, *Armies and Politics*, p. 42.

35. Nzongola-Ntalaja, *Class Struggles and National Liberation in Africa* (Omenana, 1982), p. 53.

36. R. Jeffries, 'Political Radicalism in Africa: the Second Independence'.

37. E. Mbuyinga, *Pan Africanism or Neo-Colonialism?* (Zed Press, London, 1982).

4: Women and the Transition to Socialism in sub-Saharan Africa

by Bie Nio Ong

The debate on socialist transition in sub-Saharan Africa has for too long failed to significantly address the role of women and women's struggles, although this is slowly being remedied. Essentially, there are two bodies of literature which address the topic. One stems from the Western Marxist-feminist tradition and another comes from within the African revolutionary movements themselves. The former have become increasingly aware that their analysis of the struggles of Third World women should be developed with some caution and on the basis of mutual respect, to avoid patronisation. Kimble and Unterhalter recently argued that theoretically, 'the analysis and objectives of Western feminism cannot be applied universally and abstractly'.[1] As we go on to argue, much the same kind of comment could be made concerning the second body of literature, which attempts to subordinate completely gender struggles to a wider class struggle. If the analysis and objectives of Western feminism cannot be applied universally and abstractly, neither can those of an overly economistic Marxism, as it does not have the necessary categories to deal with gender oppression. But both traditions have important contributions to make, as we will argue using examples drawn from Angola, Mozambique and Zimbabwe.

Maxine Molyneux has discussed the claim of socialist parties and governments that they alone can bring about the full emancipation of women. In her comprehensive analysis, she comes to the conclusion that the mere development of the productive forces is not sufficient to bring about changes in women's position; a theoretical, practical and political break with orthodox socialist policies is needed.[2] In this chapter we follow her suggestion by analysing the theoretical statements made by Mozambican, Angolan and Zimbabwean leaders on the women's question and considering their practical implications. Inevitably, we have to discuss certain inadequate theoretical conceptualisations and their consequences. The unity of theory and practice will be unambiguously clear when we move on to discuss the limitations placed upon women's struggles as a direct result of theoretical misconceptions of the role of women in society.

Conceptualising women's oppression

The revolutionary movements of Africa have defined the women's struggle as being part and parcel of the struggle for national liberation. Men and women are seen as products and victims of an exploitative society. Urdang, in a recent article on Mozambique, summarises President Machel's statement of this position: 'socialist transformation is the *only* basis for (the) liberation of women'.[3] The question remains, however, whether it is a *sufficient* basis. Roberts questions President Machel's claim that 'the antagonistic contradiction is not found between man and woman, but rather between women and the social order, between all exploited women and men and the social order'.[4] She argues that, with this statement, Machel makes clear that women's oppression by men is a secondary issue in the task of liberating women, and that he delegitimates the struggle around issues such as the marriage system and the brutality of husbands by implying that feminism is a bourgeois deviation and an aspect of cultural imperialism.

It is extremely important to consider the theoretical premises on which the socialist liberation movements base their analysis of women's oppression. Socialist societies have tended to adopt an orthodox Marxist–Leninist position on women, based essentially on Engels' text *The Origin of the Family, Private Property and the State* and Lenin's work *On the Emancipation of Women*.[5] The main thesis in both tracts is that women's oppression is economically determined and is inextricably linked to the rise of class society and the state. As Engels argues, 'as long as women are excluded from socially productive work they cannot be emancipated'.[6] What stems from this premise is the prognosis that giving equal opportunities in productive work will, of itself, produce gender equality.

The unchallenged acceptance of these two theoretical premises has led to serious misconceptions of women's oppression in sub-Saharan Africa. Apart from *The Origin of the Family, Private Property and the State*, the main body of Marx and Engels' work is concerned with an analysis of capitalism. Applying this analysis in Africa cannot yield sufficient insight into women's situation. Women's oppression there is embedded in a complex context of pre-capitalist and capitalist social relations co-existing with gender relations which are economically and culturally determined. In using a strict Marxist framework, sub-Saharan socialist states have kept gender oppression off the agenda. In contrast, an increasing number of authors have provided evidence that the interaction of an analysis of women's subordination to men with an analysis of production is crucial to a fuller understanding of women's oppression in its widest sense.[7] The analysis of gender relations largely falls outside the realm of class analysis, which tends to be 'sex-blind'.[8] Barrett argues that one has to 'point to specific factors which distinguish women's relation to the class structure from that of men, yet not at the cost of abandoning the corpus of a marxist approach...'[9] She also stresses the importance of an historical approach to the question of class and gender. We do not intend to pursue here a complex discussion on class in sub-Saharan

Africa, but with Barrett, we want to point out that the orthodox Marxist position on women overlooks the historical aspects of women's oppression which emerged prior to class society and which continue to exist outside class relationships.

The political strategy of incorporating women in production cannot resolve women's oppression. Given the colonial legacy of economic under-development of countries such as Mozambique, Angola and Zimbabwe, it is understandable that emphasis is placed upon the development of productive forces. The argument is made even by women's organisations. The Organisa-tion of Angolan Women (OMA), for example, stated at its First Congress that 'the struggle for the emancipation of women necessarily depends on their parti-cipation in the tasks of national reconstruction'.[10] However, subordinating women's struggles to the success of development strategies poses enormous problems for women and their organisations.

The second misconception lies in describing women as being excluded from socially productive work.[11] Defining women's work as being outside the sphere of socially productive work does not correctly characterise women's work. Beneria argues that orthodox and Marxist economics have an overly narrow focus in which the 'production of exchange values is viewed as economic activity whereas use value production is normally not viewed as such'.[12] She goes on to say that 'despite the fact that Marx talked about all labour producing use-values as productive labour, the most prevalent position within the Marxist tradition has been in accordance with his contention that "use value as such lies outside the sphere of political economy"'.[13]

The adoption of this position in countries such as Mozambique, Angola and Zimbabwe, has led to serious misconceptions of women's labour. For in reality, use value production outside market exchange takes place both in the household and in the subsistence sector. Defining work in the subsistence sector as socially non-productive, and devising a strategy of drawing women into production, is a distortion of reality. Believing that the liberation of women can be measured in terms of their participation in production ignores their contribution to the production of use values and their oppression related to that production. It is crucially important, therefore, to reconsider the analysis of productive labour and the strategies for women's emancipation which derive from it.

In Mozambique, Angola and Zimbabwe, the official political line is that women's oppression can be defined in mainly economic terms. They focus strictly on women's role in production, they assume that most of women's labour is not productive as it does not create exchange value, and that women's oppression is directly linked with the emergence of class society. Yet, at the last OMA congress, there was a growing awareness of the inadequacy of the orthodox position: 'the domestic economy is essential to the functioning of the economic system. This function of women is often under-estimated and is one of the factors which leads to discrimination and the exclusion of women as economically active labour'.[14] At the same time, this statement has to be seen in the context of a continuing acceptance of the primacy of the national reconstruction policy. It remains unclear whether this analysis of women's labour will be pursued to the point of formulating alternative policies.

Analysing rural women's labour

Ester Boserup's *Women's Role in Economic Development* has been widely accepted as the landmark which re-opened the debate on women's labour in African agriculture. Since then, many authors have taken the issue further.[15] The work carried out on labour budgets, by people such as Guyer, has been particularly illuminating in showing that women provide most of the basic food stuffs for domestic consumption.[16] Women are farmers, frequently also producing for the market, processors of food, domestic workers and child-rearers. If we are to analyse accurately their role in the process of socialist transformation, we must consider in greater detail the content and amount of labour that rural women carry out.

Beneria's argument can be used as a point of departure. She writes that 'any conceptualisation of economic activity should include the production of both use and exchange values, and that active labour should be defined in relation to its contribution to the production of goods and services for the satisfaction of human needs'.[17] The evidence for this argument can be found in empirical work on domestic labour, reproduction and subsistence production. In the economies of sub-Saharan Africa, these three sectors overlap. Domestic work and subsistence production are closely intertwined:

> Domestic work extends itself into activities such as gathering wood for the domestic fire, picking vegetables for daily meals, and baking bread in village public ovens for family consumption. Domestic work also becomes part of the agricultural labour process when, for example, the meals for agricultural workers are cooked in the home, and transported to the fields. Similarly, the agricultural labour process extends itself into household production, as when cereals are dried and agricultural goods are processed for family consumption.[18]

Studies of Zimbabwe show that the African farming system, in its predominant reliance on women's labour, produces the same picture of domestic and agricultural work contributing to most subsistence needs.[19] Here, we touch upon a second overlap whereby 'the separation between productive and reproductive activities is often artificial'.[20] Reproduction—understood as biological reproduction, reproduction of the labour force and social reproduction—can be reconceptualised in terms of production. The reproduction of the labour force requires a high level of production of use values in a subsistence economy, notably goods and services consumed within the domestic unit. This work is not commoditised, but it does satisfy basic human needs and as such, Beneria argues, it should be valued accordingly.

The reproduction of social relations does not only take place in the realm of commodity production. Relations between people within the domestic unit are social relations generated by the production of use values. They are equally important to those generated in commodity production, as they have their own pattern of oppression and exploitation. They need to be understood as gender relations and require a separate analysis. Taking this as our point of departure theoretically, it can be seen how a differentiation emerges between that part of the labour force that produces exchange value, and that part that is engaged in the production of use values.[21]

Recognising women's labour as producing use value, therefore, has profound implications for redefining their role in society and in the process of socialist transition. The distinction between production and reproduction thereby loses its former meaning, and the assertions that women are 'economically inactive' and that they should be drawn into *production* to solve gender inequality, are seriously called into question. They do not describe the daily reality of rural women in sub-Saharan Africa, who are producing use values (and often exchange values as well).

However, in the economic policies of Mozambique, Angola and Zimbabwe the assumption that women are 'economically inactive' is still effectively accepted. The implications of this are twofold. First, the economic contribution of women in the subsistence sector is not valued. The crucial importance of women's labour in reproducing the peasantry and therefore the vast majority of the population (which also happens to be the majority class base of the revolutionary governments) remains invisible. Women are not accorded economic power and are consequently limited in their political power. Secondly, women's burden of work is increased. Their production of use value is not recognised, while at the same time they are encouraged to take part in the production of exchange values. They have to maintain the level of subsistence production whilst also participating in commodity production. As a consequence, they are unable to develop their full potential in commodity production, because part of their labour (as measured in both time and energy) continues to be used in subsistence production. Again, this has adverse effects on their economic and political power, as women are much more limited than men in their participation in decision-making processes. The 'double burden' of women hampers them in two ways therefore: in production and in political participation.[22] As long as women are required to secure the means for societal production and at the same time participate in 'real' production, they will be unequal to men. Many women in sub-Saharan Africa are aware that the 'double burden' stands in the way of full emancipation. We will discuss this issue further when addressing the question of female cadres.

Transforming gender relations

Over the last decade, feminist scholarship has posed new questions about the application of Marxist theory to an analysis of women's position. Increasingly, it has been demonstrated that Marxist theory cannot adequately deal with the question of women's oppression, either under advanced capitalism or in the Third World, as it has no conceptual basis for understanding gender relations. An approach that has its theoretical underpinnings in both feminism and Marxism might have as its objective the identification of how gender relations operate. It should understand where they are distinct from, or connected with, the processes of production and reproduction. Concretely, this means that Marxist feminism explores the relationship between domestic production, the household, sexual relations and the mode of production and the systems of appropriation and exploitation, based in their historical context.[23] In the fields of sociology and anthropology this approach has proved especially fruitful and has given important insights into the interaction between gender relations and modes of production.[24] In this chapter, we wish to address the specific question of the transformation of the social relations of production and gender relations.

In socialist societies such as Mozambique, Angola and Zimbabwe, the transformation of the social relations of production is an explicit priority, but in their definition, only the social relations underlying commodity exchange are included. Where policies for subsistence farming are the subject of debate, as in the case of Mozambique's socialisation of the countryside, there is little regard for their impact upon women. Hence there is no awareness that gender relations need to be changed. Societies which have a longer experience of socialism, such as the Soviet Union, China or Yugoslavia illustrate the pitfalls of this approach. There, gender relations have not changed fundamentally and in certain ways have become even more entrenched.[25]

The strategic problem for women in sub-Saharan African socialist societies is whether to wage a relatively independent struggle or to be subordinate to the overall struggle for socialist transformation. Generally, as we have argued, the latter position has been adopted, and the implications of this choice will be discussed later. Of course, both the women's organisations and the revolutionary parties recognise that women are subject to oppression by men. They clearly state that the transformation of gender relations is part of the overall struggle. But they also argue that it is subordinate to that 'wider' struggle.

Like most socialist societies, Angola, Mozambique and Zimbabwe have made a commitment to removing women's oppression in the law. Extreme forms of patriarchal domination such as the payment of bride-price, polygamy and child marriage have been tackled immediately. Legislation has been passed, for example, concerning equal rights for women at work or in education. Yet legal changes alone do not necessarily imply removing women's oppression. An example from Zimbabwe shows the limitations of legal change. Since independence, Zimbabwean women have attained the legal age of majority at the age of 18. With the Legal Age of Majority Act, women's former perpetual status as minors was abolished and the way was opened to other far-reaching reforms. One of the most important of these was that women could enter into legal contracts and marry without consent. This means that there is now the possibility of marrying without having been paid for. However, many fathers oppose the effective abolition of the bride-price and continue to pressurise their daughters.[26] Thus male domination, as embedded in traditional culture, stands in the way of implementing legal changes. It is clear that formal limitations, such as discriminatory legislation, can be removed, while subjective informal limitations, such as cultural values, continue to exist.

Other constraints on women's emancipation are the underestimation of women's productive role or the lack of understanding of gender oppression in marriage and the family. Traditional women's roles continue to be seen as the base for women's political action. In Machel's words: 'married women especially must concern themselves with setting a positive example to the younger single women and show them in practice that marriage is an incentive for the pursuit of revolutionary tasks',[27] and 'if we consider the basic need for the revolution to be continued by the new generation, how can we ensure the revolutionary education of the generation which will carry on our work if mothers, the first educators, are marginal to the revolutionary process?'[28]

Women's social responsibility continues to be primarily determined by her relationships with men and children. Her possible emancipation in the sphere of production (in agriculture or industry) is not matched by a transformation of gender relations. It is too easy to dismiss, for example, concern for sexuality, oppression by husbands and fathers, or the binds of motherhood as 'bourgeois feminist' concerns. They do constitute the daily reality for many rural women. The objective conditions of work are clearly determined by how women's role within society is perceived, and these perceptions are derived from cultural values predating socialist transformation. The dialectical relationship between gender relations and women's role in socialist transformation must be recognised if new ways forward for women are to be developed. Without this recognition, women's participation in commodity production, in political organisations and in education cannot be equal to men's.

Women's consciousness is limited ideologically and materially. Full emancipation is blocked by both the underestimation of women's economic role and the oppressive nature of gender relations. Women's struggles should, therefore, be an integral part of the process of socialist transformation and continually question class and gender relations. Women's organisations have an important role in keeping these questions on the political agenda and we will discuss their interventions to date using our three country case studies.

Women and agriculture: social transformation in Mozambique

In the run up to Frelimo's Fourth Party Congress held in April 1983, Mozambique's agricultural policies were the subject of heated debates. Since independence in 1975 agricultural policy has undergone a number of changes.

In the early days, the development of 'communal villages' was seen to give an impetus to the development of co-operative production. The emphasis was on involving poor peasants, workers and exploited labour. In reality only 2 percent of total agricultural investment was pumped into the co-operatives. Also, from the middle of 1978, after the Third Congress, the policy appeared to change in favour of state farms. Much effort was put into expansion of that sector, without necessarily achieving an increase in productivity. This approach did not yield the expected results and in the following years the government slowly realised that it had made mistakes.[29] The most important of these was the neglect of the co-operatives and the marginalisation of the peasant family sector. The meagre growth of co-operatives was illustrated by their membership of only 37,000 people, constituting a tiny percentage of the active rural population. The relative neglect of the peasant family sector led to a dramatic fall in production, not least because the policy of low fixed prices had become a disincentive for production. Moreover, the availability of commodities in the rural areas was extremely limited, leaving the peasants with nothing to buy with their cash.

The Central Committee realised that a change in policy was needed if food production was to be increased. 'Small scale projects' were introduced as an important contingency measure to solve the problem of low productivity. Leaders of the Party saw it also as a method to mobilise the people and utilise local capacities. However, it is not clear to what extent this policy is guided by socialist principles of encouraging participation of the masses and consciousness-raising, or whether it is simply a policy of necessity. The war in Mozambique is an important consideration. The South African-backed rebel MNR (Mozambique National Resistance) had made substantial inroads in rural areas, destroying social and economic structures and seriously affecting production. Many people are hungry as a result of the disruptive influence of the MNR and the severe droughts of the last three years. Even after the signing of the Nkomati Accord, a non-aggression pact between South Africa and Mozambique on 16 March 1984, the MNR has not been effectively curbed and continues to hamper production.

Are the new policies effective in improving production? In particular, what is their impact on women and their struggle for emancipation? In order to answer these questions, we first have to go a step back in history and discuss the relationship between co-operative development and women's participation.

In 1977, Mozambique began a major campaign to restructure the rural areas. The main strategy was to organise communal villages and to turn large abandoned plantations and white settler schemes into state farms. The development of communal villages was planned to run parallel to the reorganisation of peasant family production into co-operatives. In the northern provinces, many of the colonial resettlements, the so-called strategic hamlets, had communal structures superimposed. In the liberated zones, also in the north, peasant consciousness had developed about the need to change the social relations of production. In the same year, parts of Gaza and

Maputo provinces were flooded and the building of communal villages was made part of reconstruction.

The Mozambican Women's Organisation (OMM) was given major responsibility for mobilising women to become Party members, and the OMM was involved in planning the campaign at all levels. Barbara Isaacman and June Stephen[30] followed the progress of the campaign closely, and found that there was a significant difference in political participation of women on the one hand in the liberated zones and the province of Gaza, and in the rest of the country on the other. Their argument is that in the liberated zones and in Gaza, women have been involved in the process of decision-making. During the war of liberation, the population in the liberated zones was mobilised to support the guerrillas, and years of political schooling had a lasting effect on women and men. This political awareness manifested itself in the response to Party recruitment. In most communal villages, female membership was 50% or more.

In Gaza the explanation for women's participation was twofold. A large section of the adult male population was migrant workers in the mines of South Africa. The working peasantry is therefore predominantly female. After the floods in 1977, decisions about reconstruction were made and carried out by women. This was an important exercise in consciousness raising. For many women it was their first encounter with planning, discussing policies and mobilising people. The transformation of ways of living in communal villages and of agricultural production were crucial factors in rapidly politicising women. The result was that women often made up over half the Party membership of communal villages.[31] This high level of women's participation, however, masked the fundamental problems which have continued to the present.

The relatively little support for co-operatives and the peasant family sector are linked to the underestimation of women's labour, and simultaneously reinforces it. There has always been an underlying assumption that the peasantry reproduces itself, and as such, relies mainly on women's subsistence work. Evidence from studies on the reproduction of migrant labourers is strong on this point.[32] The policy of promoting state farms also relies on female subsistence labour. The wages paid in the state farms tend to be too low for the reproduction of the worker and his family and there was less and less to buy in the shops with the currency. Thus, women often had to continue to provide basic foodstuffs; wages could serve to buy such commodities as were available or were used to invest. The classic misconception of rural labour as female subsistence farmers continued to exist in Mozambique; women were not considered to be productive workers. The call by Felimo *and* the OMM, that women should engage in production, created the well-known problem for women: the double burden of work in the subsistence *and* productive sectors, linked also with the responsibility for domestic and childcare duties. The limits placed on women's political participation are obvious. According to Urdang, 'Women's workload is recognised as an unfair burden but as the sexual division of labour is not confronted as a structural problem, it is not dealt with strategically'.[33] As a result of economic underdevelopment, there are few wage labour jobs, and the integration of women in production is therefore uneven. The official policy of stimulating women to participate in commodity production remains, however. Urdang states that 'the contradiction between women's work in reproductive labour and their work in the productive sector will be heightened.'[34]

In the years when concentrated mechanisation of the state farms took place, the implicit assumption was that the peasantry did not need help. This assumption was based, as argued previously, on the familiar premise that female labour secured the reproduction of the peasantry. This was far from the truth. During this period in Mozambique, access to agricultural implements was extremely limited, not only because of shortages and the war, but also because of ministerial prioritisation.[35] No increases in production were possible as long as the available technology was relatively primitive, and, with commodity shortages and a fixed pricing policy, incentives for production were largely absent. These factors contributed to a stagnation, and often to a degeneration, of the peasant family sector. For women, this meant that they could not reap the rewards of the process of socialist transformation, as they remained locked in the underdeveloped peasant family sector.

In 1983, following the realisation that agricultural production in Mozambique was in crisis, the government changed its policy. A rapid increase in food production became the top economic and political priority. This implied support for the peasantry, in terms of providing them with agro-technical assistance, seeds, agricultural tools and essential consumer goods. Another priority was support to co-operatives and communal villages.[36] The peasant family sector, mainly producing for subsistence, still accounted in 1982 for one third of total marketed production. However, current production levels are well below pre-1975 levels, and of the planned food increase, the peasant sector is asked to provide 20%.

This new emphasis can work out for women in two opposing ways. If peasant family production is redefined so that *both* the production of exchange values (marketed produce) and subsistence produce are considered to be productive, the recognition of the production of use values as a corner stone of the economy is a logical consequence. Instead of urging women to *join* production, it will be clear that women are *already* incorporated and constitute the main productive force in peasant family agriculture. Their role in the process of socialist transformation then moves centre-stage, giving a major impetus to their economic and political participation. With a fundamental progressive shift in their material conditions, the struggle for change at the level of gender relations as embedded in traditional culture and present politics will gain in strength. Hence women's emancipation has to be tackled from two different angles: the first, setting women free from material constraints by removing their double burden of work and the second, engaging in consciousness-raising about women's role. The latter has many different facets. For not only does it encompass an understanding of women's productive role, but it makes possible a fundamental attack on the sexual division of labour and gender relations. Legal access to education, technology, leadership and so on, can only become a reality when stubbornly pervasive cultural values are successfully challenged.

The other way this new policy initiative may work out for women is more negative. If the change of policy were fuelled by necessity, without due consideration being taken of women's role in economic development, then nothing would change, or it would change for the worse. In this situation, women will be pressed to increase production for the market, with or without technical and material assistance, but objectively their burden of work will rise. A redistribution of responsibilities within the peasant family sector will be unlikely to take place. Indeed, a sharpening of gender divisions may occur, notably with men dominating the production for the market and women being locked into the subsistence sector. For the peasant family unit, conditions can improve, but the sexual division of labour and the oppressive nature of gender divisions remain unaltered. Material progress alone does not necessarily imply emancipation of women.

It is too early to make any statement about the direction of the new policy, leaving aside any assessment of its impact on women's emancipation. Here, we can only discuss the different possible consequences of the change in policy and point out the importance of the analysis of labour in the peasant family sector.

The State, the Party and women's organisations

The literature concerned with women in socialist societies has often addressed the question of the relationship between women and political structures.[37] In theory women are equal partners in the political arena; in practice, none of the socialist states have achieved anything resembling equality. Women's participation can be estimated in two ways: firstly, by looking at their representation in Party and State organs at all levels; and secondly, by analysing their relative strength and their relationship to the Party.

Female representation in the political structures of Mozambique, Angola and Zimbabwe is still limited. For example, less than one quarter of Frelimo's 110,000 members consists of women[38] and the proportion in Mozambique's highest state organ, the National People's Assembly is just 12.35 percent. At the Fourth Congress, the Central Committee of the Party could boast only 14 women out of a total membership of 130.

Strategically more important than the numbers of women in political structures, is their actual political strength. In all three countries, women have their own organisations, which are technically considered mass organisations, but remain under the auspices of the Party. As Egero[39] points out, mass organisations should be functioning as creative participants in the democratic process. The women's organisations in Mozambique, Angola and Zimbabwe all have a history going back to the armed struggle, and in differing ways can rely on their grassroots structures. However, the relative strength of the organisations at base level is not a sufficient condition for broad political participation. Two factors play a role in this. The first is the authority of the Party. In all three countries national reconstruction and changing social relations of production are made, verbally at least, the priority. From the Party's perspective, the women's organisation is a medium through which the process of socialist transformation can be stimulated and economic development encouraged. As such, the women's organisation is clearly subordinate to broader political aims. Participation of women, therefore, falls within the remit of general political strategies, and women are not necessarily able to identify their *particular* contribution or have sufficient confidence to put *their own struggle* on the agenda. The subordination of women's struggles to the overall struggle happens at all levels and the transformation of gender relations is secondary in both local and national contexts.

The second factor is that the women's organisations themselves are often rather cautious in developing their political activities. Especially at the grass-roots level, they often engage women in 'gendered' activities, such as hygiene campaigns, or when organising co-operative production they choose vegetable gardening, poultry rearing or sewing. The obvious danger is that such activities can be seen as 'women's work' and therefore fail to be recognised as equally important contributions in the socialist development process. They can still be perceived as unequal and remain defined by traditional cultural values.

The problem of female participation is thus twofold. On the one hand, it concerns access to political structures and on the other hand, consciousness-raising on various levels — in the Party, in the leadership of the women's organisations and at the grassroots. Achieving an equilibrium between the goals of national development strategies and those for women's emancipation has not thus far been achieved in the three countries under discussion. We will now illustrate these issues with two examples, one drawn from Angola and the other from Zimbabwe.

Angola

The OMA (Organisation of Angolan Women) held its First Congress from 2 to 8 March 1983 on the central theme of development. The main speeches, one by the President, one by the Secretary for Organisation of the Central Committee and one by the newly elected Secretary-General of the OMA, all addressed this one issue. The context of the emphasis on women's role in the process of national reconstruction is all-important. At present, not only Angola, but also Mozambique and Zimbabwe are still in a state of war. The aggression by South Africa — frequently through the use of surrogate internal forces — profoundly affects all strategies for progress. Peace is the number one priority and women's role within that struggle is clearly underlined. At the OMA Congress, women were urged 'ever more actively to take part in all aspects of national life',[40] a life necessarily shaped by strong external forces, but also by internal factors. In spite of the recognition that women's problems were in part separate from the war situation, the emphasis of the congress was very much women's role in the struggle against imperialism. The war situation thus profoundly affected the agenda of priorities, and women's emancipation once again was defined as being achieved through national liberation. In this context, no autonomy, however relative, of women's struggles could be allowed. It is only through participating in the overall struggle that women are expected to create the fundamental conditions for their own emancipation.

Experiences of re-integrating female guerrillas into society after the liberation wars show that the issue is far from simple. In a war, men and women fight alongside each other, and in this extreme situation equality can exist. Comrades in struggle face the same life or death predicament. Once these abnormal circumstances are removed, one can then assess whether more permanent changes in gender relations, if any, have taken place. Often, traditional cultural values re-emerge. Equality between men and women may then be defined as being clearly limited to the war context. People returning to their communities want to rebuild their lives, which in most cases consists of a family life. Male ex-combatants looking for wives may see female ex-combatants as unsuitable partners, as they are too independent, 'rough' and therefore not 'feminine'.[41] It has proven difficult for female ex-combatants to be reintegrated into society precisely because their changed perception of women's role has not been accepted as valid outside of the liberation struggle. It is clear that a qualitatively different struggle has to be waged to effect a more fundamental change in attitudes concerning women. This cultural revolution requires material and ideological change, and above all, an analytical clarity, to construct a strategy for women's emancipation. In Angola, the renewed emphasis on women's role in the struggle against South Africa carries the same danger as outlined above, notably of creating setbacks to emancipation. Culture and values have to be continuously assessed if gender relations are to be altered, and a separate analysis of those issues remains a necessity.

Turning to the specific issues discussed at the Congress, four main areas were defined: the emancipation of women, women and the family, working women and the OMA statutes. The resolution passed on the emancipation of women proposed legal changes which would enable women to exercise their rights in the areas of political life, marriage and fertility. Women's integration in co-operative production was seen as an important factor in facilitating women's entrance into education, as their burden of work would be alleviated. Most importantly, the resolutions emphasised the essential function of female peasant labour in the economy.

These resolutions show that the crucial elements in an analysis of women's role in society are recognised. Yet, there appears to be a lack of coherence; recommendations in one section are not fully taken into account in another. For example, there is much emphasis on changing the legal context of marriage and paternity. The rights of women and children are spelled out and provisions are made to protect them. Yet there is little attention paid to the fact that men will be resistant to such changes, and no strategy is drawn up for tackling that problem. Similarly, the observation that women carry a heavy burden is phrased in individual terms. The solution to this problem is seen to lie in co-operative production. However, this automatically challenges the sexual division of labour when women are drawn into co-operative production. The socialisation of childcare and domestic tasks is as yet incomplete; conflicts within the household over the division of labour can therefore be expected. An analysis of male dominance must be included in the development of alternatives for women, because gender relations are defined by material, political and cultural conditions. Changing the structural context can still leave the cultural realm untouched, and a coherent and integrated strategy is necessary.

In the section on women and the family, resolution number 14 states: 'Traditionalist ideas on fertility of women need to be combatted, and the commission already set up to implement a family planning programme should start its work immediately, as one of the ways of reducing infant mortality'. This resolution conflates women's fertility and women's sexuality. In resolution number 12, this conflation is clearer, because it argues that women should have the right to freely consented motherhood. Thus, women's sexual relations are directly linked with motherhood. The discussion centres around the issue of women's procreative function and the degrees of freedom she can have in deciding if and when to have children. What is to be combated are the ideas that women should have many children, and that the decisions are made by men. However, an important aspect is not debated in all this, namely sexual relations between men and women. Men's power in imposing their sexuality on women is closely related to the question of fertility. In the Angolan context (indeed, in many underdeveloped countries) women's access to contraceptives is partial or ineffective. With men imposing their sexual will on women, the choice about fertility beomes seriously jeopardised. Women find it difficult to deny men sexual relations, yet are in danger of having an unplanned pregnancy as a result. Thus arguing for freedom from forced motherhood requires a broader discussion on freedom in sexual relations. Separating a discussion about fertility from one about sexuality can cause misinterpretations about the degrees of freedom women have. A discussion on changing gender relations is indispensable if the proposed changes are to take place.

Another issue related to resolution number 14 is the link made between fertility and infant mortality. Child spacing and reducing the number of children is important if healthy children are to be born. A woman's health depends on freedom from continuous childbearing. The missing link in this resolution is an understanding of the social implications for women. Women have a responsibility for their children's health, but they also have a social responsibility in being active members of society. In that sense, child spacing is important, because women have more opportunity to participate in production and decision-making (with socialised childcare, however, this argument would become largely redundant).

The emphasis in these resolutions on women as mothers has to be understood in the light of the social meaning of motherhood in African societies, which is different than in the West. The 'institution of motherhood', however, is an issue on which we cannot elaborate in the present chapter and we refer to other work.[42]

The discussions at the OMA Congress were to a great extent determined by the Party's national priorities. Women's production and education were the main concerns and measures to encourage women's participation in these areas were clearly formulated, mostly in legal and structural terms. The proposed changes create a context in which further struggles can take place. We have argued that an understanding of social relations between men and women have to be considered at the same time, if integrated and comprehensive strategies for women's emancipation are to be developed. We take issue with the position that women's liberation will take place with national liberation alone – a parallel, but separate, struggle also needs to be waged.

Zimbabwe

Women's organisations under the leadership of a Party may often reflect the struggles taking place within that Party. Such struggles can centre around the definition of priorities, or may reflect the conflicts between different interest groups or power blocs. A good example of a mixture of the two is to be found in the 1984 Women's League Congress of the ruling ZANU party in Zimbabwe.

Prior to the signing of the Lancaster House agreements in 1979, which laid down the terms of the transition to independence in Zimbabwe, the two nationalist movements formed the Patriotic Front. From the time of the elections, for reasons beyond the scope of our discussion, the two parties have gone their separate, and often conflicting ways. ZANU enjoys a majority support based on the Shona-speaking northern, middle and eastern provinces of the country, whilst ZAPU's support comes from the Sindebele-speaking west.

In 1983, ZANU started preparing for the creation of a one-Party state, to be endorsed by the 1984 Party Congress and realised after general elections in 1985. A crucial element in the political strategy was the creation of a popular base in the ZAPU dominated Matabeleland provinces. This has been a difficult task, and Party officials from ZANU in Matabeleland North were recruited from the Shona province of Masvingo in the south-eastern part of the country. In addition to the ZANU versus ZAPU conflicts, clashes took place within ZANU itself. Regional sub-groupings within the Shona – notably the powerful Karanga group, the Zezurus, the Manyikas and others of lesser importance – were jockeying for positions of power in Party and state. These general issues formed a powerful background to the Women's League congress in March 1984. At this Congress, the leading officers of the organisation had to be elected. These officers automatically would become members of the Party's Central Committee, formed at the Party's Congress held in August of the same year. Thus the elections were important for both the Women's League and the Party.

At first, the result of the Women's League Congress were hailed by Party leaders and the media as a great success:

> If there is anything that the people of Zimbabwe learnt from the recent ZANU Women's League conference it is the fact that a one-Party state can work if properly administered. There is no doubt that the conference was a one-party state at work. There was more than one candidate for each post except for the secretary which went unopposed. The 3000 delegates made their choice democratically.[43]

This initial enthusiasm was not to prove longlasting. The first intimations that all was not well appeared on 26 March 1984, when a Party leader made allegations that the elections at the Congress were carried out on a 'tribalist' basis. Two weeks later, these remarks were endorsed by the Prime Minister himself, who said that the elections 'were characterised by regional voting blocs which kept some candidates from getting positions'.[44] It appears that a voting bloc had developed, consisting of the delegates from Masvingo, the Midlands and Matabeleland North provinces. With Matabeleland North being represented by officials from Masvingo, this province was drawn into the power bloc dominated by the Karanga group. Responding to this move, the other provinces united to form an opposition bloc.

The Women's Congress, therefore, appears to have been dominated in its electoral procedures, at least, by power struggles within the Party. Conflicts over substantive issues, as they relate to women *per se*, seem to have been subsumed by wider Party in-fighting. In the local press, the women were portrayed as having fallen victim to 'some smart alecs (who) may have manipulated the women to further their own evil machinations at the peril of Party unity'.[45] The perception seemed to be that the women were easily manipulated by (male) Party members. Whether or not this is true, it is clear that much of the decision-making did not take place within the confines of the Congress. A fundamental question was raised of the extent to which there was 'free expression' by the delegates to the Women's League Congress. The gap between the leadership and the rural representatives seemed great and participation from the floor was limited.[46] This alone would account for making the fronting of candidates a 'closed' affair between people at the top. Whether or not the election was 'tribalist', the lack of democratic participation in itself was a grave problem.

In the political debate that followed, stress was laid on the negative consequences of these revelations for the Party's strategy for building a Sindebele-speaking ZANU structure in Matabeleland. The Party's problems in establishing a base in the Matabeleland provinces are great and the emphasis is therefore on giving the Ndebele full opportunities to become members of the Party and to rise within it. The Women's Congress was seen to jeopardise this strategy. The Women's League was criticised in not following the Party line, in that the alleged regionalist elections were considered detrimental to the

Party's image and to have undermined the effort to attract Ndebele members. The Prime Minister voiced his disapproval: 'Although the Party had accepted the women leaders elected, it strongly condemned such practices. . . What had happened at the Women's League conference was quite disgraceful'.[47]

The examples of both Angola and Zimbabwe show the close link between Party and women's organisations. In spite of policies dealing with specific women's issues, and aimed at transforming gender relations, overall Party policies are dominant in the women's organisations. They are technically and practically mass organisations guided by the Party. As the Zimbabwean example illustrates, it can even serve as a battleground for intra-Party conflicts. Developing a powerful political force able to fight for causes not always directly in line with the Party's prime concerns appears to be difficult for women's organisations in socialist states. It is, of course, important to be linked with the Party, but subordination does not make for a creative and radical movement for the emancipation of women.

Women and democratic participation

Women's participation at the grassroots level is an important indication of how widespread and far-reaching a struggle for emancipation is. However, female political leaders do not always maintain their roots in the base. Often they fail to have strong links with the majority of rural women. Gwendoline Konie, the Permanent Secretary in the Cabinet Office of Zambia, states the problem clearly:

> As I see it, a lot of us women have been put in high positions alright. However, because of the nature of the politics of our day, we have been swallowed up by general politics and forgotten that the majority of our sisters are not capable of standing up for themselves. We have thus failed to take up the crusade for them, and consequently failed to improve their quality of life.[48]

Several issues stand out: firstly, the political structures themselves are 'gendered'; because men dominate politics, they have created structures in their own image.[49] Secondly, women who are political leaders do not necessarily have contact with women at the grassroots. Thirdly, because of the sexual division of labour, women find it difficult to enter the arena of public decision-making. Fourthly, women are, on the whole, less educated than men, and thus have difficulty in understanding political processes or in developing confidence in their ability to deal with politics. Finally, women are held back by traditional values concerning their role; under African customary law, women have been perceived as the subordinate sex.

Enthusiasm about the number of women involved in grassroots politics can be dispelled when casting a more careful glance at the figures. Urdang provides us with a very clear example for Mozambique. She writes:

A member of a FRELIMO cell in a communal village. A woman member of the People's Assembly, perhaps even on the Executive Council. A woman on the council of the Agricultural Co-operative. An active OMM secretary who plays an energetic leadership role in the village. A woman on a special four-months leadership and literacy course. When presented thus, it would seem that there is a wide involvement of women in political activities. But what the listing masks is the frequency with which multiple positions are held by the *same* women.[50]

Women's political participation is subject to many constraints; active women are more the exception than the rule. Again, the reasons have to do with the issue of women's role in production, as an example from Zimbabwe clearly illustrates. During the 1980 ceasefire, the ZANU(PF) District Committee covering the area around Bondolfi mission in Victoria (now Masvingo) province initiated a basic preventive health scheme. A health worker at the mission drew up a syllabus for the first course. The 28 branches in the district each elected two prospective health workers to go on the course. All the popularly elected health workers were women, and in the years to come the majority remained women. The workers received six months training, including theory and practice. A system of regular meetings between health workers was set up, as well as refresher courses. The project proved to be very popular and demand for more workers increased. The people decided to expand the health programme and selected and trained over the next two years a total of 293 Village Health Workers (VHWs).[51]

After independence, the Zimbabwean government began to restructure the health service.[52] Part of their programme was an expansion of health services in the rural areas, and in 1981 the government started their own VHW scheme. It was not intended to have the same intensive coverage as the Bondolfi scheme, which provided a VHW for almost every village. Yet, one principle was the same, namely the election of VHWs by their own communities in consultation with the District Council. In some areas this was realised, but in many cases it was the District Councils themselves that selected people and 'there [was] some nepotism, councillors chose their wives and friends. . .'[53] In contrast to the Bondolfi scheme, the government VHWs received a compensation of 33 dollars a month (the national minimum wage was officially set at 56 dollars).

By 1983, two thirds of the Bondolfi VHWs had dropped out. One reason was that the paid work of the government VHWs contrasted with the voluntary work of the Bondolfi VHWs. However, this seems to be only a partial explanation. The government has never given much support to the scheme, in spite of some initial interest. More important, though, were the structural constraints upon the women, who constituted the majority of health workers. These rural women carried out their health work along with their normal daily tasks of farming and domestic labour. Their health work, being preventive and educational in character, involved a certain amount of travelling and was thus time consuming. Most VHWs therefore devoted one or two full days to their health care responsibilities, which consisted in the main of educational work concerning the need to build latrines and the importance of clean water and good nutrition.

The Chinese, who pioneered this grassroots approach to health care in their barefoot doctor scheme, provided health workers with a supportive structural context. Barefoot doctors operated within a co-operative set-up, and were compensated for their health work by crediting them equivalent workpoints. In the Zimbabwean case, co-operative development has been uneven and underdeveloped. Thus, individual peasant family production is still the base. The VHWs were mostly women working in the peasant family sector. They secured subsistence production as individuals; if they went out to do their health work, no-one took over their jobs. Thus there was no form of compensation for lost labour time. With the peasant family sector hardly producing any surplus, and certainly not during the years of severe drought (1981-83), this 'diversion' of labour could not be afforded. Even while the government's payment was not a living wage, the government's VHWs' 33 dollars could be seen as acceptable compensation. In the Bondolfi scheme the women were politically motivated, but material hardship inevitably had an adverse effect. The argument that there was a period of stagnation and discouragement of independent community organisation is undoubtedly true,[54] but it is the lack of understanding of women's work which lies at the root of the problem. In the VHW programme, there was insufficient recognition of the productive nature of women's work, in that no serious consideration was given to the loss in labour time or to the increase in women's workloads. Either the VHWs worked harder than before they became health workers, or they dropped out. In any case it was not understood that the female VHWs *needed* real compensation if they were to carry out their job effectively. In contrast, the government scheme lacked a political base, and in spite of its financial reward (which, by the way, was not based on a recognition of women's work, in that it did not provide a living wage) it has failed to be a success.

The problem of female participation at the grassroots remains a problem in countries such as Zimbabwe. There is a slowly growing awareness that the peasant family sector, mainly based on female labour, is essential to economic survival. Yet, this consciousness is only just emerging and its application in political practice is hardly developed. Women's political participation is still considered as being 'additional' to their daily burden of work. Women's vitally important contribution to peasant production is therefore underestimated. If women's commitment to the overall process of socialist transformation is to develop, a closer look at women's labour and material conditions is needed. Women want to put their political commitment into practice, but they are limited by their burden of work and oppressive notions of women's role in society. For women to realise their participatory potential, therefore, it is of utmost importance that their labour is valued accurately.

Conclusion

The achievements of socialist states in sub-Saharan Africa over the past decade should not be underestimated. These achievements continue, despite the enormous pressures of war and destabilisation. The progress made for women is inevitably shaped by this overriding context and the limitations that it imposes. These limitations, however, do not mean that women's struggles need to be continually subordinate to national political struggles. We have argued in particular for theoretical and political clarity in the analysis of women's oppression and the nature of women's labour. In our analysis, we have drawn on both Marxist and feminist theories in order to define women's role in production and reproduction. In this way, we come to a re-appraisal of women's productive labour. The political and practical implications of this redefinition are that women should be considered the economic linchpins of society.

The examples from Angola, Mozambique and Zimbabwe illustrate the problems women encounter in their struggle for equality. We have emphasised the importance of changing the social relations of production in conjunction with changing gender relations. Women's participation in political processes is contingent upon those changes, upon the degree of 'independence' of their organisations and again, upon the correct scientific 'valuation' of their labour. We cannot stress sufficiently the importance of theoretically accurate analysis. Our examples have shown how inadequate conceptions of women profoundly affect both women's struggles and development strategies generally. There is, however, a growing awareness and practice of this new theoretical approach. In Mozambique, the 'green zones' policy, providing co-operative food production around Maputo, is one such example. Women workers have a creche for their children and have lunch at the co-operative. They are freed from childcare and cooking—which is one step forward to equal participation.

Women are aware of their political potential and those who have lived through a war of liberation know what their contribution to the struggle has been. Now, the conditions have to be created and maintained in which women can realise their aspirations. As a woman from Nariva communal lands in Zimbabwe says: 'I think we women in this new Zimbabwe want to progress more than men. We want to show that our heads are the same. We want to consolidate the power that we shared during the war.'[55]

Notes

1. J. Kimble and E. Unterhalter, 'We Opened the Road for You, You Must Go Forward: ANC Women's Struggles, 1912–1982', *Feminist Review*, 12, 1982. Our analysis of women's role in the process of socialist transformation is firmly embedded in this context. Yet our attempts to under-

stand the experiences and aspirations of the women in these countries does not mean that we uncritically accept their analyses and strategies. Our discussion aims only at furthering an understanding of the complex issue of women's role in the process of socialist transformation.

2. M. Molyneux, 'Women in Socialist Societies: Problems of Theory and Practice', in K. Young, C. Wolkowitz and R. McCullagh (eds), *Of Marriage and the Market* (CSE Books, London, 1981).

3. S. Urdang, 'The Last Transition? Women and Development in Mozambique', *Review Of African Political Economy*, No. 27/28, 1984, p. 10 (emphasis added).

4. P. Roberts, 'Feminism in Africa; Feminism and Africa', *Review Of African Political Economy*, No. 27/28, 1984, p. 183.

5. M. Molyneux, 'Women in Socialist Societies', p. 176.

6. Cited in Ibid., p. 177.

7. K. Young, et al., *Of Marriage and the Market; Critique of Anthropology*, No.9/10, Vol. 3, 1977.

8. H. Hartmann, 'The Unhappy Marriage of Marxism and Feminism: Towards a More Progressive Union', *Capital and Class*, No. 8, 1979.

9. M. Barrett, *Women's Oppression Today* (Verso/NLB, London, 1980).

10. M. Holnes, 'First Congress of the Organisation of Angolan Women (OMA)', *People's Power*, No. 20, Summer 1983, p. 7.

11. L. Beneria, 'Conceptualising the Labor Force: The Underestimation of Women's Economic Activities', in N. Nelson (ed), *African Women in the Development Process* (Frank Cass, 1981).

12. Ibid., p. 16.

13. Ibid., p. 17.

14. M. Holnes, 'First Congress of the Organisation of Angolan Women (OMA)'.

15. I. Palmer, 'Rural Women and Basic Needs', *International Labour Review*, Vol. 115, No. 1, 1977; C. Obbo, *African Women: The Struggle for Economic Independence* (Zed Press, London, 1980); and M.R. Cutrufelli, *Women of Africa: Roots of Oppression* (Zed Press, London, 1983).

16. J. Guyer. 'Dynamic Approaches to Domestic Budgeting: Cases and Methods from Africa', a paper given at the conference on Women and Income Control in the Third World, New York, 1982.

17. L. Beneria, 'Conceptualising the Labor Force', p. 17.

18. L. Beneria and G. Sen, 'Accumulation, Reproduction, and Women's Role in Economic Development: Boserup Revisited', *Signs*, Vol. 7, No. 2, 1981.

19. O. Muchena, *Women and Work: Women's Participation in the Rural Labour Force in Zimbabwe* (ILO, 1982).

20. L. Beneria and G. Sen, 'Accumulation, Reproduction, and Women's Role in Economic Development', p. 292.

21. L. Beneria, 'Conceptualising the Labor Force', p. 21.

22. M. Etienne and E. Leacock (eds), *Women and Colonisation* (Praeger Special Studies, 1981); N. Hafkin and E. Bay (eds), *Women in Africa: Studies in Social and Economic Change* (Stanford University Press, Stanford, 1976); ISIS, *Women, Land and Food Production*, No. 11, Spring 1979; H. Saffioti, *Women in Class Society* (Monthly Review Press, New York, 1978); K. Young et al., *Of Marriage and the Market*.

23. M. Barrett, *Women's Oppression Today*, p. 9.

24. A. Kuhn and A. Wolpe, *Feminism and Materialism* (Routledge, London, 1978); C. Meillassoux, *Femmes, greniers et capitaux* (Maspero, Paris, 1976); *Critique of Anthropology*, Vol. 3, No. 9/10, 1977.

25. E. Croll, *Feminism and Socialism in China* (Routledge, London, 1978); M. Morokvasic, 'Sexuality and the Control of Procreation', in K. Young et al., *Of Marriage and the Market*; M. Molyneux, 'Women in Socialist Sociëties'.

26. J. May, *Zimbabwean Women in Customary and Colonial Law* (Mambo Press, Harare, 1983); J. Kazembe, 'More on the Legal Age of Majority, *Social Change and Development*, No. 8, 1984.

27. S. Machel, *Mozambique: Sowing the Seeds of Revolution* (CFMAG, London, 1974) p. 33.

28. Ibid., p. 24.

29. B. Munslow, 'State Intervention in Agriculture: The Mozambican Experience', *Journal of Modern African Studies*, Vol. 22, No. 2, 1984.

30. B. Isaacman and J. Stephen, *A Mulher moçambicana no proceso de libertação* (INLD, Maputo, 1982). See also S. Kruks and B. Wisner, 'The State, the Party and the Female Peasantry in Mozambique', *Frontiers*, Vol. VII, No. 2, 1983.

31. Ibid., p. 34. For example, in the province of Gaza, seven sample villages had the following percentage of female Party members: 59.3, 50+, 50+, 50, 50+, 37.5, 50+. Figures on female members for the People's Assemblies were more or less the same.

32. R. First, *Black Gold: The Mozambican Miner, Proletarian and Peasant* (Harvester Press, Brighton, 1983).

33. S. Urdang, 'The Last Transition?', p. 19.

34. Ibid., p. 23.

35. B. Munslow, 'State Intervention in Agriculture'.

36. Frelimo, *Directives economiques et sociales*, Maputo, 1983.

37. D. Davin, *Woman-work: Women and the Party in Revolutionary China* (Oxford University Press, Oxford, 1979).

S. Urdang, 'The Last Transition?'; B. Isaacman and J. Stephen, *A mulher moçambicana no proceso de libertação*.

38. See the chapter by Bertil Egero in this volume.

39. Ibid.

40. M. Holnes, 'First Congress of the Organisation of Angolan Women (OMA)', p. 5. See also *Angolan Women Building the Future: From National Liberation to Women's Emancipation* (Zed Press, London, 1984).

41. K. Weinrich, 'Changes in the Political and Economic Roles of Women in Zimbabwe Since Independence', in *Cultures*, 8, 1982, p. 4.

42. J. Kimble and E. Unterhalter, 'We Have Opened the Road'; A. Oakley, *Women Confined: Towards a Sociology of Childbirth* (Martin Robertson, Oxford, 1980); A. Rich, *Of Woman Born* (Virago, London, 1978).

43. *The Herald*, 19 March 1984. I am grateful to Professor T.O. Ranger who gave me access to his collection.

44. *The Sunday Mail*, 8 April 1984.

45. *The Herald*, 9 April, 1984.

46. See T.O. Ranger, *Fourth Review of the Zimbabwean Press* (for the period 17 March to 26 April 1984).

47. *The Sunday Mail*, 8 April 1984.

48. G. Konie, *Women and Political Structures: The Grassroots to the National Level*. A statement made to the Conference on Women in Southern Africa: Strategies for Change, Harare, 1982.

49. This goes equally for Western institutions. A symbolic example is the fact that the men's lavatory in the British House of Commons reads 'members only', erroneously implying that all members of Parliament are male.

50. S. Urdang, 'The Last Transition?', p. 15.

51. D. Sanders, 'The State and Popular Organisation', in *Social Change and Development*, No. 8, 1984.

52. S. Thornton, 'Health Administration in Zimbabwe', *Hospital and Health Services Review*, January 1984.

53. Quoted in D. Sanders, 'The State and Popular Organisation', p. 8.

54. Ibid., p. 8.

55. Zimbabwe Women's Bureau, *We Carry a Heavy Load: Rural Women in Zimbabwe Speak Out* (Harare, 1982) p. 7.

5: Practice and Theory: Guinea-Bissau and Cape Verde

by Basil Davidson

As large in the recent history of Africa as they are small in population and territory, Guinea-Bissau (formerly the Portuguese 'overseas province' of Guiné) and the nine inhabited islands of the Cape Verde archipelago (another part of the Portuguese empire), suffered colonial enclosure as a process of impoverishment in every field of life. The capitalism of this enclosure, as it would be easy to show in detail, produced an immiseration that was not relative, but absolute.[1] In cultural terms, less than one-half of one percent of the population of the mainland, and perhaps twenty percent of the population of the islands were effectively literate by 1950. Against this small 'enrichment' (if one may call it that, given the narrow provincialism of this literacy in Portuguese), was the assault on the consciousness and confidence of these peoples by decades of a viciously instrumental racism on the part of their colonial rulers and their 'metropolis' in Europe.

Political deprivation may have scarcely worsened since the early 1920s, but by that time, and then with the onset of the military dictatorship which gave rise to Portuguese fascism[2], the last political rights and claims of these peoples all but disappeared, before they were altogether destroyed in the 1930s. Economic subordination — marginalisation, 'peripheralisation' — meanwhile grew steadily greater, until, in the 1940s, Guiné had become little more than a helpless victim of Lisbon's trading monopolies, while Cape Verde in the 1930s was about to enter one of the harshest periods of its colonial misery.

No doubt this impoverishment was felt in varying degrees of pain. If Portuguese-appointed chiefs of Fula and Mandinka groups on the mainland lived worse than their genuine predecessors, they nonetheless lived better than those over whom they were placed to rule on behalf of colonial masters. If *dyula* traders had to be content with the crumbs let fall by Portuguese traders, they were still able to extract a profit that could seem enviable to their customers. If small landowners living in Cape Verdean towns had little wealth or comfort, they remained a lot better off than the sharecroppers or tenants who cultivated their lands. Practically all these people felt the pressures of impoverishment in one way or another; but their social stratifications were many and complex.

It followed from this that the cause of anti-colonial liberation was seen and shaped as a protest against specific forms of exploitation, just as it followed that a minority — as it transpired, a small minority — would always prefer the personal gains of colonial privilege, in so far as these were available, to the risks and perils of revolt. As many have pointed out, the result would have been neocolonialism if the Portuguese system had possessed the economic strength to make concessions: to admit the transfer of direct political control over these 'overseas provinces', but without serious change in the nature of the system produced by the colonial period.

It was Portuguese intransigence that posed the question of system. An exploitation that almost universally was felt as hateful and oppressive could not be diminished, much less removed, without abolishing the colonial system root and branch. This became ever more widely understood as the initial 'protest movement' of the PAIGC (African Party for the Independence of Guinea and Cape Verde) developed after 1959 towards insurrection and anti-colonial warfare.[3] Few had faith in any prospects of that kind; but the lesson was driven home, especially in 1962, by new and more bloody waves of police persecution and administrative violence. Clearly, compromise was not going to be remotely possible. The solution had to be removing the Portuguese, together with their taxes and their servitudes, their forced labour and their trading greed. Having done that, people could begin to live decently again, treading once more in the paths of their ancestors, and restoring to themselves the self-respect that foreign rule had taken from them.

It was always evident that the struggle for anti-colonial liberation could in no direct or conscious way pose the issue of socialism. The road to an acceptance of a socialist perspective would have to be a long one. And if a few were tempted to lose sight of this stubborn fact and condition of progress, every now and then during those embattled years, Amílcar Cabral, the leader of the PAIGC, was quick to bring them to earth again. 'Keep always in mind,' he advised in a well-known passage of his *Directives* of 1965, 'that the people are not fighting for ideas, for the things in anyone's head. They are fighting to win material benefits, to live better and in peace, to see their lives go forward, to guarantee the future of their children.'[4] Anyone who ran ahead of the majority's willingness to follow would soon be running alone.

The struggle's influence

What proved repeatedly renewing and creative, as the war spread and grew and grimly continued, was precisely the majority's willingness to follow — to perceive the need for their liberation, to accept the challenge of meeting that need, and to join the effort of the PAIGC in answering that challenge. Exemplary leadership went into developing this popular response, and much patience. Above all was the importance of the influence of the struggle itself. Wherever adequate security from colonialist attack could be achieved in wide rural zones, their inhabitants increasingly found themselves drawn, not into retreading the paths of their ancestors, but into building a new way of life. This new way of life had to be revolutionary because it had to be democratic. It had to call for a revolution in consciousness as well as structure. Two ever-present pressures ensured this.

It was seen that the war could not be sustained, much less won, without a steady conversion of mass sympathy into mass participation; this was the first pressure. Mere sympathy would soon shrivel in the face of enemy reprisals and the hardships that a war of liberation could not but impose. Only when people took themselves beyond the stage of sympathising with revolt and made the revolt their own, consciously, and comprehendingly, would the necessary self-sacrifice and moral power be forthcoming. This certainty drew out another. That kind of active and voluntary participation, whether in fighting the enemy or helping those who fought, would respond only to a far-reaching and increasingly systemised practice of democracy. At the grassroots; at every level. For who would risk their lives and all that they held dear so as to exchange one set of exploiters for another?

The lesson was taught again and again: as often as it needed to be taught. In Guinea–Bissau it was taught most painfully and convincingly during 1963 with the initial emergence of local bosses and bullies in newly-liberated zones, and with their overthrow at the crucial party congress of early 1964.[5] Comparable confrontations occurred in the experience of Frelimo (Front for the Liberation of Mozambique) in Mozambique and of MPLA (Popular Movement for the Liberation of Angola) in Angola; and I think that they have occurred, in one form or another, in every recent war of anti-colonial struggle.

The essential means of surviving and winning, in other words, imposed the need for a profoundly democratic system, one different from the old system — from any previously known system — in its organisation, quality and aims. Out of these imperatives there came, gradually and unevenly according to the difficult nature of this enlightenment, the practice and then the theory of socio-economic change that were to give these movements their political resonance. For 'it was in the process of struggle that we synthesised the lessons of each experience,' Samora Machel has told us, 'forging our ideology, constructing the theoretical instruments of our struggle.'[6] Or, as Cabral liked to put it, this was the process through which participants came to know that national liberation, if it were to be more than 'simply a matter of raising a flag or singing an anthem', had to mean a revolution in conscience and objective structure.

The launching of the process, unavoidably, was 'substitutionist'; the long-term task was to displace this 'minority substitution' by mass participation. 'When they began, like every other minority of their type, the pioneers of the PAIGC were obliged to substitute themselves for "the will of the nation". They had to do this all the more because then, and for a long time afterwards (as they also say, recalling those days), they were "nationalists without a nation".'[7] The central duty of revolutionary leadership was therefore to promote mass participation; and their steady success in achieving this extremely difficult development was indeed the core of their eventual victory.

'Today'—as seen at the end of 1972—'the process of making participation gain over substitution, but without the vanguard's in any way abdicating from its task of leadership, has gone very far. Five years ago I heard an old man in the Quitáfine sector describing that process. He began by talking about life under Portuguese rule. He said it was "like living in a cave". But "we didn't think it could be different. Party work and Party talk: it's like a big lie at the beginning. But in the end it's the real truth." It is an explanation that Cabral liked to recall. That old man, he would tell you, had got to the heart of the matter with a minimum of words.'[8]

'So it appeared to a visitor [to this liberated zone in 1972] that nothing happened or could happen, save for accidents or defaults of duty, without the active participation of local people, and this was true even down to the organisation of canoe-transport for crossing creeks or to the handing out of permits to visit relatives in towns still garrisoned by the Portuguese.'[9] Village assemblies and their executive committees, together with their local militias for self-defence and their law tribunals and other instruments, had begun to embrace mass participation within an organised *system*.

This achievement, profoundly liberating though it was, innovating and fertile of renewed innovation, had nonetheless to be limited to the political and cultural aspects of everyday life. It could and it did mobilise the rural majority for national unity, irrespective of internal class and sub-class conflicts; but while the war lasted it had to stop short of moving into the field of economic reorganisation. Lars Rudebeck has put this well:

> It proved to be possible, in Guinea–Bissau, to carry out a successful and even exemplary struggle for national liberation. But this was based on the *political* interest of almost all Guineans in ending alien rule in their country. It was only based in a very embryonic way on the interest of the majority of them in transforming the economy into a popularly ruled economy, able to sustain the production of a surplus for national development after the achievement of independence.[10]

Thinking back, it seems clear that Amílcar Cabral and those closest to him (whether inside the liberated zones or at the external office in Conakry) were entirely aware of the limited nature of the process achieved by 1972. At this time, however, they were convinced that the stage of the struggle, as well as the manifestly weakening ability of the dictatorship to continue its colonial war, imposed an urgent need to complete the building of the political institutions they had launched in the middle 1960s. To that end, during 1972, the PAIGC began a major political campaign, committing many of its best militants, for the preparation and holding of a general election throughout the liberated zones, and by universal adult suffrage, of candidates to a People's National Assembly. The Assembly was envisaged as the supreme legislative arm of the existing complex network of local assemblies and executive committees, and as the body which would give the new state its right, constitutionally and *vis-à-vis* the world as well as the Portuguese, to assume a national independence. I saw the final stages of that memorable election campaign. Its success was such that in the following September, no more than eight months after losing Cabral by assassination at the hand of agents of the dictatorship, a popularly elected Assembly was able to proclaim the independence of the Republic of Guinea-Bissau and win immediate recognition across the world.

I have heard it argued (though not by any participant) that Portuguese collapse would have come more favourably, for the development of this infant state, in 1976 or 1977 (as many expected, including myself) and not, as actually happened, early in 1974, only seven months after the Assembly had proclaimed the new state's constitutional existence and independence. A delay might have helped the building of new structures in the economic field. But this is doubtful, because the last phases of the war were extremely painful and destructive as the dictatorship's commanders made their final and desperate effort to stave off defeat. As it was (and I think, in any case, must have been), effective movement towards economic transformation in the then large liberated zones could not be a realistic project; there was no time, and fighting was fierce throughout 1973. Yet this is not to say that the need for it was not perceived by those who looked ahead, and above all by Amílcar Cabral himself. Rudebeck has reminded us of Cabral's 'characteristic admonition' of cadres in 1971, or, as Rudebeck puts it, his heartfelt cry for deeper understanding:

> We have to make greater efforts to create collective fields in the villages. . . Regardless of specific responsibilities the comrades should help our people to organise collective fields. This is a great experiment for the future, comrades. Those who do not understand this have not yet understood anything of our struggle, however much they have fought and however heroic they may have been.[11]

The PAIGC and the new state thus entered independence, swiftly realised and politically complete, without possessing the economic structures of mass participation. Other forms of participation, often remarkably advanced, had won the liberation war and cleared the way for further progress; but now it would be the weight of economic influence, as between sectors and as between classes, sub-classes or privileged groups, that would be decisive in shaping the future. In a population that was ninety percent rural, and entirely dependent on rural production for its viability, the countryside would have to continue to lead the towns (or rather the town; the only one of any size was the capital of Bissau). Continued transformation would be otherwise impossible.

Cabral believed that the test of independence, when it came, would be the extent to which the interests of the rural populations were placed and were kept in front of any other interests. 'The general approach that we have,' he said in 1967, nearly seven years before victory came,

> is that all structural decisions are to be based on the needs and conditions of the peasantry. . . Our new administration will be strictly without those

chains of command familiar in colonial times – governors of provinces and so on. . . Above all, we want to decentralise as much as may be possible. That's one reason why we're inclined to think that Bissau will not continue to be our capital in an administrative sense. In fact, we are against the whole idea of a capital. Why shouldn't ministries be dispersed?. . . Why should we saddle ourselves with the paraphernalia of a presidential palace, a concentration of ministries, the clear signs of an emergent elite which can soon become a privileged group?

Agriculture would come first: 'We shall put our whole priority on agriculture. . .'[12] Within three and a half years of independence (and just over five of Cabral's murder), as it turned out, a new presidential palace was nearing completion in Bissau, and leading party cadres, appointed to be administrative heads of districts, were beginning to be called governors, and were certainly enjoying it.

After independence

It is tempting to be wise after the event, but I think that most qualified observers, including myself, were aware by 1977 that something was going wrong. A visit to the old liberated zones of the south, during early 1976, had shown that the wartime committees were still valid and in place; and if nothing had been done to improve rural facilities in these remote areas the answer was that there had as yet been no time. The answer at that time was convincing. 'But naturally,' a political commissar remarked to me on Como Island, 'if people remain isolated by bad communications, they could quickly become demoralised now that the war is over.' He added that 'as yet, there is no political problem here,' and I judged that he was right about this. After all, the time was still less than two years after the collapse of the dictatorship, and only eighteen months since the completion of Portuguese withdrawal.

Another eighteen months later, with the congress of November 1977, a change had begun to appear: a subtle change, hard to define, little more perhaps than a change of political atmosphere. On the surface all seemed well, but a closed session nonetheless had to give the floor to sharp criticism by delegates from the old liberated zones where the war had been fought and won. Its drift was that the danger of 'Bissau swallowing the rural areas' was no longer a remote one, but an issue that had really begun to count. A long report to the congress by Secretary-General Aristides Pereira (who had also become President of the Cape Verde Republic upon its proclamation in July 1975) seemed to confirm this, at least by implication. More exports were needed – and needed desperately, given the economic crisis left behind by the Portuguese – 'but the movement of our economy must, above all, be activated by an internal dynamism, arising from the activation of our own resources, whether human or material, and not relying on a merely mechanical expansion won through spending foreign aid'.

'Foreign aid must remain complementary to a dynamic dictated by the needs of an independent internal development,' continued Pereira's statement of November 1977, at a time when foreign aid had become large, even abundant, and from many sources. Such aid, he emphasised, could not be accepted as a substitute for self-generated expansion of the economy. But that kind of expansion could come only from 'the active participation of the most deprived sector of our population, and above all of our rural producers'. Otherwise, if policy were to benefit the few at the cost of the many, 'our economy might grow, but it would not develop'. As to Bissau, the capital 'must not be allowed to monopolise our action, but must function only as a motor of development, as a catalysing element for the activities of the regions'.[13]

Less official warnings were more direct. A planning paper prepared for the November 1977 congress by the relevant commissariat (ministry), then headed by Vasco Cabral—on the 'left' of a party leadership which was now beginning consciously to have a 'right'—drew attention to the growing predominance of the capital city, and its absorption (actual and prospective) of a major part of new investment. For example, Bissau disposed of 12.15 million kWh while all the rural zones together had only 1.85 million kWh; yet the accepted plan for 1980 was that Bissau would have 24.7 million kWh and the rural zones still only 3.5 million. No doubt there were strong arguments for building up a capital city left with few facilities and no industries. But the case for building up the rural zones was not only far stronger—it was the case for which the PAIGC had, in no small measure, fought the war. And with Bissau receiving priority, there would be increasing exploitation of rural producers to the advantage of an urban population nourished by foreign aid and rural exports. How could this be more than a variation on the familiar neocolonialist recipe?

Warnings went unheeded. Having settled in Bissau for reasons of necessity in September 1974, the leadership stayed in Bissau. This in itself might have mattered little, for the country is small and many of the chief roads (thanks to Portuguese military requirements during the war) were paved and in good condition; the government also had the use of helicopters provided by foreign aid (Soviet, in this case). Ministers travelled about the country, and kept in touch with regional centres. Plans were laid to make the little provincial 'town-lets' of Bolama and Farim into centres of development that could offset the attractive pull of Bissau.

Paradoxically, the large quantity of foreign aid—still arriving at a rate comparatively higher than that of any other African country, a major token of the prestige won by the PAIGC—was near the root of the trouble. The wartime leadership had depended on the rural majority for life, survival and eventual victory; this dependence, as anyone who was there at the time knew full well, was always a prime factor in every major decision of policy that was taken. Now it faded into the background. More and more, the reverse became true; it was the rural majority who depended on a leadership equipped with state power and with access to large supplies of foreign aid. Nothing during the wartime struggle could be done without standing on the sure and ready base of 'people's power', of mass participation, of 'mobilisation', as the PAIGC called it. But now, it appeared, everything could be done without it.

Mass participation might still be an honoured theme and something to be praised, but too often, the practical affairs of daily life no longer made it seem essential.

Increasingly, policy was formed without reference to the institutions of *participação* by a central government dazzled by the mirage of aid-funded capital-intensive projects, which themselves offered little or no benefit to the rural populations. At the same time, much continued to be done with foresight and good intentions. Yet the fact of 'growth without development', against which Pereira had so clearly warned in November 1977, soon bulked larger on the scene. In spite of continued declarations of support for rural producers, only 5 to 6 percent of budgetary expenditure and state investment were devoted to agriculture during the closing years of the 1970s.[14] The ill fortune of drought again lowered rural production, and even rural productivity, in the staple food of rice; in consequence, food imports pressed harder than ever on the chronic deficit inherited from colonial times.

Bissau grew insistently in size and influence, and with a population of which a large part had never possessed any of the ardent political commitment of the rural zones. The infections of decay, and very obviously in the case of some leading elements on the right of the party-government spectrum, began to smell and even stink. 'They import champagne for themselves,' an ambassador *en poste* in Bissau disgustedly remarked to me in July 1979, 'and they expect you to serve them with champagne when they visit you.'

So it came about, at first imperceptibly and then more and more as a matter of course, as a thing accepted while officially unknown, that dependence on foreign aid supplanted dependence on the labour and initiative of the rural populations. 'The country's internal and external resources,' in the words of a well-informed and sympathetic observer, Ladislau Dowbor,

> were concentrated in the city without, however, any significant increase of production: either in the countryside, which had no access to adequate resources, or in the city itself, where application of those resources was not productive... And so it evolved that external finance, instead of constituting the initial means of development, became ever more the crucial axle of the economy, dragging the country into a difficult posture of dependence.[15]

That posture, as elsewhere in Africa, was made ever less tenable by soaring oil prices and, structurally, by the adverse terms of trade inherent in the whole South–North relationship.

It is difficult at this stage of inquiry to be sure when these various seeds of decay were first sown, although I think myself that 1977 was probably the crucial year. Writing in 1982 after several visits, Rudebeck found rural situations in which 'PAIGC organisation and the whole structure of mass participation [*mobilisation populaire* in the original French text] had been liquidated since 1976–77'. More and more, these zones had been left to themselves, and had reverted to their 'traditional' economy. A village like

Kandjadja, he added, 'looks fairly autonomous within the framework of the state—as well as depoliticised. They have been waiting a long time for a new political commissar. "It's the state that decides. So we wait." Distrust of the regional authorities is great'.[16] The wartime system had evidently gone into disuse.

There was criticism from the rank and file, from the rural militants, from the 'left' in the leadership; but it met with silence. There was protest; more and more, after 1978, it met with police repression. The very basis of the PAIGC's legitimacy—that it represented a highly democratic system of political power—was now eroded. When rice shortages in the capital became acute, and other tensions grew insistent, the military coup of November 1980 quickly followed. There was next to no opposition. The government had self-destructed.

After the coup

It was obvious in the early weeks that the right had taken over, and was much more to the right than had seemed likely before the coup. Wild accusations of 'Cape Verdean colonisation' reproduced the wartime propaganda of the colonial dictatorship, and the project of union with Cape Verde was denounced. The misdeeds of the overthrown post-independence leadership were lavishly rehearsed, and, as later evidence suggested, were considerably exaggerated. The effective rejection of 'people's power' seemed, now, to become deliberate policy. Had Portugal at last managed to achieve its own 'neocolonialist solution'? It appeared very possible.

Then it was seen that matters were not so simple. There is no space here for details, but within six months or so the initial description of the coup as the 'victory of the right' became doubtful. As a party of mass participation, schooled in the lessons of a long struggle, the PAIGC could not so easily be shoved aside. Gradually, there came an at least formal return to 'the policy and ideology of Cabral' — meaning, of course, Amílcar and not his dethroned younger brother—while the new President, the ex-military commander and Prime Minister Nino Vieira, made it repeatedly clear that he himself, at least, had no intention of turning his back on the aims and ideas of the past.

But was it now possible for existing trends opposed to the realisation of those aims and ideas to be reversed? There was little to suggest, at least in 1984, that the institutions of mass participation were being revived and reinvigorated, much less extended into the economic field. There were repeated calls for 'a struggle without compromise against corruption'—as reported, for example, in the newspaper *Nô Pintcha* on 10 September 1983—and for a greater investment of resources in agriculture and the rural zones; Nino himself seemed especially committed to that aim. Tolerable relations with the Cape Verde Republic were renewed, although still at arm's length. Guinea-Bissau remained a member of the African lusophone community, whose heads of state met there in late 1983. But the overall outcome, in real terms, now seemed more than doubtful.

If atrophy of the organs of people's power appeared to have set in, what had become of the PAIGC as a dynamising force, as a political vanguard, as a critic of the state and its government? No reassuring answer was to hand. In spite of its name, the PAIGC had remained a movement rather than a structured party, and its identification with the state had continued: the 1977 congress, after all, had defined the PAIGC as 'a national liberation movement in power'. In contrast to post-war evolution in Cape Verde, as will be seen (and other such contrasts could be made for Mozambique and Angola), there was no emergent separation of party power from state power or as between militants and those 'members of the public' (above all, in the old liberated zones of wartime organisation) who continued to regard themselves as belonging to 'the party of Cabral'.

Some efforts at restricting PAIGC membership to properly constituted members, and a systematic listing of those members (and counting of such members), were certainly made in 1977, and possibly later. But here, too, the signs were of atrophy, or even worse than atrophy. One may note in this respect that Nino Vieira, when addressing the national council of the PAIGC seven months after his coup, could urge that 'the party's return to the masses is necessary and urgent, for through seven years we have witnessed the gradual liquidation of our party'. The party apparatus, he continued, was threatened by loss of 'one of its foremost characteristics: that is, its close ties with the people and its profoundly popular roots'.[17]

Which was not to say, as yet, that the PAIGC had ceased to exist as a broad grouping of militants, most of whom were still the veterans of the armed struggle and its intense political experience. On the contrary, there were some signs of political activism 'at the base'. A new congress in November 1981 was attended by 301 delegates elected by regional party assemblies, of whom 163 were peasants and 44 were women.[18] For all that, the following period brought no sure evidence of 'the party's return to the masses' in the sense that Vieira had undoubtedly meant, while the leadership appeared to give additional authority to the right in spite of Vieira's repeated exhortations on the need to pursue 'the line of Cabral'. It was already difficult to resist the tentative conclusion that the PAIGC had subsumed itself into the apparatus of the state, had thus become an appendage of government, and, as such, had ceased to exist as dynamising vanguard. Equally, though, nothing had yet proved that this was the end of the story.

From certain angles it might seem that regressive trends had gone beyond reversal; but on the evidence of the congress of 1981 and later trends, this might be going beyond the evidence. A more hopeful conclusion has been suggested by Ladislau Dowbor. 'It seems to me,' he wrote late in 1983, 'that Guinea–Bissau is in furious debate with itself, and with the combination of adverse forces... Who will win? Nobody knows.'[19] There may be much to make one think that the profoundly liberating legacy of the struggle before 1977 will not and even cannot be cancelled out, and that wrong choices can eventually give way to right political choices. In this respect, though dourly, and perhaps more grimly than Amílcar could have foreseen even in his most pessimistic moments, *a luta continua* (the struggle continues).

In Cape Verde

If the building of a viable economy which should reduce and remove 'the exploitation of man by man', and give a leading place to the producers of wealth, was difficult in Guinea–Bissau, it could well seem beyond solution in the Cape Verde of 1975. Throughout decades of colonial neglect or indifference, emigration had offered the only alternative to starvation. Especially since the onset of severe drought in 1969, the population had lived on charity from Portugal, on the *apoio* hand-out system which had no constructive value but was rather, in Silva's well-justified words, 'a truly generalised instrument of corruption'.[20] When the PAIGC was swept to power in July 1975 by a general election held while the Portuguese were still there, local production provided no more than 15 percent of basic food needs; imports had to provide the rest. This meant, of course, that large emigration filled much of the gap.

A land-holding structure derived from the long period of slavery added another set of problems. Whether by sharecropping (*parceria*) or a primitive system of tenancy (*arrendamento*), 'about 60 percent of peasants had to procure the land of others in order to provide for the minimal needs of subsistence'.[21] An obscure process of social fission had divided the population (more than 90 percent rural) into a bewildering variety of forms of dependence, and these, in turn, were rendered still more complex by the fact that emigrés continued to hold land at home and to support families at home by the return of earnings. Meanwhile, foreign aid continued to be indispensable to basic food needs, as well as to any infrastructural tasks the newly independent regime might wish to undertake. A helpless slide into neocolonialist subordination and its consequences seemed all too possible. This could appear all the more likely to happen, even certain to happen, because the largest concentration of emigrants was in the USA, and the bulk of this American population of Cape Verdean origin (sometimes, of very recent origin) had been opposed to the PAIGC.

Yet no such slide came about. The Cape Verde Republic of the mid-1980s proved that even the smallest and economically most vulnerable country can defend its self-determination and its policies if the appropriate political choices are made and maintained, and can progress towards a widening mass participation in the conduct of its government and the reorganisation of its economy.

The PAIGC came to power in Cape Verde with overwhelming popular support. It possessed some of the most effective and experienced militants of the wartime struggle on the mainland. All but one or two of these returned at once to the islands, where they were joined by another handful of veterans, this time of the clandestine struggle on the islands which had begun, effectively, in 1958, and for which some of them had long sat in colonial jails.

They made their capital in Praia, but in this respect they had an advantage over the mainland. Praia was (and is) a small town on a small island (although the biggest town on the biggest island of the archipelago). Besides this, a far-reaching decentralisation was built into the geography of the country, for each of its nine inhabited islands has a history and identity of its own and is divided from other islands by more or less wide ocean channels. Cape Verdeans have a strong and even passionate sense of Cape Verdean identity, but each island has its own pull of local loyalty, and the pull is a powerful one.

As on the mainland, a new political system had to be built from ground level up, for the Portuguese left nothing behind save unusable fragments of their dictatorship. How was this to be done?

Building from ground level

On the one hand, there was a vivid local patriotism and pride in the capacity of Cape Verdeans to extract a living, however fragile, from their volcanic rocks and from the ocean around them; on the other hand, history had imposed a metropolitan culture that was deeply weakening of self-assurance. It was Cape Verdean good fortune, at this unique moment in the islands' history, that independence arrived with the banners of a party, of a political movement, of volunteers returning from a war of freedom they had helped to win, with a clarity of aims and self-confidence that immediately became a magnet for distracted or scattered loyalties, and a focus for common effort in a *national* dimension never known before, or even, save in the poetry of romance, so much as dreamed before.

'Substitution', at the outset, was complete and unavoidable. A few dozen men and women—at the most, a few hundred—may have known what needed to be done and how to do it. For the rest, it was 'rhetoric and euphoria'. Opposition there was none, save for some insignificant handfuls of colonial bourgeois; but of organisation there was also none. Just as no armed struggle had been possible here, so there had been no liberated zones. Lacking these, there had been no means of launching even the beginnings of mass participation. Yet—the words are those of a leading Cape Verdean militant—'there could not be, nor ever was, a national liberation without mass participation'.[22]

The problem was to build a system that would depend upon mass participation and *systematically* ensure its further development. The solution was approached by various initiatives. Two were politically crucial: the building of a vanguard party from the foundations provided by veterans who were few in number but, fortunately, large in experience; and, secondly, the building of participatory institutions and structures. The first had necessarily to precede the second, since the second was necessarily dependent on the first. The leadership's line of thought was that the mere building of a van-guard party could guarantee nothing in itself; on the contrary, if wrongly built, it could act as a shield and buttress for elitist substitution. The need, accordingly, was to build a small but devotedly competent party of unpaid volunteers (aside from a few fulltime and paid workers) who, while being able to rely on the support of state power, would themselves possess no state power, nor, outside their own ranks, any executive power of any kind. Its central function would be to lead the development of a 'national revolutionary democracy'[23] based on, and legitimated by, the institutions of *participação popular*.

This determined separation of party power from state power contained an ambiguity, for the persons at the head of the party were the same persons as those at the head of the state, a situation epitomised after 1975 by Aristides Pereira, at once the veteran Secretary-General of the sole political party and the new President of the Republic. That ambiguity was both unavoidable and desirable. There could be no other way of building a democratic system from the ground level, much less a system vowed to far-reaching structural change; and it would obviously continue. The guarantee against substitutionist abuse of power and policy, or ossification of democratic initiative, or the sort of decay symbolised elsewhere by 'importing champagne', would lie in the very needs of the evolving system. This was because the system could neither function nor grow, or even take shape, without the continued development of a real and effective mass participation; and the organs of this mass participation, as they expanded further, would possess the suprene legislative power. I will return to this cardinal point a little further on.

Building the Cape Verdean party was a priority of the years immediately after independence. A carefully selected and tested membership—selected and tested, that is, by the veterans of 1975—had grown by 1980 from a few score at the time of liberation to somewhat over 4000, or about one in 75 of the total population (and to around 4500 in 1983, for the time being, probably the desired maximum). Sixteen percent were wage-workers and 38 percent 'small peasants' or sharecroppers (the latter category due to become small peasants after the then-prospective Land Reform), while 30 percent were state employees (in a country virtually without private enterprise in services or industry), and the rest were students, professional persons, or the like. A little more than 46 percent were under 30 years of age, another 36 percent between 30 and 50.

They were organised in *grupos de base*, 'base groups', scattered throughout this highly dispersed population. By mid-1980 there were about 400 of these *grupos*, or about one for every 750 souls (although this average can be mis-leading, since some islands were more advanced than others). These 400 groups elected representatives to 73 section committees which, in turn, elected 15 sector committees culminating in one regional committee for each of the nine inhabited islands. Much of this structure was still being "run in"; women members still formed only 16 percent of the total membership in a culture where male chauvinism is no less obstructive than elsewhere in Africa (or wherever). Here again there were interesting contrasts: whereas the island of Fogo had only 10.7 percent of women members at the end of 1979, Maio had 36 percent.[24] But the decisive advance on 1975, whether in terms of individual quality, spread of membership, or the capacity that derives from practical work, was well secured.

In any case, the advance was enough, by 1979, to set about tackling the task of building structures of mass participation: of drawing the whole adult population into assuming an organised and permanent responsibility for the government of its own affairs, whether local or national. This task was difficult, as it always must be, but the difficulty here was enlarged by the complex nature of class division, notably as between landholders living on rent (often set at extortionate levels) in towns or villages, and small peasants and sharecroppers whose meagre surplus provided that rent (in cash or in kind). Many of the former were 'petty bourgeois' who had no least thought of 'committing suicide as a class' by joining themselves to the cause of the hungry masses, while many of the latter found it hard to understand just what was possible and what was not. Others, again, were disturbed by 'tales from America', where many had close relatives, which warned against the 'communist evil' being brewed by the new regime. A few, among the young, fell victim to 'far left' illusions.

The necessary principle of organised and permanent mass participation was laid down, or rather further defined, on the basis of wartime practice in the liberated zones of the mainland. At the congress of November 1977, held in Bissau, the agreement was that there must come into existence, alongside every executive committee of local self-government, an assembly which elects and controls it. To gather these assemblies was easy enough among a people whose communities, often formed in physical isolation by the nature of these islands, have traditionally known a strong internal cohesion. The problem was to cause the assemblies to produce effective committees of men and women who, giving their free time and varied experience or talent, would be able to speak and act for their communities: doing things, that is, which no previous state power had asked or allowed them to do. To this problem, as anywhere else, there was and there can be no final solution, since the reality of an active and purposeful participation has to call for continued political struggle; but this, after all, is in the nature of the human condition. The need—and the choice—was to create a dynamic system, and then to promote its further reality and evolution.

A start was made in 1980. Village or locality assemblies were asked to produce *commissões de moradores*, residents' committees, in each of the islands. They were created initially by unprompted election or, more often, by nomination until habits of election were learned in the next year or so. These executives were endowed with considerable powers of decision over local affairs and services. As they evolved and multiplied, they would become the spine of government, served by state administration rather than serving it, flanked by three mass organisations representing the interests of wage-workers, women, and youth, and advised and promoted by local party *grupos*. In 1980, for example, the approximately 50,000 people of the island of Santo Antão had 22 *commissões de moradores* and a party membership of 430 militants organised in 55 *grupos*.[25]

More research into all this is much to be desired; but even without, it can be seen just why and how (as I wrote above) the 'system could neither function nor grow, or even take shape, without the continued development of a real and effective mass participation'. In the single matter of law and order, for example, state power had to rely, in Santo Antão, on nine people's tribunals for the handling of civil and criminal offences (apart from homicide and other major crimes, where higher courts take over), and, otherwise, on exactly twelve regular policemen. But perhaps there were soldiers instead of police? No, but there were village militias raised and controlled by *commissões de moradores*. State power, in short, was people's power.

This was the process, chosen and promoted, through which the initial 'substitutionism' of the executive had begun, even by 1980, to be overtaken and replaced by a complex and intensive system of democratic representation, capped by the election of a People's National Assembly with legislative power. What is portrayed here is not, of course, any smooth march into utopia or the growth of angels' wings, but the steady construction of a living and egalitarian democracy where nothing remotely like it had ever existed. Much, even most, of the work remained to be done. Many assemblies and their executives did not function consistently and well. Human frailties were as common as one should expect. But the system had come into being, and would be reinforced and enlarged.

Class issues

This achievement, nonetheless, would not hold its own unless the legacy of class exploitation were rapidly reduced and, at least in some measure, brought to an end. First and foremost, this called for the reduction and at least partial removal of the exploitation suffered by the rural majority through the agencies of sharecropping and the like. A far-reaching land reform had always figured in the Cape Verdean programme of the PAIGC, and Amílcar Cabral, himself an agronomist by training and practice, had given it a high priority. Now, at last, it could be realised.

The work began with preliminary study of land-holding and land-usage, for little reliable and exact information was to hand. A dramatic situation was revealed. It was found, for example, that 39 percent of all Cape Verdean peasants owned no land at all, while another 30 percent, while owning some land, owned too little for subsistence and were obliged to lease land from proprietors usually living as absentees. Summarising in 1983, Silva wrote that: 'The majority of Cape Verdean landowners receive revenues from the agricultural sector, appropriate an important part of the surplus work necessary from the landless peasants, and consume outside the agricultural sector to which they contribute nothing.'[26] Coupled with emigration, this disinvestment was defined in 1978 as 'economic desertification', and became one of the central targets of the land reform.

A series of decree-laws launched the process of reform after 1976. With the first of these, as Silva has written,

> the government nationalized the various large landed estates belonging to absentee landlords and traitors [most of them in Portugal]. Later, it

banned sub-tenancy farming in new tenancy contracts; it also forbade the breaking up of certain properties for the purpose of leasing plots of less than one hectare in the rain-fed zones, or half a hectare in the irrigated zones; and, further, strengthened measures allowing for the reduction of rent in case of bad harvests or crop failure.[27]

With these and other preliminaries designed to improve peasant income and facilities, such as the launching of a co-operative movement, the government was able on 25 March 1982 to present its Basic Law on Agrarian Reform. This important measure, after further discussion and modification, came into force on 1 January 1983. It provided for 'an apparently slow but sure rhythm' of structural change so as to avoid any collapse of production or social upsets. There appeared, by 1984, to have been only one serious upset. This occurred when a handful of landholders on Santo Antão, evidently stirred up by hostile critics in emigration, set going a rumour that emigrés were to lose their land. 'In the ensuing melée, one man was killed and several injured. The ringleaders were arrested and at their trial were sentenced to between six months and ten years in prison for their part in the tragedy.[28] The rumour was baseless because the law provided for no such thing; the emigrés in question were regarded as temporary absentees with continuing rights to hold land. Silva summarises:

> At the end of this process [set going by the decree-laws and the Law on Agrarian Reform] about 74 percent of the Cape Verde peasants will have cast off the bonds of dependence which bind them today to one or more landed proprietors. . . [and] Cape Verde agriculture will be based on a system of organisation having, at its base, the small peasant enterprise which, on its side, will be integrated into various types of service and productive co-operatives.[29]

What was the effect, meanwhile, of large quantities of foreign aid, from many sources, arriving here as it was arriving in Guinea–Bissau? Such quantities were entirely necessary to food needs and to every aspect of infrastructural or non-agricultural development. But did aid, as in Guinea–Bissau, have the effect of discouraging investment in agriculture and peasant needs, and thus of deflecting the regime from its declared policies? Some consideration of the year 1980, five years after independence, will help to answer these questions.

By that time, the state had been able to invest a total of some four million contos (about £600,000) in various ways—an investment at an annual rate that was three or four times' larger than ever envisaged by the colonial regime.[30] With industry able to provide no more than 2.5 percent of the national product, and unemployment at a very high level, some of this investment laid modest industrial foundations in fish-refrigeration, power-production, ship-repair facilities and comparable activities. Other investment went into the improvement of inter-island communications, rural roads, and the launching of a small ocean-going cargo fleet (planned to be developed in co-operation with Angola). Money was put into health facilities and public education; by 1980, about 99 percent of all Cape Verdean children between 7 and 13 were attending school (and the big majority of these, of course, were rural children), another great advance on 1975.

But agriculture and the peasant sector received the lion's share. 'Rural development,' Pereira could report in mid-1980, 'has absorbed between 25 and 30 percent of all investment' in the five year period since independence, and has employed between 12 and 15 thousand workers in islands with an agricultural potential [several have none] on various projects, some of large dimensions' concerned with soil and water development or the like.[31] But there was more. A major effort was also invested in a general ecological improvement of islands long deforested and deprived even of elementary means of reducing the loss of precious rain through precipitous 'run off' into the sea. There were foreign donors who liked this idea and thought they should hand out money for the purpose, copying, however unintentionally, the *apoio* system of the Portuguese.

The government thought otherwise. From aid monies thus made available they created a wages fund. This they used to employ some 30,000 unemployed in conservation work (perhaps one-third of the total work-force, though still only half the total unemployed, such was the wretched inheritance of want left by the colonial regime). By 1980 this labour force had constructed 7,200 sturdy stone barrages across hillside gulleys and other rainwater courses, and some 2,400 kilometres of earthen dykes and retaining walls, the object in all cases being to cut down the 'run off' loss of (normally torrential) rainfall. At the same time, some two million drought-resistant and fodder-productive trees, mostly varieties of acacia, were planted with good success and in part by voluntary effort. Many new trees were lost in the continuing drought, but many more have since been planted. The drought, in 1983 in its fourteenth year, was not going to last forever; when the rains fall regularly again, Cape Verdean agriculture will be better placed to conserve and use them.

The party in 1983 could claim with good reason that the eight years since independence, however burdened by endemic poverty and severe drought, had begun to achieve a major and *systemic* shift of advantage to the benefit of the poorest majority of the population: the 60 percent of peasants who possessed no land or not enough land to guarantee subsistence, and the poorest stratum' (relatively, a large one) of towndwellers. These were the sectors which were completely illiterate in 1975, and which for years, even for generations, had provided the bulk of emigrants to America or elsewhere, and of *contradados* for plantations in Angola.[32] The party could also claim that the further process of this shift was now inherent in the nature of the new state and its people's institutions, since the regime, in respect of the actual workings of the state, depended on the further development of the organs of popular rule. Well seated in the people's loyalty, this party could look forward to the future with a confidence unique in Cape Verdean history.

This is not to say that all class issues will be ironed out in the foreseeable future, or that acute problems of underdevelopment will not long persist and dominate the scene; any such claims would be regarded as absurd. What this Cape Verdean experience demonstrates, above all else, is that even the most vulnerable of ex-colonial countries, virtually bankrupt on the day of independence and bereft of almost every modern infrastructure, can none-theless make and maintain policy choices which provide for the economic and cultural expansion of its people, enlarge their independence, and endow them with an increasing command over a democratic future. And in another dimension, that which concerns our debate in this book on the prospects for socialism, this experience, together with the linked but contrasting experience of Guinea-Bissau, may have an especial relevance. For it may offer a most valid and instructive contribution to a realistic view, for the 1980s and after, of the means and potentials of the socialist project in Africa.

Notes

1. For a general introduction to the mainland territory, see L. Rudebeck, *Guinea-Bissau* (Scandinavian Institute of African Studies, Uppsala, 1974). No comparable work in English exists for the archipelago; there, the population in 1980 totalled about 300,000 or about three-eighths of that of the mainland. For a summary of statistics see *Africa South of the Sahara* (London, edited annually). For historical background, see A. Carreira, *The People of the Cape Verde Islands: Exploitation and Emigration*, translated and edited by Christopher Fyfe (Hurst, London, Archon USA, 1982); and its indispensible (but unhappily very rare) forerunner, A. Carreira, *Cabo Verde: Formação e Extinção de uma Sociedade Escravocrata* (Bissau, 1972).

2. I use the term 'Portuguese fascism' in a strictly lexical sense. In so far as it was more than an excrescence from earlier Portuguese structures, it derived from the example of Italian fascism in the 1920s, and was further developed from the example of German fascism in the 1930s; the dictatorship was proud of these antecedents.

3. Partido Africano de Independência de Guinea e Cabo Verde, founded clandestinely by Amílcar Cabral in Bissau in 1956.

4. My translation from the Portuguese original.

5. For the fullest available report on the PAIGC crisis of 1963, see B. Davidson, *Africa in Modern History* (Allen Lane/Penguin, 1978) chapter 30; US title, *Let Freedom Come* (Atlantic, Boston, 1978).

6. In his *Report* to the standing political committee of the 4th session of the Central Committee of Frelimo, Maputo, 2 August 1978.

7. B. Davidson, 'Further Report on the Liberation of Guiné', *Socialist Register* (London, 1973) p. 294.

8. Loc. cit., p. 295.

9. B. Davidson, 'African Peasants and Revolution', *Journal of Peasant Studies*, Vol. 1, No. 3, April 1974, p. 283, and generally.

10. L. Rudebeck, 'On the Class Basis of the National Liberation Movement of Guinea Bissau' (mimeo, Uppsala, 1983) p. 2.

11. A. Cabral, *Sobre alguns problemas práticos...*, 1971, quoted here from Rudebeck, *Guinea-Bissau*, pp. 9 and 18.

12. Quoted from B. Davidson, *Liberation of Guiné* (Penguin, London and Baltimore, 1969) pp. 136–7; reprinted in enlarged edition, as *No Fist is Big Enough to Hide the Sky* (Zed Press, London, 1981) p. 102.

13. PAIGC 3rd Congress, Bissau, November 1977: *Relatório* by Aristides Pereira on behalf of Conselho Superior da Luta, quoted here from my summary in *People's Power*, 10, Oct.–Dec. 1977 (Mozambique, Angola and Guinea Information Centre, London) p. 8.

14. L. Rudebeck, *Problèmes de pouvoir populaire et de développement: Transition difficile en Guinée-Bissau* (Scandinavian Institute of African Studies, Research Report 63, Uppsala, 1982) p. 15. The whole report is a valuable contribution to understanding this 'difficult transition'.

15. L. Dowbor, *Guiné-Bissau: a busca de independência econômica* (Editora Brasiliense, São Paulo, r. general jardim 160, 1983) p. 40.

16. L. Rudebeck, *Problèmes de pouvoir populaire*, p. 41.

17. *Nô Pintcha*, 27 May 1981.

18. Quoted from Rudebeck, *Problèmes de pouvoir populaire*, p. 48. His discussion of this Congress (pp. 49–60) is of great interest.

19. L. Dowbor, *Guinée-Bissau*, p. 25.

20. João Pereira Silva, 'The Role of Rural Institutions in Agrarian Transformation for Rural Development: The Case of Cape Verde', paper presented to workshop on agrarian transformation in Africa, Arusha Tanzania, October 1983, p. 35.

21. Ibid., p. 46.

22. O. Pires, *Sobre a Democracia Nacional Revolucionária*, Praia, 1980; a speech at the 8th legislative session of the People's National Assembly by its first vice-chairman and secretary of the Conselho Nacional do PAIGC (then about to become PAICV), p. 11.

23. O. Pires, supra, p. 9.

24. These and other relevant facts derived from my inquiries of 1980; see also article in *People's Power*, no 17, of Spring 1981.

25. It may be noted that Santo Antão, by tradition, has been often regarded as the least developed of the islands: its population in 1980 lived in four large villages or 'towns' and a multitude of scattered hamlets and homesteads, niched into the steep hillsides of its volcanic and often astonishing mountains.

26. J.P. Silva, 'The Role of Rural Institutions', p. 45.

27. Ibid., p. 40.

28. C. Foy, 'Cape Verde: Land and Labour', *People's Power*, no. 20, Summer 1982, pp. 28–29.

29. J.P. Silva, 'The Role of Rural Institutions', pp. 59–60.

30. A. Pereira, programmatic presidential address at the fifth anniversary of independence, Praia, 5 July 1980, p. 14 (my translation).

31. loc. cit., pp. 14–16.

32. On the dimensions and coercive conditions of Cape Verdean contract labour, see A. Carreira, *The People of the Cape Verde Islands*, edited and translated by Christopher Fyfe, London, 1982, *in extenso*.

6: People's Power: The Case of Mozambique

by Bertil Egero

In April 1983, nearly eight years after independence, Frelimo held its Fourth Party Congress.[1] Major problems were unfolding in all parts of society. Production was low, import deficits were growing, food supplies were lacking and a third of the population was threatened by drought and starvation. South African-trained MNR (National Resistance Movement) units operated over large parts of the country and black market trading appeared to dominate commerce in the cities. The number one requirement of a socialist society, to provide a minimum material standard of living to all its members, was far from being fulfilled. The Congress took a frank and honest look at the problems, attempting to identify their origins not only in the external economic and political conditions but also in the internal class struggle. Critical observations were made, especially regarding the state, its organisation and methods of work. A number of the decisions taken reflected either directly or indirectly the party concern to revitalise *Poder Popular* (People's Power) as a major political force in society.

Poder Popular, as a concept and as a form of socio-political organisation, was a reality of the liberation struggle from 1964 to 1974 against Portuguese colonial power. In the liberated areas of the north, it was a popular defence against corruption and the abuse of power in local production and commerce. After victory had been won, it provided the general framework for political organisation, notably with the *Grupos dinamizadores*, or dynamising groups, the People's Assemblies and the Production Councils (see Figure 1 for a list and description of the most important structures of people's power). It paved the way for strong popular participation in the nomination of members to these organs, as well as in the selection of candidates for party membership. *Poder Popular* remains a central point of reference in current attempts to master the problems hampering development.

The case of Mozambique raises anew some basic questions concerning the problem of socialist transition in an underdeveloped country. These include the special forms required for the assumption of state power in the absence of a strong working class; the political aspects of planned economy/market economy and central/local relations; and the possibility of a dynamic perspective on the relation of party/state supremacy to worker–peasant democratic control of power. Some of these issues will be addressed in the present account of *Poder Popular* in Mozambique.

114

Figure 1
Key structures of *Poder Popular* in Mozambique

Frelimo
Mozambique Liberation Front, created in Dar es Salaam on 25 June 1962. Led the guerrilla struggle up to negotiations on independence with the colonial power in September 1974; and shared power in the transitional government up to independence on 25 June 1975. In February 1977, it was transformed from a front organisation to a Marxist–Leninist vanguard party. The old cadres (from before September 1974) were readmitted automatically, others only after submitting their candidatures before a public hearing. By 1983, it had an estimated membership of 110,000 persons organised in 4,200 cells over all parts of the country.

Dynamising groups
Called DGs, were founded during the transitional government (1974–75) as local representatives of Frelimo, administrative centres and centres of local popular defence. Gradually they were replaced by other structures, and today basically remain in the city neighbourhoods as the lowest level state authority.

People's assemblies
Constitutionally, the highest body of the state with authority to pass legislation, take resolutions on economic development plans and control the functioning of the state apparatus in accordance with Frelimo Party directives. National elections for the creation of assemblies on all levels from subdistrict to nation, were held in 1977. A second round of elections at local levels was held in 1980 (see Fig. 2).

Production Councils
The workers' organisation. Initially set up in 1976–77 in Maputo-based industries, later extended to all medium and large production units as well as to the public sector. Industrial branch organisations have been erected, and in October 1983, the Mozambican Workers' Organisation, OTM, was created as the national embodiment of about a dozen unions. Subordinated to Frelimo, the unions are responsible for worker training and discipline, work security and hygiene, defence of workers' rights, control of plan elaboration etc.

Mass organisations
Created to mobilise for popular participation in, and support of, national reconstruction and development, as defined by Frelimo, including recruitment into party ranks. Most important are: OMM, Mozambican Women's Organisation, created before independence; OJM, Mozambican Youth Organisation, created in 1977; ONP, National Organisation of Teachers, established in 1981.

Poder Popular and Third World socialism is a term used both in Mozambique and Cuba. More than its simple literal translation, which means 'people's power',[2] this term denotes something common, something popular; it embraces everybody. Its class content, its relation to the concept of dictatorship of the proletariat, is more complex than indicated by the established English translation. *Poder Popular* relates to the essentials of democracy as a form of political organisation, to people's participation in, and direct influence on, decision making and implementation.

Cuba is the country perhaps most commonly associated with *Poder Popular*. In relation to other socialist countries, its history is somewhat unique. The struggle against the Batista regime was carried out without organs of popular mobilisation and control. In fact, it took about fifteen years of national independence before institutional reforms were initiated which allowed for broader participation under conditions of a certain autonomy.[3] Until then, democracy had been exercised informally, and was highly dependent on the strength and orientation of the national leadership.[4] According to one interpretation, the reforms should be seen as being introduced *from above*, as part of a political strategy to reduce the direct participation of the national leadership.[5]

This experience contrasts with those of other recently independent socialist countries such as China, whose long peasant war was transformed, after independence, into a variety of strategies for rural development based on local political and economic organisation. In Vietnam, the long war forced an increasing degree of autonomy on the part of the peasants, in co-operative production as well as in defence. In Mozambique, *Poder Popular* grew out of the material conditions of the anti-colonial war and the ideological contradictions emerging within the liberation movement.[6]

Today, profound and in many ways similar debates are being carried out in a number of Third World socialist countries on issues related to the political economy of transition, the organisational forms of agricultural production, the role of the private sector and the state, and decentralisation. The debates, particularly in Vietnam and Mozambique, demonstrate that experiences gained in the course of the nationalist struggle are not easily transferable into the situation of the nation--state. This is not least the case concerning forms of political organisation or *Poder Popular*. The factors that brought about broad participation in the days of the struggle are themselves changing. What then, is the significance of *Poder Popular* as a principle of political organisation in socialist transition?

Poder Popular must be seen in the context of a profound social transformation. The strategy for this transformation may have grown out of a long struggle, but it will not be part of the ideology of workers and peasants in general. The need, therefore, is to mobilise broad popular support for the implementation and class-based defence of that strategy – in other words, to make *Poder Popular* a nationwide reality.

Poder Popular is also significant in another and more far-reaching sense, namely in the creation of conditions for popular government and social control of the means of production. To get out of the tight grip of dependency and poverty, socialist governments tend to emphasise the necessity of industrialisation and agricultural mechanisation in their development strategies. While linked to processes of working class formation, industrialisation also implies plan centralisation, technocratisation and growing management power. Nationalisation as such does not necessarily change the social control of production, i.e. the role of the worker in the production process. This fact provides a bridge to some of the problems of socialist economies, including problems of productivity and the quality of production. MacEwan's recent work on Cuba suggests that 'moral incentives and non-market mechanisms in general can only be effective if applied in a situation where the workers have participatory institutions which involve them in the process of production'. Thus 'If centralized planning is applied and labour is mobilised through moral means it is the working class who determine the effectiveness of the strategy.'[7]

MacEwan is no doubt aware of the risks of decentralisation in the absence of strong organised workers' representation. Until such representation has been established, the major instrument of economic and social development is the state apparatus—an institution which is dominated by representatives of class interests other than those of workers and peasants on the one hand, and on the other is the central institutionalised articulation of the divergent interests of these two major classes.

A weakly organised working class and an equally unorganised peasantry are common characteristics of socialist Third World countries. Objectively, this situation implies that conditions do not exist for their assumption of power in the state or party. Who holds the reins of power initially, therefore, becomes a question of the party or national leadership, whose short-term need for an 'alliance' with the bureaucracy (and petty-bourgeoisie) has to be linked with a long term strategy for changing the balance of class forces in favour of workers and peasants.

Not all socialist Third World regimes chose the vanguard party as the supreme political guide to this process—Guinea-Bissau is a case in point. But those which do, have to face up to the problem of a party departing from a weak class base amongst workers and peasants, and face the risks of elitism and bureaucratisation. The central issue for the party, to get peasants and workers to trust the revolutionary process and give it their active support, is no less complicated by the intimate links between the party and a bureaucratic state machinery.

The sceptic might argue that the case inevitably is lost, that the cadres, 'whether they be politocratic, bureaucratic or technocratic, they still have much to lose from genuine democratisation in terms of concrete interests and are ideologically armed to resist it, whether in terms of "Party leadership", the supremacy of the state or the "neutral" requirements of rapid modernisation'.[8] However, two counterforces might exist: the still living traditions of a popularly based liberation struggle; and the very fact that economic crisis can politically weaken bureaucratic power. This is the case we will investigate in the Mozambican revolution.

Transitional government and after

Unlike the process of decolonisation in most British or French colonies, political independence for the Portuguese colonies was not preceded by a period of transitional adjustment in either the centre or the colonies. The Portuguese political system up to 25 April 1974 did not and could not permit any process of planned reform. Although an exodus of Portuguese from the colonies at war had started already in the early 1970s, the settler communities were bent on turning developments in their own favour, perhaps through modified versions of the 1965 Rhodesian UDI (Unilateral Declaration of Independence).

Though forerunners to the 25 April coup were by no means lacking, the coup and its immediate aftermath caused a great deal of confusion in the colonies. Frelimo's rapid advance during the following months and the internal conflicts in Portugal leading to the fall of President Spinola, forced the unconditional capitulation of the old colonial power. In the midst of frantic efforts to unite the settler front or create a black puppet regime, the numbers of Portuguese leaving the colonies rose rapidly, concomitant with rising waves of destabilisation and material destruction. Of the approximately 200,000-strong Portuguese community living in Mozambique at the time of the coup, at least half had left before independence a year later. The majority of the remainder left within the first year of independence.[9]

The intimate financial, commercial and other links between Mozambique and Portugal, and the Portuguese near-monopoly on 'know-how', meant that the massive exodus dealt a blow to all sectors of society far deeper than caused by the destruction alone. Chaos was inevitable, or so it seemed.

Following the Lusaka agreement between Portugal and Frelimo in September 1974, a transitional government was installed in Maputo (then known as Lourenço Marques). The organisational decisions taken by the new government reflected the need to resolve three fundamental and urgent problems:

Establish Frelimo all over the country. The war had never reached the southern parts of the country, nor the main urban centres. A substantial and politically important part of the population had only vague notions of Frelimo, its ideology and methods of work. A rapid recruitment of reliable cadres was necessary, through which authority could be extended and established.

Replace Portuguese administrative and managerial authority. The rapid exodus of colonialists meant that factories, farms and shops were abandoned, commercial chains were broken and government functions fell apart. New forms of local authority had to be erected to uphold these functions and control the take-over of abandoned units.

Contain material destruction, sabotage and destabilisation. The exodus was accompanied by a wave of material destruction, the export of vital production components and the removal of essential written knowledge about property and processes. Popular defence was the only method available, and it would serve a good political purpose in the process.

In what could now be described as a key decision, the leadership called for the creation of dynamising groups (*grupos dinamizadores*, or GDs, first called party committees) in every place of work or residence. With the exception of military defence, the GDs came to be involved in virtually every aspect of society: local government, production and workers' organisation, commerce, health, literacy and other social functions, mobilisation, information and popular defence. GD members, drawn from the local community, and where possible having the political confidence of Frelimo, were selected or elected in general meetings which could last for days.

The composition and methods of work of the GDs made them important instruments in the break with colonialism and the creation of new relations of power and influence. Participation, not only in the implementation of common tasks, but also in discussion and decision-making, had important political effects. 'It created a new sense of confidence in the oppressed masses and it helped convince them that they had the capacity to transform Mozambique. . . This is the very essence of *Poder Popular*,' as one top national leader summarised the experience.[10]

We will return below to the development of the GDs and their relations to other organs of political or state power. Here it is important to note that the GDs' initial all-embracing roots meant that they embodied general problems of political organisation in society, specifically, the (non)distinction between party and state and the problem of vanguard leadership and mass participation. The leadership would later direct itself to resolving these issues in a process of moulding and remoulding policies which were not always so easy to handle at the local level.

Creating the organs of *Poder Popular*

From the outset, the GD system was part of the explicit intention of the leadership to create democratic structures of collective participation, institutions which in their form and methods of work allowed for popular control of national reconstruction. There were several serious problems to be dealt with in this process:

The extreme lack of cadres of all kinds. The Portuguese monopoly on 'know-how' had been extreme; independent Mozambique was hopelessly short of competent cadres. There simply were no people around to fill political, governmental and managerial positions, let alone the new structures of voluntary work.

The individual search for career outlets. The embryonic lower middle strata of Mozambicans suddenly found themselves in great demand. The temptation was great, not least for those whose past links with the colonial power were not altogether spotless, to try to obtain positions of power. The GDs offered one possible outlet, whilst other new structures such as the factory administrative commissions or the production councils (see below) provided others.

The lack of acquaintance with democratic procedures. At no time in the history of Portuguese colonial rule have democratic processes been utilised, not even within the metropole itself. Traditional local systems of decision-making through, councils etc., had been eroded by the integration of local chiefs (called *régulos*) into the colonial state. In the 'modern' sector, hierarchical authority together with lack of employment security (in particular for the blacks) combined to prevent even the rudiments of democratic collaboration from emerging.

The supremacy of party authority. The collapse of colonial structures left a vacuum of authority, both locally and centrally. Unless this was filled by Frelimo, the vacuum could permit various local actions with counter-revolutionary effects. Frelimo's grassroots organs, though popularly based, therefore had to exercise an authority derived from above, from the Frelimo leadership. Here, as with all institutions, whether political or state, the question was of the limits of local or popular authority in relation to central authority.

The definition of democracy was firmly based in the concept of party supremacy. Democratic procedures were aimed at defending the revolution and finding popular solutions to local problems within the general strategy of development. As explained to the district GD representatives in February 1975:

> It is important to keep in mind, that when we talk about a People's Democracy, then we talk about a democracy within the discipline of Frelimo, which is contrary to any anarchy and ideological liberalism, we talk about democratic centralism. To talk about a 'light spirit democracy' could compromise our line, because then some people could under the name of democracy assert their personal ideas which have nothing to do with our objective to implant Poder Popular. . . For us, democracy is the realisation of the national objectives. . .[11]

The period of the transitional government was a period of debate over, and development of, such concepts as democracy, democratic centralism and leadership. Given the impossibility of exerting day-to-day control, the government had to trust the local organs, and this in turn implied a great emphasis on the process of selecting members of GD secretariats. Universal participation was aimed at in order to expose those compromised by earlier actions, or whose possessions made them biased against Frelimo's policies. At the same time, collective leadership was strongly recommended. This was a line which was to be pursued throughout the first years of independence. Machel set the tone when he addressed the 7th Central Committee meeting just before independence, about the new society to be erected: 'we want to appraise the energies, the capacities of each one of us, we want to appraise our talents, we want to have collective discussion, collective leadership. . .'[12] Echoes of this concern appeared in subsequent debates—over leadership methods in the state apparatus, in the creation of productivity control commissions in departments of government and, perhaps more well known, in the formation of ward commissions in hospitals to run the wards with the participation of the entire staff. The value of such reforms has been subject to debate and was indeed later reconsidered by the government. Nevertheless, as with the GDs, workers' shared responsibility for their place of work was seen as a learning process and a means of breaking with the past:

> It is where they work that the workers first of all must get organised. It is there that we must urgently destroy the colonial structure, based on individualised, bureaucratised and antidemocratic management, and substitute for it a new democratic and collective structure, which permits an organised participation of all the workers in the study and solution of the problems. . .[13]

Workers' production councils

The necessity for a separate workers' organisation had been indicated by the President at the 7th Central Committee meeting in June 1975. There were grave problems in industrial production all over the country. Factories were being abandoned, or sabotaged, and production levels were dropping. Administrative commissions were set up where the factory management had left, drawing their membership from amongst the employees. GDs were formed to fulfil political functions, establish literacy classes and provide the link between the party and the workplace. However, a historically unstable workforce, an almost complete lack of organisational and managerial experience amongst non-whites, combined with local acts of opportunism and sabotage, all contributed to creating serious problems in the new structures being set up in the factories.

In a long speech to the workers in October 1976, President Samora Machel related some of the experiences of the GDs. He gave a vivid picture of the 'ambitious and opportunists' who, believing that the GDs were a new form of management, virtually flooded these groups, frequently creating several competing GDs in the same workplace which then fought each other and dealt out competing unrealistic promises to the workers. Seeing that they were not supposed to manage the firm, that administrative commissions were set up for this purpose with a membership separate from that of the GD, those who had entered the GDs for reasons of ambition, left, and tried to find ways into the new management structure.[14]

Thus one immediate aspect of the malfunctioning of the GDs was that they were often not controlled by the workers, but were instruments or springboards for individual careers. Their intended political functions amongst the workers were not fulfilled; in firms under private management they posed no serious threat to continued malpractices of the traditional colonial type. Nor were they able to organise an effective front against the diverse forms of sabotage taking place within the industrial sector.

It was necessary to stop the fall in production, and to restore production and productivity to earlier high levels. The production councils created shortly after the presidential address were not intended to be substitutes for the political structures, i.e. the GDs. Nor were they to substitute for the management of the firm. Their activities were directed towards the workers themselves, at organising them to increase work discipline and order, ensure the maintenance of machines and rolling stock, identify and resolve obstacles in the production process—in short, to account for the workers' side in getting production going again.

Starting in forty-six Maputo-based industries, the programme of establishing production councils was soon extended to other industrial areas. During the first six months, four national meetings were held to discuss the councils' experiences. Documents from these meetings record the hostility of both private and state-appointed managements to what they perceived as a threat to their hitherto unchallenged authority and monopoly on information, planning and decision-making. The GDs still had a leading role in the nomination of candidates for the production councils, which could have between three and twenty members depending on the size of the firm. The nominations had to be confirmed in general meetings of workers, similar to those held for the election of people's assemblies, where all workers could voice their opinions about the candidates.

By 1983, production councils had been extended to the whole country. Periodic meetings evaluated their progress and decided on the steps to be taken towards eventual national integration, through the formation of industrially organised branches with local as well as national representation. When, in October 1983, it was considered that sufficient satisfactory progress had been made, the Organisation of Mozambican Workers (OTM) was created as the coordinating body of a dozen different unions. Members are organised according to workplace, and membership in principle embraces all employees.

The change, it appears, is basically one of organisation. The new trade union structure will continue its work on the formation and training of workers, labour discipline, security and legal questions. In principle, it is subordinated to the party cell of the workplace, although in practice they often seem to work as one. In recent years, stress has been laid on workers' participation in the drafting and implementation of production plans, within the framework of the already established divisions of responsibility between management, party and workers' organisation. However, even if the state department concerned still nominates each management director, 'we can now conceive of the situation where the director is elected by the workers themselves,' as a representative of the national office asserted, pointing to the fact that several directors have been drawn from the ranks of the factory employees.[15]

The true reality of labour relations in industry and in the state farms remains to be systematically explored. A 'presidential offensive' carried out in 1980 against obstacles to increased production (see below) disclosed the weakness of workers' organs and the reluctance of management to accept any closer collaboration with party and workers' council. The remedy offered to problems in the organisation of production was to reinforce the power of management, at the apparent expense of other organs.[16]

There is no simple way out of this classic dilemma of socialist industrialisation. Various mass media reports confirm the weakness of workers' organs in, for instance, control of production losses to the black market, or even in securing legally determined wage levels.[17] The creation of a trade union structure might be the beginning of a search for methods to tackle such problems more efficiently, while reaching a role for worker participation in management.

People's assemblies

The history of Mozambique is remarkably free from any semblance of democratic process. Whatever rights that did exist were the exclusive preserve of the Portuguese community and of those few blacks accepted by the colonial government—the *assimilados* (those assimilated into Portuguese customs and values).[18] In the last elections under the colonial government in 1973, only 160,000 people out of a total population of 9 million had the right to vote. The vast majority were Portuguese, and their low degree of involvement is evident from the fact that one third of the voters stayed at home on polling day.[19]

In the People's Republic of Mozambique, democratic processes were an essential part of leadership methods guided by 'democratic centralism'. Democracy was also vital to the selection of leaders for political and state organs. Whether in the party or in the state, gaining and maintaining the confidence of the people depended in a very direct way on *who* (in a personal sense) held positions of responsibility. In terms of the state, a structure of popular assemblies was intended to provide the representative safeguard against the bureaucratic machinery itself.

Elections were set for the latter part of 1977, after the Third Congress decision to transform Frelimo into a party but before any party reconstruction had really started. Popular assemblies were to be created at all levels, from the subdistrict or 'locality' to the nation. Local government structures were more or less erected down to the district level, but vertical links remained weak. Perhaps it is for this reason that the electoral law is quite vague on the intended structure at the base level. As a measure of the degree of local responsibility in organising the elections, no less than 612 of 894 'locality assemblies' were created during the campaign itself in new population centres and communal villages.[20] Loyal to its historical experiences from the armed struggle, Frelimo requested maximum popular participation in the first stage of the elections. The GDs were important in the initial selection of candidates, who were later subjected to public scrutiny in large meetings. The success of the operation must have varied considerably over the country,[21] but there is no denying that it did command a great deal of support. It represented the first real shake-up of the GDs themselves, exposing some of their members as being unsuitable for the functions assigned to them. Ten percent of the local level candidates were rejected as a consequence of the meetings; slightly less were rejected at the district and city levels.[22]

Elections at all levels above the base were conducted by 'electoral conferences' composed in part of locality deputies and in part of representatives of political, state or defence organs. No steps appear to have been taken to ensure a representative distribution of those elected, in terms for instance of the lower-level assemblies or settlements. No figures have been published showing the percentage of party members or members of other organisations.

Provincial and national assemblies were elected for a period of five years, the others for two and a half. In 1980, new elections took place in districts, cities and localities. It was an extremely busy period. Recuperation from the recently ended war with Ian Smith's Rhodesia, implementation of the first annual state plan and an excellent nationwide change-over to a new currency, the Metical, competed with preparations for the first national population census in drawing resources from the elections. This made the voting process less of a rehearsal and educational exercise in democracy than was intended, and reporting on the results was almost completely lacking. It became clear, however, that many of the local assemblies, especially at the base level, were defunct or operating only infrequently. In the election process, the number of local assemblies increased from just under 900 to over 1,300, mainly reflecting a change in agglomeration patterns in the countryside. The number of elected deputies grew slightly faster, from 22,000 to over 38,000. About half of the former were re-elected, or—to put it another way—about two thirds of the deputies after the elections were new to the assemblies.

Creating a functioning representative democracy based on universal franchise is a long and difficult process. Unfortunately, the lack of any systematic studies of the assembly structure in Mozambique makes it difficult to comment on their actual status and contribution. However, interviews conducted both at local and at national levels,[23] along with other relevant material, leave us with the following picture. Inherited structural weaknesses have inflicted deep marks on the operation of democratic processes. High or very high levels of illiteracy in the local assembly are matched by a general lack of understanding and competence amongst the cadres appointed to guide the process of work. Their control of the conduct of local assemblies is infrequent, as is the reporting of the assembly deliberations to the higher structures. Written instructions are few and not very helpful.

The word 'representative' often does not seem to carry a clear meaning. For instance, district assemblies appear primarily oriented towards the problems of the district centre or town. The task of the delegate is not generally seen as representing or defending the interests of one's 'electorate', be it the communal village in the locality forum or the locality assembly in the district forum. In organisational terms, the goals set for the assemblies do not accord with the terms of their work. To defend the interests of the people in relation to the state machinery is not an easy thing if you are semiliterate or illiterate, meeting in an assembly presided over by the local senior government functionary, who is at the same time the local party head. Things are made no easier, if, as often happens, some of the state functionaries also hold posts as deputies. Given this organisational structure, with the party as the supreme body defining priorities and laying out programmes of work, the tendency is for the assemblies to become executing bodies, or rather channels of labour recruitment, for the tasks defined by party and state machinery. This tendency can be observed even at the level of the National Assembly.

The National Assembly meets regularly, usually a few days after the party central committee meeting. Its principal tasks are enacting legislation, approving state budgets, overseeing state activities and approving state plans. But apart from these tasks, how do the assemblies fit into the structures of People's Power? In his opening speech to the Provisional National Assembly preceding the 1977 elections, Samora Machel stressed that the assemblies must direct themselves to solving the concrete problems in people's lives. They should concern themselves with such problems as the 'difficulties in water supply to a communal village or communal suburb, difficulties in outlets for goods produced by the people, the school that must be opened, the road that must be cut in the middle of the bush'.[24]

These tasks obviously require mobilisation for joint efforts to solve local problems. But assembly responsibilities also include looking after the state, and guaranteeing 'that all citizens get effective support and a non-bureaucratic solution to their problems, within existing possibilities, from the state services. The assemblies must punish severely those civil servants who, by their behaviour, show neglect, incompetence or insensitivity towards the people'.[25] The contradictory nature of the goals set for them, coupled with the other problems outlined, may be a major reason for the assemblies' initial difficulties. It is certainly still too early to predict their longterm development in the hands of peasants and workers, now allowed, for the first time, to participate in a context of free democratic discussion.

The party Frelimo

For those who had followed the progress of the liberation movement in the armed struggle, it came as no real surprise when Frelimo was transformed into a vanguard party in February 1977. Signs of a party structure within the movement had emerged long before independence, along with the ideological change from a pure nationalist to an anti-capitalist position. In 1973, party committees had been formed in the military structures of Frelimo. In January 1974, the party school had been inaugurated, 'to synthesise and generalise our experiences and provide a theoretical base for our cadres and militants'.[26]

At this stage, as John Saul notes, 'the movement was party, state administration and representative institution all in one. . .'[27] The reordering of these functions into new and separate structures required both deep reflection

Figure 2
Some Results of the 1977 and 1980 elections to people's assemblies

Number of assemblies and elected deputies

Level	No. of assemblies		No. of deputies		% women deputies	
	1977	1980	1977	1980	1977	1980
Locality	894	1 332	22 230	38 660	28.3	24.5
District	112	101	3 390	3 324	23.8	16.6
Town	10	12	490	672	20.9	17.0
Province	10	11	734		14.7	
Nation	1	1	226		12.4	

Social composition of elected deputies (in %)

Level	Workers	Peasants	Members of Defence Forces	State Employees	Others
District					
1977	20.0	38.0	17.1	16.0	8.9
1980	12.7	43.0	8.2	26.6	9.5
Town					
1977	38.9	10.7	15.4	24.8	10.2
1980	30.8	6.8	8.3	28.1	25.9
Province					
1977 ·	26.3	22.2	16.5	26.2	8.8
Nation					
1977	31.4	28.8	15.5	11.1	13.2

Sources: *Boletim da República*, I Série, No. 150, 24 de Dezembro de 1977; *Relatório da Comissão Nacional de Eleições*, Assembleia Popular, Maputo, Julho de 1980.

and experience, provided in particular by the GDs and by the Frelimo militants found in all strategic sectors of society from the transitional government onwards.

Indeed, the new role assigned to Frelimo and the political institutions as a whole must have been developed in the light of a growing understanding of the social structure of Mozambican society, in particular the situation of the workers in industry and agriculture. Given the relatively small size of the industrial sector and the relative numerical significance of the workers, their lack of training, organisation and stability as a workforce, would make the workers a real political force for socialist transition only in the long term. The peasantry, relieved of colonial coercive exploitation, but still scattered in part-subsistence production, would be accessible as an organized class force only through major transformations in both its forms of settlement and production relationships.

Embarking initially on the strategy of economic production and increased self-reliance through industrialisation and mechanised agriculture, Frelimo had to create the vanguard leadership necessary to control this process in all sectors, not least in the rapidly growing state apparatus. The creation of the party is a key part of the Frelimo ideology of socialist transition which, as Joe Slovo summarises, postulates: the existence of a modern industrial sector; state control of the means of production; intensified class struggle against hostile forces within and outside the state; a revolutionary political vanguard guided by scientific socialism; and a gradually reduced dependence on the world capitalist economy.[28]

The Mozambican conception of the party is that of a vanguard body which assumes national leadership on behalf of workers and peasants, controls the state's economic policies, and ensures that the state creates the conditions for the assumption of real power by the working classes. This conception is reflected in Frelimo's identification of phases or stages in the passage to socialism. The position entails a series of problems which only recently are becoming more openly exposed to the party, and to which we will have reason to return below.

In the first period after independence, the definition of membership in the front was vague, not least because of problems related to the political status of the GDs. Frelimo's answer was to readmit into the new party only those who had been members of Frelimo before the signing of the 1974 independence accord, and who still fulfilled the conditions for party membership. All others had to be recommended by at least two party members, and had to stand as candidates for one year. Only those with a clean record in relation to the colonial government and with no income except that gained from their own work, could be accepted for party membership.

The building of the party proceeded somewhat slowly during 1977. At the end of the year, a national campaign was started, aimed at the creation of more cells in the state apparatus, productive units and in the countryside. Party brigades went around to inform people about the campaign and to collect applications. These were then discussed with the local GDs, workers' councils, mass organisations and other bodies. The final selection of candidates was presented to general meetings where everyone was encouraged to speak freely about the candidates.

Not unexpectedly, the creation of the new organisation caused some confusion at the local level. What was the difference between the new party cell and the GD, the workers' council and the mass organisations? What was required to become a party member, and what was expected of the new member? Eventually, the campaign had to explain to people that a party member 'does not have to be a doctor, does not have to have a high theoretical education'.[29] But every potential member had to have a 'clean' past. Some candidates had collaborated with the Portuguese secret police PIDE, served in special colonial military units or participated in puppet political organisations. These activities were revealed and discussed publicly, with the purpose of freeing the candidates from the burden of former complicity and from the risk of being blackmailed into counter-revolutionary work.

No results, in statistical terms, of the 1977–78 campaign were ever published. The following few years showed that the growth of the party as a political force in society was linked not so much to the rhetoric of its role, as to the day-to-day politics of party-state relations. The state apparatus was expanding rapidly. By the end of 1978, serious work began on the first annual economic plan, under the direction of the newly created National Planning Commission. Seemingly all party cadre resources went into the state, whose work was directed at the highest level by the party leadership in ministerial positions in government.

The first annual state plan took shape in 1979. The liberation struggle for Zimbabwe, which had resulted in a situation of open warfare in the central parts of Mozambique, was by then drawing to a close. Samora Machel proudly announced that the decade of the 1980s would be the decade of economic struggle, during which great advances would be made. The measures necessary to fulfil this goal were declared to be the streamlining of management and administrative leadership, the identification of individual responsibility in place of more collective forms and the introduction of a hierarchy of authority and subordination.[30]

Following official exhortations on the need to reinforce management power, the President initiated a dynamic 'political and organisational offensive' in the whole state sector, particularly related to production. It was directed against 'the internal enemy'—all those who, deliberately or not, put obstacles in the way of economic and social recovery, including cases of irresponsibility, incompetence, corruption or outright sabotage. The offensive exposed problems far more serious than originally anticipated. Its effect was that of a boomerang, hitting back at the very structures of political and state power, and forcing a reconsideration of the issue of popular participation and, even more broadly, of *Poder Popular* within the Mozambican revolution.

Firstly, there was a gap between party directives and actual state policies, a gap which did not disappear simply with the presence of top party people in leading state positions. Secondly, in all the departments and other units visited, the party was seen to be too weak to tackle, or even report on, the often serious state of affairs that existed. The policy of executing party control through individual party members busy in their state functions simply did not work. The party itself was in disarray:

> This error [of not giving more attention to the party] meant that leading structures of the party, both at central and local level, were not filled, that party work was carried out as a secondary task and that the party did not concentrate on the principle task, the economic battle. Consequently the work of the party cells was weakened and militants frequently remained without tasks. The necessary impetus to get patriotic citizens and honest workers into the ranks of the party was missing. The party press became routine and lagged behind events. Economic, social or international questions are not discussed. . .[31]

Amongst the steps taken to rectify the situation was to free two top party functionaries, Marcelino dos Santos and Jorge Rebelo, from all government duties and to supply them with a number of experienced cadres at lower levels to work solely in the party. In this way, a few immediate improvements could be made, and the party secretariat started to probe the condition of Frelimo. The results were quite alarming. The party appeared to embody all the problems threatening any vanguard body: elitism, bureaucratic methods, and increasing insensitivity to the people and their problems. Many local party cells' activities were affected by the leadership's emphasis on administrative power as well as by the *de facto* unity of party and state personnel at every level of government.

The new resources injected into the party were directed towards raising the qualifications of party members—which included everything from literacy training to political formation. New campaigns to increase membership were launched, leading to a better implantation of party structures in the countryside. Hard data about the party was released for the first time during the Fourth Party Congress in April 1983. The preparations for the congress involved a far-reaching campaign of cell revitalisation and membership recruitment. The party was reported to consist of 110,000 members, active in over 4,200 cells. Of the total number of members, 19 percent were workers and 53 percent peasants, whilst women made up one quarter of the overall membership.[32]

Party/state structures at the base

In the beginning, as we have noted, there were the GDs. What became of these with the creation of new structures? The production councils formed in workplaces did not replace the GDs, which remained the workplace political organisation until such time as the party was directly represented. As Marcelino dos Santos explained in a radio broadcast in 1977:

> We are now in a transitional phase in which the GDs are everywhere our Party. This should remain the character of the GDs until the formation of the party cells. . . In work places the GDs will give way to Party cells. In other words, from the GDs in the places of work the Party cells will be born.[33]

This, apparently, was not just a simple change of name. One of the best accounts of the process as it occurred on the ground is provided by Peter Sketchley, relating his experiences in the large steel rolling mill, CIFEL, in Maputo.[34] There, a party team moved in to take a close look at all aspects of the GD's operations. Workers' criticism led to the dissolution of the existing GD and the replacement of a ministerially appointed administrator. Through a laborious process of meetings and controls, six factory workers were eventually selected and accepted for provisional party membership in the new party cell.

CIFEL is one of the country's strategic industries, and the attention given it by the party certainly could not be repeated everywhere. However, in principle the process was meant to be the same throughout the economy, in the state apparatus and, though generally only after the seventh session of the Central Committee in July 1980, in communal villages. In the villages, administrative responsibility was to rest with an executive council formed within the popular assembly, and with its president as chairman. In very large communal villages, like those in Gaza, with 1,000 households or more, GDs would exist as 'residents' organisations' in the different village wards.

The city GDs were extremely important in organising the urban neighbourhoods in the first years of turmoil. Their relation to the party was somewhat different. According to Marcelino dos Santos in 1977: 'the GDs will remain. They are the mass organization in the suburbs, they are the residents' organization'.[35] In reality, the official position of the state shifted in favour of turning the GDs into the lowest level of government, responsible for the implementation of higher-level decisions. This new policy, however, presupposed the urban GDs' existence as relatively stable and capable organs enjoying the support of the residents.

During the national population census in August 1980, many cases were discovered of weak or even defunct GDs in the city suburbs. Only in 1981, however, in the context of the formation of militia units in the suburbs of Maputo, was the situation investigated more carefully. Delegations were sent out to all parts of the capital. They returned to give some of the background concerning the fate of the GDs:

> After the party restructuration campaign [in 1978], there followed a period of almost complete lack of activity on the side of the GDs, which lost their dynamism, prestige and authority with the masses. . . The majority of the GDs function as offices for receipt and emission of messages and authorizations. . . In practice, the circumstances require that the GD is at the same time an administrative organ and a party organ [in fact the only one at ward level], but it is not capable of doing so, for lack of clarity concerning its role and duties. . .[36]

Since then, matters have been clarified. The GDs have been incorporated into the local government organisation, with paid functionaries and a growing number of administrative duties, such as registration for food rationing, residence permits and, lately, the eviction of the unemployed to rural areas. The party, meanwhile, is putting its efforts into creating a viable network of cells in the city wards. Here it is stumbling over one serious obstacle: who is going to staff these cells when all the dedicated militants are politically active at their places of work?

Democratic mass organisations

The mass organisations represent an important response to the problem of democracy under the supremacy of a vanguard party. How are they to ensure the participation of the revolutionary classes, not merely as objects of mobilisation but as creative participants in the whole process?[37] Their formation was anticipated by President Machel in the 7th Central Committee meeting before independence. In the new party programme, the mass organisations' relation to the party is clearly spelled out:

> The democratic mass organisations are the most perfect connecting link between the Party and the People. . . The mass organisations are a great school where the consciousness. . .is developed. They are the base for the recruitment. . .of Party Militants. . .[38]

Angoche District — a case study

Angoche is a small and densely populated district in the province of Nampula. Situated along the coast, it was the site of the old Sultanate of Angoche, whose descendants successfully resisted Portuguese domination right into the present century. Untouched by the armed struggle of Frelimo, Angoche today is an important district in economic terms, not least because of the three big cashew factories situated there. The situation in Angoche is illustrative of local progress and problems in political development. Data refers to a visit to the district by the author in August 1981.

The district has about 200,000 inhabitants, perhaps one tenth of whom live in the district centre of Angoche. Most of the over 6,000 workers and other wage earners are found there, in cashew factories and allied industries, in fishing and in wood processing. Cashew trees are an important part of the peasant economy and, being immovable property, an obstacle to the formation of communal villages. These number twenty-six, with a total population of around 24,000 people. Thus the majority of the rural population lives scattered in the four localities (sub-districts) of Angoche district.

The day-to-day affairs of the district are directed from party headquarters more than from the local council. The party has all data on the local economy and production. The state representative responsible for communal villages turns up every now and then to discuss problems. A district party meeting gives most of its attention to economic plans, production and social development.

In the locality of Namaponda, the executive council had folded with the transfer or leave of the three most important office holders. Two party candidates have taken it upon themselves to get the locality administration on its feet again, through the secretariat and the committee of the party. Work programmes elaborated in these bodies are passed over to the popular assembly for ratification and for the recruitment of deputies for tasks to be resolved.

Two communal villages visited, Mepapata and Mucopola, were both created in the first year of independence. Both had their Frelimo party cell, elected assembly and mass organisations. The assembly had elected its executive council from among the deputies. Not surprisingly, all the members of the council were party members, some of them even in the cell secretariat. What then, is the difference between party and state in the life of the village? The answer comes slowly and with hesitation,

'We too have some problems sorting out the difference. Perhaps it is that the party discusses all the issues of the state, whereas the opposite does not occur. . .'

Between 1977 and 1980, eight party cells were formed in the district. The party cell of Mepapata was the only one outside the district centre. The party campaign of 1980–81 led to the creation of another eighteen cells, this time with priority to communal villages. Eight hundred and sixty new candidates were registered in the campaign, in addition to the already existing 520 members. But the party organisation is still weak in the rural areas, not least in the locality centres where party committees were formed only in 1980.

The lack of resources is a serious obstacle to all development. The shortage of office equipment and transport is matched by an equally serious scarcity of educated people capable of preparing a document. The district party secretary comments: 'Frankly speaking, the assembly work has been very poor so far. To start with, there was much confusion on the limits between party and assembly. Nobody had any experience in the procedures of formal meetings, in agendas, or minutes. The district assembly did not receive any reports from lower levels, and spent most of its attention on the district center itself. Only lately has it been possible to give local leaders some formal training, and results are definitely forthcoming.'

The political role given to workers in Frelimo's strategy is well reflected in Angoche development. The factories were given priority in the creation of party cells and other organs. Today, the workers are on the whole more advanced politically, and special monitors are recruited from their ranks to help in information and mobilisation in rural areas. Their job is also to talk to people and learn about their needs, in order to give district leaders a better understanding of the situation.

Of the two major organisations, the women's organisation, the OMM, with its background in the women's detachment of the armed struggle, is the most successful in the local context, even if at the central level it still proves rather cautious in its approach to certain key issues. On the other hand, the history of the youth organisation, the OJM, is important, for the insight it gives into tendencies within the party itself and therefore into the problem of the autonomy of the mass organisations *vis-à-vis* the party.

Two circumstances influenced the formation of OJM. First, young people all over the country showed uncontestable enthusiasm for the new tasks and opportunities offered by the revolution. Second, the crises in employment and in education led to a gap between youth expectations and the means for their fulfilment. The new organisation was discussed during several months of preparation, before its formal creation in November 1977. The OJM was defined as an open, broad-based organisation with minimum requirements for membership, developing various youth-related activities including voluntary work and training. In practice, however, it did not develop along these lines.

Unable to tackle in a serious way the problems of youth, such as unemployment and poverty, probably devoid of any resources for sports or training activities, its leaders withdrew more and more into formalism and elitism. Membership was generally equated only with the secretariat of OJM, which in some areas was viewed with outright hostility because of its arrogance and isolationism.

The problems of OJM surfaced in the general review of political organisations carried out in the follow-up to the 1980 Presidential offensive. The criticism was in many ways similar to that directed against the party itself. In fact, OJM leaders were said to 'see the OJM as a mini-party for young people, with the requirements, the discipline and the rigor of the party Frelimo. Thus they try to copy in a mechanical way the structures and methods of work of the party and impose them on the youth. . .'[39]. There are no indications as yet that this insight has led to any lasting changes in the life of OJM.

The development of OJM becomes more comprehensible if we take into account that most—if not all—of its leaders are party members, participating in local party work and perhaps aspiring to posts in the party itself, with the OJM being the main springboard to the party for young people with little work experience. In this sense, the problem is one of the party itself, or the party/state, with its emphasis on authority, administrative efficiency and hierarchical discipline. Party leaders are today very aware of the need and urgency to tackle elitist tendencies within the party. Whether a greater autonomy is required for the mass organisations to gain strength is a matter which remains to be discussed.

Poder Popular and the strategy for socialist transition

The Fourth Party Congress in April 1983 had before it the experience of nearly eight years of socialist construction. On the one hand, there was the creation of political and state structures, the restructuring of the economy, the development of central economic planning, the emergence of new social relations of production, the extension of health and education to embrace a majority of the population—in short, the fulfilment of basic and necessary conditions for the transition to socialism. On the other hand, there existed the failure of the state to provide for even the basic consumption needs of the majority of the population, the growth of trade deficits, and the rapid spread of black market dealings.

Two factors have contributed decisively to the poor economic record: international economic relations, which since the mid-1970s have gone from bad to worse, and the almost uninterrupted state of war caused by Rhodesian and later South African military aggression. It could, of course, be argued that the aggressions, like the inevitable deteriorations in economic relations with South Africa, were to some extent foreseeable results of post-independence conditions of national development. But it is not equally clear what effect this insight would have had in determining national development strategies.

Frelimo inherited an economy shaped to suit the needs of the colonial power, Portugal, and of its economically powerful neighbour, South Africa. A large peasant sector provided labour to South African mines, Rhodesian farms and capitalist farms within Mozambique. It produced one third of the cash crops while ensuring its own reproduction on low-yielding family plots. A semi-proletarianised workforce of unskilled labour served the needs of the comparatively large industrial sector, which had weak links to agriculture and a corresponding dependence on imported materials. When the Portuguese left in massive numbers at the time of independence, a complete breakdown was averted only through state intervention. In agriculture, nationalisation of abandoned farms and plantations prevented the emergence of an indigenous capitalist sector.

The cornerstone of Frelimo's economic strategy was the introduction of 'state farms', created out of the nationalised modern sector. Politically these were intended to be centres for the formation of an agricultural working class. The state farms were expected to feed the urban population, produce raw materials for industrial production and generate foreign currency through exports. Thus the peasant would be relieved of the worst of colonial exploitation, and could sell his labour to the state farms, whilst organising communal villages and co-operative production. Market regulation and subordination to the state plan would ensure the necessary transfer of surplus.

In reality, things did not go this way. Health and education received a sizeable share of the budget and expanded rapidly in response to common expectations. Industrial recuperation on the other hand, proved stubbornly difficult. Centralised import controls and poor factory management would probably have kept production low even without the ever-present economic sabotage, frequently carried out via the international linkages of companies. In addition, relations between management, the party and workers' production councils did not always run smoothly. Management problems were equally apparent in the state farms, which, despite heavy investments, could not achieve satisfactory yields or even cover their costs.

Of all investment in agriculture, only a few percent went to the relatively small co-operative sector. The millions of peasants engaged in familial agricultural production also received negligible amounts. This policy, which was in conflict with party directives, reflected more general problems concerning the state's competence in its dealings with the peasantry. The aim of commercialising agricultural products was complicated by poor transport, poor organisation and payment problems. Exchange relations were not favourable to the peasant, who found tools and consumer goods increasingly scarce. Re-privatisation of the 'people's shops' and parts of the trade network led to some improvements. As long as industrial production was low, however, shop shelves remained empty.

On the whole, state planning and market regulation had failed to satisfy the needs of the majority of primary producers. The result was a reduction in the volume of publicly marketed products, and the clandestine re-emergence of private traders. The problem has not gone unnoticed by the government, which a few years ago began to create the conditions for private enterprise in a specified number of areas, and also to hire the services of old established wholesalers for the purchase of products from the peasant sector. The state itself tended to become the embodiment of an ideology of *gigantismo*, going for advanced technology and large-scale projects.

Data about the process are found in the Central Committee report to the Fourth Congress, where it is analysed as being a part of the class struggle within the state. There exists today an 'aspiring bourgeoisie' consisting basically of those who enjoyed certain privileges during the colonial period, including that of education, and whose values were formed more by Europe than by their own country. Operating within the state, they

> try to distort the class character of our revolution by transforming it into a technocratic process through which they can control power. This social stratum actively opposes any measures that aim at simplifying organisation and methods, democratising the leadership or increasing the workers' share in the planning and control of production.[40]

The Central Committee report points to a key problem in the party/state model — that of the *de facto* alliance between a revolutionary leadership and a basically non-revolutionary (or even counter-revolutionary) social stratum within the state. We would prefer, however, to characterise the problem of *gigantismo* and the neglect of *poder popular* in slightly different terms. Firstly, the Portuguese exodus caused an immense dearth of knowledge and experience in the ranks of the state apparatus. The composition of the party leadership reflected the few career outlets available to the Mozambicans under colonialism: they were basically social and health professionals and humanity students. Secondly, in Mozambique, even more than in Portugal, the gap between urban and rural, like that between the white-collar strata and the worker in his *fato macacu* (literally, 'monkey dress') was almost unbridgeable. The new state functionaries were simply unable to relate to the conditions of the majority of Mozambicans.

The confusion that occurred around the time of independence was to a large extent cultural, sometimes leading to a near-paralysis in the face of the new demands on management-worker relations. Into this knowledge-gap moved *cooperantes* of all nationalities, with those from Eastern Europe and the Soviet Union carrying by far the highest prestige. Their advice, supported by aid and co-operation agreements, was well received. In fact overambitious projects both in industry and agriculture met little resistance in the generally 'triumphalist' climate following the unconditional victory of Frelimo. The party/state leadership itself was certainly not free from feelings of optimism about the Mozambican revolution and its unbounded potential.

The Fourth Congress deliberations represent a sober and realistic assessment of the possibilities compared to the visions of the past. Its resolutions mark, in a fundamental sense, a rehabilitation both of the peasantry and (to a more limited extent) of the private sector. The Congress also openly admitted the failure of state farm policies and the—at least temporary—need for a very different strategy. It was the government's first serious confrontation with the fundamental problems of the state and of central planning.

Behind this reorientation lay a series of factors: the precarious balance of payments situation and the need to reduce imports; the necessity of generating more food supplies within the country; the problem of the party's popular support and the maintenance of the revolution in the face of deteriorating material conditions and increased banditry; the persistent lack of returns to the vast investments made in the state agricultural sector. With the government having addressed these problems, the question now is to what extent international support can be mobilised, and how far the state machinery will adjust itself to the radical demands of the new strategy. These include the following points:

Centralisation has gone too far and the central state machinery is too big and costly. Budget reductions are necessary together with the decentralisation of staff. Direct state interventions should be reduced in favour of a policy of offering general guidance and support.

State planning should make the district its point of departure. District plans based on local resources and capacities are to be the building blocks in central planning.

This requires the reinforcement of local democratic organs working under a certain autonomy and with budgetary resources of their own. Stronger involvement of the workers in all aspects of planning production is strongly recommended.

Local initiatives should be stimulated and given the necessary state support. Small projects and simple technology, artisanship and small scale industry are to be encouraged.

While state farms have to be consolidated and made economically viable, state resources should be redirected into the cooperative, private and family sectors of agriculture. Concomitantly, state policies on prices and salaries should be more actively directed towards the re-establishment of market mechanisms in society.

Immediately following the congress, a general government reshuffle was announced, together with a remodelling of the state structures. Soon thereafter functionaries were called up to work outside Maputo and to help create the conditions for the urban unemployed to be sent to rural districts in search of productive work.

Conclusion

The experience of Mozambique, though inevitably reflecting its particular geopolitical situation in Southern Africa, provides important lessons for other countries. As a Third World country, Mozambique suffers under the heavy burdens of deteriorating international terms of trade, the so-called oil crisis, and reduced domestic food supplies. Its socialist strategy makes Mozambique vulnerable to the apparently general problems of agricultural production in a planned economy: the role of market relations, of the state, and of co-operative or private agriculture. With these problems still remaining essentially unresolved even in the advanced socialist countries, the search for new perspectives inevitably is left to the Third World socialist countries themselves.

But these countries, operating under hostile conditions and with serious economic problems, are acting under pressure. 'Material scarcity exerts a stifling grip – the parameters of innovation are narrow,' is the conclusion of one recent study.[41] The scarcity is reflected everywhere in society, from the communal village lacking sufficient human resources to keep even simple records of their work, to the state machinery basing its interventions on only the very scantiest information about the reality of the country it is hoping to transform.

The particular historical context of revolutionary struggles in the Third World, and their deep reliance on popular mobilisation, tend to make the problems of popular participation, democracy and leadership, areas demanding special attention. In national liberation struggles to date, the strength of popular will and motivation has made possible advances far beyond the mere technological level of the war machinery employed. This is the general historical experience of any popularly based struggle. Nevertheless, little work has been done on its significance for succeeding phases of the struggle, those of the transition to new forms of social organisation and a new mode of production. Here, a vital issue is that of establishing a relation to the technology and means of production formerly dominated by the enemy. Their control and development must be achieved in the midst of a general scarcity of trained and qualified labour. If the former upholders of technology had not left (as they did in Cuba, Angola and Mozambique), they would have endangered revolutionary progress by being both indispensable technical cadres and ideological enemies of the revolution.

The burden of the struggle in both the economic and political fields must therefore, even now, be borne by the same strata as before, the exploited workers and peasants. It seems to us that a profound reflection on the significance of this fact could lead to reconsiderations of the dominant strategies of industrialisation, of the nature of party/state organisation and of methods of work. The strength of the Mozambican revolution is that the links to the ten years of liberation struggle have never been allowed to dissolve. Today, when economic problems have made a deep and disturbing imprint on society, these very ties have made possible a strategic reconsideration in favour of the peasantry, of local resources and initiatives, and of *Poder Popular*.

It is the dynamic of the political processes, the open character of the class struggle and the ability of the leadership to view theory in the light of its own social reality, which give countries like Mozambique a central position in the unfolding theory and strategy of socialist transition.

This chapter was researched and written whilst on a research grant from SAREC in Sweden.

Notes

1. The creation of a vanguard party out of the front in 1977, meant that the name Frelimo, no longer an abbreviation for The Front for the Liberation of Mozambique, is written in small letters.

2. See for example *People's Power*, the publication of the Mozambique and Angola Committee (MAC) in London.

3. A. MacEwan, *Revolution and Economic Development in Cuba* (Macmillan Press, London, 1981).

4. M. Honecker, *Cuba: Dictatorship or Democracy*? (Lawrence Hill & Co., Westport, 1980).

5. R. Carciofi, 'Cuba in the seventies', in G. White, R. Murray and C. White (eds), *Revolutionary Socialist Development in the Third World* (Wheatsheaf Books, Brighton, 1983).

6. B. Munslow, *Mozambique: The Revolution and its Origins* (Longmans, London, 1983).

7. R. Carciofi, 'Cuba in the seventies', p. 201f. (discussing the conclusions of MacEwan).

8. G. White, 'Revolutionary Socialist Development in the Third World, an Overview', in G. White, R. Murray and C. White (eds), *Revolutionary Socialist Development*.

9. D. Wield, 'Mozambique – Late Colonialism and Early Problems of Transition', in G. White, R. Murray and C. White (eds), *Revolutionary Socialist Development*.

10. M. dos Santos as recorded by A. Isaacman in *A Luta Continua: Creating a New Society in Mozambique* (State University of New York at Binghampton, 1978) p. 38.

11. J. Chissano, address to a meeting in Mocuba, 16–21 February 1975, published in *Datas e Documentos da História da FRELIMO* (Maputo, 1975) p. 288.

12. S. Machel, opening address to the 7th Central Committee meeting in Inhambane, 19 June 1975, published in Ibid.

13. 'Transform the Central Hospital into a People's Hospital' in B. Munslow (ed), *Samora Machel: An African Revolutionary. Selected Speeches and Writings* (Zed Press, London, 1985) chapter 10.

14. S. Machel, speech to industrial workers, 13 October 1976, published in *Organização dos Conselhos de Produção* (CNICP, Maputo, 1977) p. 64f.

15. Interview with Felizberto Mondlane, Vice-Director of the CNICP, Maputo, 20 July 1981.

16. See the party organ *Boletim da Célula*, No. 1, July 1980.

17. Examples of such reports are those published in *Notícias* (Maputo) 3 December 1982 and 16 March 1983.

18. The requirements on *assimilados* are well described in E. Mondlane, *The Struggle for Mozambique* (Zed Press, London, 1983) p. 48.

19. *The People in Power: Mozambique's Elections*, AIM (Mozambique Information Agency), Maputo, 1977.

20. *Boletin da República*, I Série, No. 150, 24 de Dezambro de 1977.

21. See *The People in Power . . .*, and *African Communist* No. 74, 1978, for accounts of the election process.

22. *Boletim da República* op. cit.

23. Interviews were carried out in August 1981 with representatives of communal villages, locality and district structures in the district of Angoche, and with the then Ministry of State, Maputo.

24. *Supplement to AIM Bulletin* (Maputo), No. 15, September 1977.

25. Ibid.

26. *Central Committee Report to the Third Congress of FRELIMO* (English language version published by MAGIC, London, 1978).

27. J. Saul, 'Politikken bag den mocambikanske socialisme' (The Politics of Mozambican Socialism), *Den Ny Verlden* (Copenhagen), No. 1, 1981.

28. J. Slovo, 'Lessons of the Mozambican Revolution', *African Communist*, No. 73, 1978.

29. S. Machel, in a speech closing the campaign, *Voz da Revolução* (Frelimo), No. 71, 1980.

30. S. Machel, closing address to the Council of Ministers, 1–4 August 1979. *A Luta Contra o Subdesenvolvimento* (Frelimo, 1983).

31. Resolution of the 7th Central Committee meeting, July 1980, *Voz da Revolução*, No. 71, 1980.

32. Report of the Central Committee to the Fourth Congress (Maputo, 1983).

33. M. dos Santos in a radio broadcast published in *AIM Bulletin*, No. 14, August 1977.

34. P. Sketchley, *Casting New Molds: First Steps Toward Worker Control in a Mozambican Steel Factory* (IFDP, San Francisco, 1980).

35. M. dos Santos, in *AIM Bulletin*, footnote 33.

36. *Notícias*, 27 April 1981.

37. J. Slovo, 'Lessons of the Mozambican Revolution', footnote 28.

38. *Programme of the Party Frelimo* (AIM, 25 March 1977).

39. *Façamos da OJM a Organização de Toda a Juventude Moçambicana* (OJM, Maputo 1981).

40. *Report of the Central Committee to the Fourth Congress* (Maputo, 1983) p. 74.

41. G. White, R. Murray and C. White (eds), *Revolutionary Socialist Development*, p. 7.

7: Establishing the Conditions for Socialism: The Case of Angola

by M.R. Bhagavan

We say, and it is easy to say, that we want to build socialism. We say so at every step. But what does socialism mean for each person? For each person? What degree of happiness can socialism give to each one of us?

We shall have socialism when everyone can say: I have my house; I have my small belongings; I have my cooperative; I have the possibility, in the area where I live, of getting what I need in the way of food, medical treatment, of getting from one place to another, that is, having transport facilities; having organised trade; being able to sell produce; and, lastly, being able to exchange goods within the country or even with other countries, so that our work really represents an advantage for everyone.

We shall be able to say we have socialism when there are no classes exploiting each other; when we no longer have a group or various groups of people in the country who want to have greater advantages than the rest.

This means that we must create conditions. What are those conditions?

President Agostinho Neto
from a speech delivered at
Calandula, Malanje province
18 August 1979.

The state of the political economy on the eve of independence

The People's Republic of Angola (PRA) was proclaimed by the MPLA (People's Movement for the Liberation of Angola) on 11 November 1975. By April 1976, with the help of the Cuban troops, FAPLA (the People's Armed Forces for the Liberation of Angola, the military arm of MPLA) had driven out the invading South African and Zairean troops. This defeat had immediate repercussions on their Angolan protégés, the FNLA (National Front for the Liberation of Angola) and UNITA (National Union for the Total Independence of Angola).[1] Any presence that the

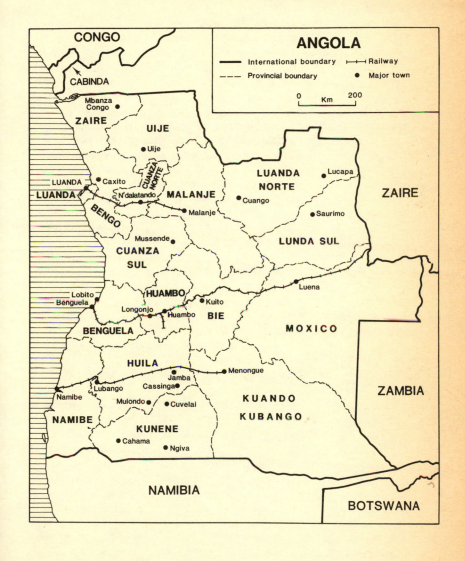

FNLA previously had in the country was eliminated. Although UNITA could not so easily be eradicated, its armed attacks were greatly reduced and its influence was restricted to certain pockets in the southern provinces. The retreating troops from South Africa, Zaire, the FNLA and UNITA plundered consumer durables, vehicles, machinery and equipment, and destroyed what they could not take with them, blowing up bridges and installations, and burning down villages and food stores.

By 1975, the number of Portuguese settlers in Angola was about 340,000. Most of them had arrived in the 1960s and at the beginning of the 1970s. Between early 1975 and early 1976, in the space of one year, about 300,000 of these settlers left Angola.[2] They too, decamped with consumer durables, vehicles, boats, machinery and equipment, and sabotaged what they could not take with them.

This mass exodus, which demonstrated all the signs of panic and mass hysteria, is understandable in light of the settlers' background. They came from the smallholder peasantry, the urban and industrial working class, and the petty bourgeoisie, to escape the hardships of the crisis-ridden and failing economy of Portugal, in the hope of a better material life in Angola. Their immigration had been actively encouraged by the fascist regime in Lisbon, as a way of increasing the stake of the Portuguese civilian population in retaining the colony, thus countering the growing successes of the MPLA. The white population jumped from 173,000 in 1960 (3.6 percent of a total population of 4.83 million) to 335,000 in 1974 (5.7 percent of a total of 5.9 million).[3] Portuguese and other Western capital followed on their heels, to take advantage of the boom conditions created in the 1960s in Angolan mining and manufacturing and construction industries, and in the commercial farming of coffee, cotton, maize, sugarcane, rice and other crops, as well as of livestock. The settlers had obviously assumed that colonial rule would continue for quite a long time, and their exploitation of the Angolan population and Angolan natural resources would be carried on indefinitely behind the 'protective shield' of the colonial army.

The coup in April 1974 by the Armed Forces Movement (MFA) in Portugal, which overthrew the fascist regime, and the announcement by the MFA of its firm intention of ending the colonial war, of withdrawing the colonial army and of 'granting' independence to Angola on a negotiated basis, shattered the settlers' dreams. Their leaders, and some top army officers of the colonial army, seriously considered staging a 'unilateral declaration of independence' along the lines of the Rhodesian UDI of 1965. But unlike Britain in the case of Rhodesia, the MFA firmly stamped on the idea and effectively killed it. That left the settlers with the choice of staying on and co-operating with the government of an independent Angola, or of leaving. Dr Agostinho Neto, the President of MPLA and the first President of the People's Republic of Angola, appealed on the eve of independence to the settlers to stay and help in the task of rebuilding the economy. But they ignored this appeal.

There were several reasons behind the massive flight of the Portuguese. Part of the settler community and the colonial army had carried out numerous atrocities and massacres against the African population from the distant past right up to the end of 1974, and now they feared that vengeance would be taken.[4] The transitional government comprising the MPLA, FNLA and UNITA was sworn in on 1 January 1975, to prepare the country for independence on 11 November 1975. But hardly was this government in place, before the FNLA and UNITA began their murderous attacks on MPLA cadres in Luanda and elsewhere in the country. Internecine violence broke out. Fearing for their life and property, many Angolan blacks and mestiços fled from the countryside to the relative safety of the cities, while the white settlers began to look to Portugal as their haven of safety.

The 'leading personalities' of the settler community, whether through lack of nerve or fearing for their wealth, were among the first to leave. They set the example for others to follow. The settlers realized that their dream of accumulating wealth rapidly through the horrendous exploitation of Angolans was over, and this undermined the original rationale for their arrival in Angola. Having regarded Africans as racially and mentally inferior to themselves,[5] it became psychologically and socially impossible for them to accept the fact that Angolan Africans had become masters in their own country and whites would have to take orders from blacks.

The material and financial loss inflicted on Angola by the retreating enemy troops and the fleeing Portuguese was truly enormous. Added to this was the severely disruptive effect of the sudden departure of most of the people who had the knowledge and the skills (although in absolute terms these were small in number) to maintain and run the economy and infrastructure. The settlers had monopolised all the skilled jobs, from the lowest to the highest, in the various organs of the state, banking and commerce, private and public industry, commercial farming, transport and energy, education and health services, wholesale and retail trade, and in the legal, medical and other professions.

Few Angolans had been allowed access to middle and higher education and technical training. In 1973, the number of pupils registered in all middle schools was 40,024 and in all secondary and higher education 40,377 (see Table 1), each accounting for only 1.2 percent of the school age population (5 to 24 years) of 3.24 million, and 0.7 percent of the total population of 5.88 million.[6] Since 85 percent of the population was illiterate, and this included virtually all of the black Angolans, one can infer quite clearly that the settlers had also monopolised all middle and higher educational opportunities. (After 1950, official data stopped giving the racial breakdown of pupils and students to avert possible criticism.)

Lest this give the impression that a large number of Portuguese immigrants and settlers were educated and skilled, it should be pointed out that this was far from being the case. The majority were uneducated. As Bender emphasises, 'less than *six percent* of the approximately 100,000 Portuguese immigrants between 1950 and 1964 who were seven years and older attended school beyond the fourth grade'.[7] He then continued:

> While the proportion of immigrants with post-primary school education rose during the 1965–72 period, it still did not exceed the 1950 level of less than 17 per cent. Moreover, the percentage of immigrants who arrived without any schooling at all during the last decade of colonialism rose to 55 per cent. Clearly, after a century of successive government campaigns to raise the cultural and educational level of Portuguese immigrants in Angola, the *fina flor* (of uneducated, poor Portuguese peasants), continued to predominate until the very end of colonialism.[8]

The severe lack of highly qualified people among the Portuguese immigrants is well illustrated by the fact that, in 1968, the total number of persons in Angola practising liberal and technical professions was only 1205 (although this was extremely widely defined to include 26 categories ranging from lawyers to insurance agents, engineers to electricians, masseurs to musicians). Of these, 69 were engineers, 340 physicians, 87 lawyers, 28 engineering technicians, 123 nurses, and 20 veterinarians.[9]

The fascist dictatorship that ruled Portugal for many decades from the early part of this century to the mid 1970s deliberately held back Portugal's economic and social development.[10] This was at a time when northern Europe and parts of Western Europe were making radical advances in inventing, developing and using ever more modern technologies and methods of socio-economic organisation and management, which now characterise the industrially developed capitalist countries. The result was to keep Portugal in a state of underdevelopment in comparison not only with the advanced countries of the West, but also with some of the industrialising countries of Asia and Latin America.

Colonised by such an economically and technologically backward country as Portugal, Angola, like the other Portuguese colonies, suffered a double burden of underdevelopment. Apart from a few urban centres where the more well-to-do Portuguese immigrants congregated, in the rest of the country there was virtually no economic and social infrastructure that could benefit the majority of the Angolan population—there were no schools, dispensaries, hospitals, rural roads, clean drinking water, sanitation, public hygiene facilities, postal services and public transport. In contrast, every population centre, however small, had at least one church and usually more. The three railways that were built ran east–west to bring primary produce (agricultural and mineral) from the interior to the ports, in the classic pattern of colonial exploitation. A similar geographical pattern existed with the three electricity transmission lines. Neither the three railway lines nor the three electricity transmission lines were interconnected in a north–south direction, for the obvious reason that it would serve no economic purpose insofar as colonial economic interests were concerned.

The condition of the people

The year 1973 is regarded as the last 'stable' year, before the disruptions set in. It is also considered to be the 'best' year (historically), from the point of view of the economy. Let us take a look at the living and working conditions of the great majority of the Angolan population around that time.

By 1973, more than half a million Angolans had fled from the northern and north western districts to the relative safety of Zaire to escape the terror and devastation unleashed by the colonial army and the FNLA bands. Of the population that remained behind, 84 percent lived in the rural areas, and they made up 80 percent of the total labour force (see Table 2). Seventy two percent of the total labour force were subsistence peasants (including subsistence fishermen and pastoralists), 8 percent worked as agricultural wage labour on farms and plantations owned by the Portuguese immigrants (see Table 3). Their nutritional standards were poor. Their staple diet consisted of cassava (manioc, mandioca), beans and dried fish in the northern areas, and maize, beans and fish in the central provinces. Only the pastoralists in the southern region (who constituted a very small part of the population) had a regular protein-rich diet of meat and milk.

The average daily wage of an African agricultural worker was 20 escudos, i.e. about 60 US cents (see Table 4). The cash income of a subsistence peasant household was even less. On average, the household of an agricultural worker and a subsistence peasant consisted of six to eight persons. This one cash income of 20 escudos per day, or less, had to supply the essential consumption requirements of six to eight persons. If we compare this abysmally low income with the prices of essential mass consumption goods prevalent in Luanda in the early 1970s, given in Table 5 (and prices in the countryside would have been higher because of transport costs and the profit margin of the retail trader), we will see how very low its purchasing power was. To buy even the basic food for a household of six to eight persons would have been entirely out of the question for the African agricultural worker. What could they afford to buy? Some salt, sugar, edible oil, soap, and very rarely some clothing. Footwear and medicine would be out of their reach, as would dairy products. If they ate meat at all, it would be only occasionally and the source would be chickens, pigs and goats that they bred themselves. Unable to survive on their wages, agricultural workers were semi- rather than fully proletarian, and growing much of their own food.

To understand the conditions under which the agricultural wage labourer and the subsistence peasant lived, one has to go back somewhat in time. Officially, the Portuguese government in Lisbon maintained the fiction that slavery had ended by 1878, and that from then onwards the African was 'free' to sell or withhold his labour. However, the settler economy as it then was, depended on the easy availability of African labour to work under slave conditions in cotton and other plantations. To dispense with slave labour meant 'modernising' the technologically and economically extremely backward and inefficient methods of production and of surplus extraction, which rested almost entirely on the very hard, unceasing manual labour of the African, in return for less than bare subsistence.

The settlers were unwilling to, and also incapable of, making the transition to even relatively moderately more efficient and advanced methods, which could at one and the same time increase their profits and ameliorate the inhuman working and living conditions of the African labourer. Amazingly, this inability and unwillingness to modernise persisted into the early 1960s, when for instance, the methods of coffee production in Portuguese plantations in Angola were the most backward in the African continent (not to say in the rest of the world), while at the same time fetching substantial profits which gives an indication of the degree of exploitation to which the African was subjected.

The formal and official end to slavery was accompanied by the institution of contract labour, a euphemism for the modern slavery of forced labour. Under the contract system, the settlers obliged the colonial authorities to supply them with African labour. In the words of Duffy,

> The employer felt less obligation to the contracted labourer than he had formerly to his slaves. The *serviçais* (contracted workers) were maintained at subsistence level. Many died or failed to return to their villages. . .and some parts of Angola were almost emptied of their inhabitants; from other areas the Africans fled deep into the interior. Some workers, driven to desperation by the distance from their villages and the inhumanity of the treatment given them, revolted and formed fierce little bands of warriors.[11]

According to a United Nations estimate,[12] by about 1954, half a million Africans had fled from Angola to the neighbouring countries to escape the forced labour system.

> Despite critical reports by Caetano, Galvão and others, Africans continued to be "given" to the *colonos*, who often treated them worse than their forefathers had treated their animals or slaves. . . Under the forced labour system, however, the employer cared little if his worker became incapacitated or died, for he could always ask that another labourer be furnished. Galvão reported that the death rate for Africans supplied by the government to certain employers reached as high as 35 per cent. . . The forced labour system was only abolished in 1961, after African nationalists attacked the coffee plantations in the north, where the greatest concentration of "contract workers" in Angola was found.[13]

As in the rest of colonial Africa, the peasant household in Angola was forced into cash crop cultivation by a combination of three factors: physical coercion by the administration, the necessity of having to pay tax (or be drafted into the forced labour system on European farms), and the necessity of buying a bare minimum of essential food items (e.g. salt, sugar, edible oil) and clothing. Needless to say, the prices paid for the cash crop grown by the African peasant were extremely low. The effect on peasant production of food crops was devastating. Soils became depleted, food production fell to very low levels and hunger became endemic.

> Many of these African families were thus caught in a vicious circle: as their agricultural production annually decreased, more men left the land to seek employment as rural wage earners; and the more men who abandoned their fields, the more African production declined. While this "proletarianization" of the African countryside proved beneficial to European planters by providing them with an increased number of cheap labourers, it had a devastating impact on African production.[14]

The situation of the unskilled workers in industry and in other miscellaneous employment in urban areas was no better than that of the agricultural wage labourer. More than 80 percent of the industrial labour force were unskilled workers and they were all African.[15] In the early 1970s, the average daily wage of an unskilled worker in the manufacturing sector was 28 escudos and in the mining sector 16 escudos, compared with 155 escudos for an African or *mestiço* (i.e. of mixed African–European parentage) skilled worker (there were very few of these), and 400 escudos for a Portuguese skilled worker (see Tables 5 and 6). The cash incomes of middle and top level employees, who were all Portuguese, were respectively 50 and 80 times that of the unskilled workers; if we include fringe benefits paid out in kind, in goods and services, to those members of the petty bourgeoisie and the bourgeoisie, their real income would be double that indicated above.

In the early 1970s, real wages of African unskilled and skilled workers fell (see inflation rates in Table 7). What the great majority of the urban and industrial proletariat could buy was the same as the agricultural wage labourer and the subsistence peasant; a few bare essentials like maize flour, beans, rice, salt, sugar, edible oil and cloth. Modern facilities for hygiene, health care, education and transport were firmly kept out of their reach. The 'best' year of 1973 was for the overwhelming majority of Angolans the same as every other year: one of unrelieved deprivation and misery.

Agricultural production

The Portuguese were wont to claim that they had a 'five hundred year presence' in Angola. This claim is hollow and ludicrous. Until the 1850s, their 'presence' was limited to a band of territory along the northern and central coastline and to the northern districts now bordering western Zaire. In the vast interior of the country, there were only a handful of Portuguese, isolated in scattered fortifications or travelling as traders. Their major economic activity was slave trading.

Two things woke them up to the fact that they had no 'presence' worth the name in the interior. First, the slave trade ended under pressure from Britain and other West European powers. Second, with the Berlin Conference of 1884 and the 'scramble for Africa', the continent was carved up among European colonial powers, and Portugal realized that without effective occupation of the interior, rival colonial powers like Britain, Germany, Belgium and France would move in.

In desperation, Portugal decided to settle the interior with *degredados*, i.e. Portuguese convicted of serious crimes in Portugal sentenced to hard labour and then sent to penal colonies in Africa. These convicts were supposed to found 'model' farms, and thus show the world that Portugal effectively occupied Angola. As the 19th century neared its end, so did the possibility of surplus extraction and capital accumulation through the slave trade. To make the colony pay, and at the same time to settle the interior, *degredados* and sundry other immigrants were encouraged to simply take over the best agricultural land that they could grab, and begin the production and export of cash crops, such as coffee, cotton, sisal, etc. Not until the 1920s did this process get fully underway; its profitability was dependent upon forced labour by Africans at starvation wages.

From the 1920s to the 1950s, two main categories of agricultural production were in evidence. First, subsistence cultivation by African households, who also cultivated and sold small amounts of cash crops (including some food crops) to obtain an essential minimum cash income; secondly, cash crop farming (again including some food crops) by Portuguese settlers, on medium to large scale plantations. Until the 1950s, the demand for food crops, dairy products, fish, meat and poultry products by the domestic urban market was very limited. The overseas export trade was the only dominant connection between the rural producer and the urban market. It was not until the early 1960s, when to counter the military successes of the MPLA, the colonial regime poured in large numbers of troops and more urban settlers, and the production of food for the growing urban market became an important economic activity for both the African subsistence peasant and the Portuguese farmer. The implication of this historically very recent 'food connection' between the town and the country, and its inherent colonial fragility will be examined when we come to discuss the contemporary economic crisis in Angola.

It is often claimed by apologists for the Portuguese colonial regime that by the 'best' year of 1973, Angola was not only self-sufficient in food but it also exported it. A cursory examination of this claim shows that the self-sufficiency was limited to the petty bourgeoisie and the bourgeoisie with their high incomes, who constituted only about 6 percent of the total population. One can infer from Tables 4 and 5 that only this tiny privileged class was able to buy regularly foods such as dairy products, fish, meat and poultry. Nineteen out of every twenty Angolans lived on the bare essentials. Food exports were possible only because of the integral connection between the exploitation of African labour, the corresponding lack of African purchasing power, and the surplus produced by its labour for European farm-owners.

On the eve of independence, the dominant marketed food crops were maize, bananas, potatoes, cassava (mandioca), rice and beans, in that order. Milk, eggs and beef were also strongly represented (see Table 8). This structure was indicative, however, only of the consumption preferences among the urban dwellers. It did not correspond to the situation in the country as a whole, where subsistence production was (and continues to be) the most important economic activity. Typically, no figures are available, either for pre-independence or post-independence years, for the volume of subsistence production. Based on the personal impressions of people familiar with rural life, one infers that the dominant food crops were cassava (in the north), maize (in the centre), sorghum and millet (in the south), bananas and rice (mainly in the north) and beans. Milk and beef seem to have been available in sufficient quantities only among the subsistence pastoralists of the south. Coffee was the most important export crop, followed by sisal, cotton, bananas, and sugar.

Industrial production

In 1973, the chief sources of export earnings in hard convertible currencies were oil, coffee, diamonds and iron ore, accounting respectively for 30, 26.5, 10.4 and 6.2 percent of total export income.[16] Angola has proven deposits of 34 minerals, fourteen of which are strategic.[17] The production figures for oil, diamonds and iron ore are given in Table 9.

The period of substantial growth in the manufacturing sector did not begin until 1960. From then on, until 1973, it was quite rapid, the real growth rate (at constant 1963 prices) being 11 percent per annum. Even though this figure must be interpreted with caution, because the growth occurred on a small initial base, it still represents a remarkable rate of growth. Manufacturing output, which was only 6.5 percent of total GDP in 1960, grew to about 16 percent by 1971.

Let us now turn to look at the social and political factors that led to this growth. Between 1940 and 1960, the immigrant white population (almost entirely Portuguese) rose from 44,000 to 172,000, and formed 3.6 percent of a total population of 4.8 million by 1960. Within the space of twenty years Angola was transformed into a settler colony. Originally, most of the white immigrants were single men, but by 1950 immigration became more balanced and more family-based, with proportionate numbers of women and children, and with an increasing proportion of permanent residents. One of the major reasons for this influx was the promise of high profits that could be made in the cultivation and export of coffee. An additional powerful reason was the lack of social mobility in Portugal, where capitalism remained under-developed and stagnant under fascist rule. Opportunities for material advancement were few in number.

There is a view prevalent among the top echelons of the Portuguese petty bourgeoisie, that during the 1950s and 1960s many of the 'most energetic, gifted and ambitious' emigrated to Angola in search of wealth and power, while the 'mediocre' stayed behind to join the Portuguese bureaucracy. This opinion should be treated with some scepticism, in view of the fact that Angola hardly attracted any 'dynamic' and 'enterprising' settlers in the earlier centuries, so much so, that Lisbon was forced to settle the colony first with *degredados* and then with poor and illiterate peasants.

The MPLA launched its armed struggle against the colonial regime in 1961. As the first war of liberation intensified and spread to different parts of the country, the regime had to fly in more and more troops from Portugal. This further swelled the number of the white population, which had already quadrupled between 1940 and 1960. By 1970 (the year of the latest census), it had risen to 290,000, i.e. 5.2 percent of a total population of 5.6 million. Both because of its size and its high income, this white population formed a sizeable domestic market. It acted as an incentive to capitalists in Portugal and to owners of coffee plantations in Angola to invest in the manufacture of consumer goods inside Angola. Domestic production was greatly helped by the demand generated by the settler population for consumer goods, which were cheaper than those imported from Portugal.

The structure of manufacturing production clearly reflected the dominant position of the white settlers in the domestic market. We recall from our earlier discussion, that the buying power of 95 percent of the population in the early 1970s was equivalent to about 25 escudos per day, as against the buying power of between 400 and 1600 escudos per day of the remaining 5 percent of the population, made up very largely of Portuguese immigrants. Correspondingly, we find that in 1973, 37 percent of manufacturing output was in luxury consumption goods, 33 percent in mass consumption goods, with the intermediate and capital goods sectors making up 20 and 10 percent respectively (see Table 10).[18]

During the colonial period, manufacturing was organised principally to cater to the luxury consumption of the petty bourgeoisie and bourgeois sections of Angolan society. This comes as no surprise, because it is precisely these sections which constituted the local ruling groups, and acted as agents of the metropolitan ruling classes, exercising political power. Self-sustaining industrialisation based on the domestic production of intermediate and capital goods was not on the agenda, as the low percentage figures for, and even more the composition of, these two sectors shows. The structure of imports (see Table 11) tells the same story.

The world market and foreign capital

Like other underdeveloped colonial economies, Angola was linked to metropolitan capitalist markets as a supplier of raw materials. In 1974, nearly all of its exports in monetary value were either unprocessed or simply-processed primary products. As Table 12 shows, oil exports dominated at 55.4 percent of total principal exports followed by coffee at 23.2 percent, diamonds 9.1, sisal 4.7, iron ore 4.5, raw cotton 1.9, bananas 1.1 and sugar 0.1 percent. These products were destined primarily for about half a dozen countries in the West, with the USA accounting for the biggest share (made up overwhelmingly of oil and coffee), followed by Portugal, the UK, Holland,

West Germany, France and Italy. This is the all too familiar pattern of a concentration both in primary commodities and export destinations. The contribution to exports by manufactured goods was entirely negligible, in monetary terms; small quantities of cigarettes, beer, textiles, sugar and preserved meat were exported to neighbouring African countries.

As the first war of liberation, launched by the MPLA in 1961, began to score successes and spread into different parts of the country, the Portuguese found that their own resources were inadequate to counter the MPLA advances. They turned to their NATO allies, who provided military and financial aid. In return Portugal had to open up Angola to a massive penetration by non-Portuguese monopoly capital. Using this opening, multinational corporations (MNCs) moved primarily into the mining of oil, diamonds and iron ore.

The resulting increase in the exploitation of these three minerals was dramatic: oil production increased from a mere 58,000 tons in 1958 to 7.4 million tons in 1973, iron ore from 106,000 tons in 1957 to 7 million tons in 1973, diamonds from about 1 million carats in 1960 to 2.1 million carats in 1973. The MNCs that moved into mining were largely American, West German, South African, British and Belgian. The largest and economically most powerful of these investors were: Gulf Oil of the USA in the Cabinda oil fields, Anglo-American and De Beers of the South African Oppenheimer group in the diamond mines of Luanda province in eastern Angola bordering Zaire, and the West German Krupps in the iron-ore mines at Cassinga in the south, whose main buyer was Japan.

The picture was quite different for manufacturing. Profits in manufacturing were much smaller than in mining, because production was primarily for the small domestic market, and the promotion of exports was not considered to be viable. Some idea of the enormous difference in profits between mining and manufacturing can be seen from the fact that in 1961 the net profit of the diamond mining monopoly Diamang was about 300 million escudos, whereas ten years later, i.e. in 1971, one of the biggest money-spinners in manufacturing, the cement producing Companhia Cimento Secil do Ultramar, was making a profit of 'only' 63 million escudos. It would be a reasonable assumption that by 1971, Diamang was making profits tens of times greater than those of 1961, given increased production, and increased sale value with respect to 1961 prices. It was not surprising, then, that the MNCs did not move into manufacturing in any big way. The non-Portuguese capital that did enter manufacturing was very modest by MNC standards: West Germans went into sisal fibres, wood products, pulp and paper; British into textiles; South Africans into meat processing; and Belgians into rubber tyres.

However, by law, at least 55 percent of the shares in each manufacturing firm had to be in Portuguese hands. Only the big capitalists in Portugal had the capacity to get into joint-ventures with large non-Portuguese capital. Six of the biggest Portuguese groups, which in Angola combined manufacturing activity with banking, insurance, trade, transport and plantation agriculture, were (in descending order of the magnitude of their total holdings): Companhia União Fabril controlled by the Mello Brothers, the Champalimand Group controlled by the Champalimand family, the Espirito Santo group, the Banco Portugues de Atlantico, the Banco Fomento Nacional, and the Grupo do Banco de Angola. The profits they made were fairly high, ranging from 10 to 35 percent of the nominal investment for the year 1971.

Portuguese big capital also collaborated with white settler capital in starting manufacturing firms. The biggest of the settler capitalists made their money through coffee exports, during the boom in coffee prices after the Second World War. Within twenty years (1945-1965), competition and government policy had reduced the number of coffee export traders from 300 to 30, thereby concentrating domestic Angolan capital into a few hands. (For instance, to survive in coffee trading, a company had to mobilise capital of about 500 million escudos.) The number of manufacturing enterprises rose from 2,490 in 1961 to 5,561 in 1972, and the total investment in this sector rose from 2,561 to 7,336 million escudos during the same period. The vast majority (85 percent) of these firms were small establishments owned by white settlers.

THE PRESENT ECONOMIC CRISIS

South Africa's undeclared war

The second war of liberation began in August 1975 with the invasion of Angola by South African troops. It ended in April 1976 in defeat for the South Africans and the Zaireans and their Angolan allies, the FNLA and UNITA. The peace that came with the victory of the People's Republic was extremely shortlived. South Africa and the USA would not allow the People's Republic to consolidate its revolution and start on the work of economic reconstruction.

Soon after April 1976, the South Africans began an undeclared war against Angola, with the tacit and covert approval of the United States. The South Africans claim that these attacks were, and are, aimed at SWAPO bases inside Angola. But an examination of their targets clearly shows that they were bent on destroying the economic and social infrastructure such as industrial plants, electricity generating stations, electricity transmission lines, oil depots, schools, hospitals, etc. in the southern provinces, while their UNITA allies were attempting to do the same in the Central High Plateau.[19]

The UNITA bands, using the weapons left behind for them by the retreating South African troops in 1976 and with the help of the military and civil material supplied to them ever since by the regime in Pretoria, have unleashed a wave of terror and destruction against the rural population in the central provinces. This includes the plunder of crops and livestock, arson, murder, rape and kidnappings. In order to contain and defeat this combined and coordinated aggression, the People's Republic has had to devote the major part of its financial and cadre resources to the war effort. This has effectively halted all reconstruction and development work (see the appendix on war damages).

Shortages of essential commodities

Before independence, 85 percent of all households grew their own food, including the households of agricultural wage labourers who made up 10 percent of the rural population. The picture remains broadly the same today, eight years after independence, with two significant changes: the first concerns the agricultural wage labourers and the second the subsistence peasants on the central plateau.

With the demise of the colonial regime and the coercive power it exercised, agricultural labourers were no longer forced to accept the earlier starvation wages and inhuman living and working conditions. It is entirely possible that if the European farmers and plantation owners had stayed on, the workers would have agitated for, and obtained, better wages, and better working and living conditions, which would have motivated them to carry on working these farms. But things did not work out that way. The Portuguese immigrant farmers and plantation owners left the country *en masse* in one year, taking with them whatever vehicles, agricultural machinery and tools they could move and wilfully sabotaging what they could not move.

The workers were faced with three choices: to organise themselves into co-operatives to run the farms; to wait for other private owners or the state to take over farm ownership and management; or to abandon the farms and return to their villages and subsistence cultivation. The first choice was historically impossible at that stage, given the state of ignorance, fear, blind obedience and total dependency into which workers had been conditioned by the settlers and the colonial regime. As for the second, no Angolan private entrepreneurial class had been allowed to grow during the colonial era which could have stepped into the shoes of the departing Portuguese to take over and manage 6,250 farms and plantations.

This left the third option. Clearly, the new state did not have enough trained cadres of managerial ability who could do the job. To bring order into a chaotic situation, the state nationalised the abandoned farms and tried to keep production going on some of them. At the time of writing, only a few hundred of these (now state-owned) farms are functioning. The great majority of the 250,000 agricultural workers had to leave the farms and return to their villages.

Commercial farms were the principal suppliers of food products to the urban population and of cash crops to the export market. But they were not the sole suppliers. The subsistence peasantry also sold part of its produce, which reached urban and export markets through Portuguese traders, who bought the produce in the villages and transported it to the towns. With the collapse of cultivation in the commercial farms, and the simultaneous departure of the Portuguese traders, both sources of supply dried up. The towns were hit by a severe food shortage. Exports of the main crops, coffee, sisal, bananas and cotton dropped dramatically, and marketed domestic agricultural production plummeted (see Table 13).

These shocking facts should not, however, blind us to two central and important facts. First, the subsistence peasantry—who constitute the overwhelming part of the population—were not and are not hit by shortages of staple foods, for they grew these themselves. Their overall consumption was no worse (and perhaps no better) in 1977 and 1982 than it was in 1973. (The exception to this is the peasantry in the Central High Plateau, whom we discuss below.) Second, the subsistence peasantry still have the capacity to produce food and export crops for the market, but they have ceased to do so for two main reasons. No traders come to buy their produce, and they lack transport facilities to move their products to the towns on their own. The other factor is the almost total lack of even simple and essential consumption goods, which makes cash income useless.

In this regard, let us consider the situation of the peasantry in the provinces of Huambo and Bié which lie in the Central High Plateau. Together they account for about 28 percent of the total population of Angola, with Huambo having 16 percent and Bié 12 percent. Huambo province has the highest population density in the country with 27 persons per square kilometre, against the national average of about 6 persons per sq. km., while Bié has 9 persons per sq. km.

The people of Huambo and Bié are Ovimbundu, an ethnic group which UNITA claims to represent, with its leader, Jonas Savimbi, being an Ovimbundu himself. UNITA has played the 'ethnic card' very strongly, harking back to the 'great' days of the Ovimbundu kingdoms, before they were subjugated by the Portuguese. In the late 1970s, misled by this ethnic appeal, part of the Ovimbundu peasantry left their villages to join the UNITA guerrillas in the bush. After a few years, this peasantry abandoned UNITA and trekked in their several hundred thousands to the urban centres in Huambo and Bié. The main reason for this was a severe lack of food. They could not cultivate enough to feed themselves in the uncleared bush, and much of what they did cultivate was forcibly taken from them by the UNITA bands. The drought of 1981 exacerbated this situation to create a state of famine. Thousands died of hunger and malnutrition. The People's Republic was faced with the task of feeding many hundreds of thousands on the Central High Plateau. It has been able to meet this challenge with the help of the International Red Cross and other overseas donors, who have been flying out food from the port of Luanda since 1981.

The agricultural lands of the Central High Plateau are fertile and receive a high rainfall. The peasantry of these areas have traditionally grown enough surplus not only to feed the urban population in Huambo, Bié and Benguela, but also several other major towns and cities much further afield. These lands were regarded as the 'bread basket' of the country during the colonial regime, especially because Portuguese commercial farmers there produced surplus for the towns. Since 1981, a large part of this subsistence peasantry has not been able to feed itself, let alone feed the urban population. They have become dependent on international assistance and government imports.

Apart from this rather exceptional situation of the subsistence peasantry in the Huambo and Bié provinces, the food shortages apply by and large only to the urban centres. (An urban centre in Angola is defined as a concentrated settlement of more than 2,500 people; there are today between 20 and 25 of these.) The supplies of food that are available to the majority of the urban population are provided by the state-owned shops (*lojas*), which sell severely restricted amounts of basic foodstuffs at low (and controlled) prices. Foreigners who can pay in hard convertible foreign currency have access to special shops, which are well-stocked. However, foreigners who work as *cooperantes* for salaries paid in local non-convertible currency (the kwanza), have their own shops, which are also state-supplied and which suffer from the same shortages as the *lojas*.

There are four types of Angolan *lojas*: people's shops (for the lower-end of the petty bourgeoisie, the working class and the urban poor), shops for the *responsaveis* (middle-level salaried employees), shops for the higher levels in state and party bureaucracy, and shops for the highest levels in state and party. The prices for the basic essential commodities are the same in all four types, whilst the purchasing power of the higher levels are two to three times those of the shoppers in the people's *lojas*.

The figures for the production of food given in Table 13 are, in effect, the production of state-owned farms. Only produce from the state farms and goods imported from abroad find their way to government shops (and directly to the defence forces). Imports are much larger than the state-farm production, perhaps five times as large. In fact, imports provide the mainstay of food in the government shops for the urban population.

So far, the state has proved incapable of organising the buying and transporting of the little surplus that subsistence peasants produce. Instead, this small surplus is bought up by a few private traders who have their own vans and lorries, especially from the peasants living near the few large towns and cities. The traders resell this produce at high prices in the open, 'parallel', markets in towns. Prices in the parallel market for the same commodities as those in government shops are between 30 to 100 times higher. Table 14 lists some of these prices, as well as the average incomes of the various urban strata, to illustrate their purchasing power (or the lack of it) in the controlled-price and open-price markets.

It is sometimes argued that the reason subsistence peasants will not sell their existing small surplus to the state or produce a greater surplus, is the low price offered by the government. In the current economic context, this argument is fallacious. Even if the government were prepared to pay far more, peasants still would not sell their produce for money, because there is virtually nothing that they can buy. In this sense, the kwanza, the Angolan currency, has lost its value. It is a mythical currency. It has a nominal value only insofar as it can buy strictly rationed basic commodities in the government *lojas*. It has no value outside of the goods and services provided by the government.

Equally mythical is the official foreign exchange rate of 30 kwanzas to one US dollar. Legal conversions take place on paper, but *in effect* convertible foreign exchange is used by the state as the currency that fuels and runs a large part of the organised monetised economy. If anyone were so foolish as to sell US dollars for kwanzas, instead of, say, exchanging them directly for goods and services, he would get (in 1983) on the parallel market one thousand kwanzas for one dollar, i.e. more than 30 times the official rate.

So the question arises as to why the peasant sells to the private trader. By and large, she does not sell for kwanzas, but for other goods, which the private trader brings with her (we use the female gender here, for all buying and selling is done by women). In other words, we are back to the ancient world of barter trade. This situation begs several questions. Where does the private trader get the goods she barters with, why can she not barter more goods to induce the peasant to produce more surplus, and why is the government unable to do what the trader is doing; and what use are all of the kwanzas to the trader, when she resells the peasant produce at astronomical prices on the parallel market? We can provide some responses to these questions, but detailed answers have to await in-depth research.

The private trader has three main sources for the basic commodities which are in high demand, namely salt, sugar, edible oil, matches, footwear, clothes, milk powder, etc. The first is the people who queue up to buy at the people's shops and resell to traders at a substantial monetary profit to themselves. The second source is the workers who sell part of the commodities they get paid in or have the right to buy at subsidised prices in factories where they themselves produce these goods; this is called 'self-consumption'. The final avenue is those workers, supervisors, or petty bourgeois elements who simply steal goods from their workplaces in ports, airports, factories, state-owned internal commercial establishments, etc., and sell them.

In turn, these individuals spend their money in the parallel open market to buy at high prices other goods and services that they need. Thus the circle is completed and one finds that a 'high price' parallel economy is functioning outside of the realm of the state. It is an economy that the state knows about, and with good sense has so far allowed to function. But since there are very definite limits to goods that can be legitimately obtained or illegally acquired for further resale, the private trader can offer only limited variety and quantity of goods to the subsistence peasant in exchange, which in turn dampens the motivation for producing more surplus food.

A substantial part of the kwanzas in circulation in the parallel economy never gets back into the official economy, because people do not put money into bank accounts (all banks were nationalised after independence). The government is thus forced to print more money to keep up the kwanza liquidity in the official economy within which salaries, wages, etc. are paid.

What happens to the huge quantities of kwanzas that therefore accumulate in the hands of private traders, and some members of the upper echelons of the petty bourgeoisie and the bureaucracy — the so-called 'kwanza millionaires'? This wealth generates its own version of the parallel economy at the luxury consumption level such as, for instance, buying air tickets for travel abroad and foreign exchange quotas for annual holidays abroad, and for buying consumer durables (e.g. cars, stereos, etc.) from departing diplomatic personnel, at super-high prices, because diplomatic personnel have the right to convert kwanzas into convertible hard foreign currency at the official exchange rate. This latter practice results in the Angolan 'kwanza millionaire' getting his consumer durables while the diplomat in question makes a tidy profit. A typical example would be as follows. A person with diplomatic status brings a car into the country, which he has bought for US $3,000. When leaving, he sells it to an Angolan national for one million kwanzas, and converts the million kwanzas at the official rate of 30 kwanzas to a dollar to US $30,000. This brings him a net profit of US $27,000 out of pure speculative activity at the expense of the Angolan exchequer. This kind of activity is an open secret, and is tolerated for political reasons, both external and internal.

Imports: the lifeline of the urban population

The volume of domestic food production reaching the urban population has fallen dramatically (see Table 13). In 1981, government shops were receiving from the state farms—their major source of domestic supply—less than one tenth of the volume of basic staples put on the urban market by domestic producers in 1973. The state farms are at present extremely inefficient and wasteful of resources. There has been no let up in the decline since 1977, the first relatively stable year after independence. Compared to 1977, the 1981 figures for basic foods have fallen by a factor of two. Although no figures are currently available for 1982 onwards, one can safely say from on-the-spot enquiries that the situation is worse than in 1981.

After independence, the urban population grew enormously. Much of this growth was due to the return from Zaire of Angolans who had fled the country during the colonial era to escape the modern-slavery of forced labour (before 1961) and the massacres practised by part of the colonial army and the Portuguese settler community (after 1961). Their years of exile in Zaire, corresponding to two waves of exodus, the first in the 1950s and the second in the 1960s, lasted from 15 to 25 years. Over the years, the peasants became urbanised; most lived in or near Kinshasa, the capital city. On their return to Angola, they naturally gravitated to the urban centres, continuing to earn their living as they had in Zaire. The largest part of these returning exiles (*regressados*) settled in Luanda, and built colonies of simple mudwalled dwellings, adding to the spread of shanty towns (*musseques*). Between 1976 and 1980, the population of Luanda increased from about 450,000 to 1,200,000.

Faced with the task of supplying basic foodstuffs to this mushrooming urban population, and unable to motivate subsistence peasants to grow and sell more food, the state resorted to importing foodstuffs from abroad to sell in its *lojas*. This is paid for with the export revenue from oil and diamonds, as are imports of essential industrial consumer goods.

Imports are kept to a bare minimum, however, both in quantity and variety. There are perpetual shortages of essential commodities in the people's shops. Queues are a permanent feature of the urban scene. Weeks can go by without sugar, salt, edible oil, rice, fish, beans, milk powder, matches and soap appearing in the shops, not to mention 'luxuries' such as meat, eggs, cigarettes and beer. Although the working class, the lower strata of the petty bourgeoisie and the poor, who make up 80 to 90 percent of the urban population are not starving, they are not getting adequate nutrition either.

The situation is somewhat better for the middle strata of the petty bourgeoisie (salaried employees) who have access to officials' shops, the *loja de responsaveis*. Weekly basic rations of essential foods and goods are assured, and there are no queues. The *responsaveis* live simply and modestly. They have no access to any luxuries.

Top officials (of the state, the party and the defence and security forces), who perhaps number only a few hundred, live better than the *responsaveis*. They also have their own shops. However, they do not live in luxury, as the term is understood in relation to the ruling groups of other underdeveloped countries. They live comfortably, with modest consumer durables that one would find in any middle class home in the West. In this connection, it is important to recall that the gap between the low and high incomes in Angola is the narrowest in Africa and one of the narrowest in the world—the differential is about 1 to 3. In this and many other profound aspects which we will discuss in the next section, the People's Republic of Angola is highly egalitarian and socially just.

Apologists for capitalism claim that there is no difference between rationing through cards and rationing through prices. This is not true. The former assures a minimum of basic necessities to everyone, however low their income. It prevents starvation, but 'free' prices do not, as the so-called food riots in Brazil in 1983 amply illustrate. Two reasons are advanced by the Angolan authorities for not having the same category of shops for everybody. Firstly, the queuing would be so bad and take up so much time, that middle and top level officials would have a good excuse for not turning up for work. Further, lacking any material incentive, they would stop doing even the minimum amount of work they now grudgingly do, bringing the state apparatus to a halt.

The collapse of industrial production

The departure of almost all skilled personnel, together with the damage caused by the second war of liberation and the ongoing undeclared war by South Africa, have caused severe disruptions in industrial production. It is no exaggeration to say that manufacturing industry has collapsed. Compared to 1972, when 5,561 manufacturing enterprises were functioning, in 1981 this number had dropped to 148 (out of which 97 are entirely state-owned, 44 are entirely private, while seven are joint-ventures between the state and private owners). In these 148 plants, capacity utilisation is down to 20 to 30 percent. Correspondingly, there has been a massive reduction in the total number of employees from 125,373 in 1973 to 38,851 in 1981.[20] (The distribution by section and ownership of the 148 factories that were functioning in 1981 is shown in Table 16. The percentage distribution of the monetary value of industrial output in 1981 among various branches is given in Table 17.)

There is generally a mistaken notion, both in Angola and abroad, that the Angolan state and the MPLA-Workers Party dogmatically oppose private enterprise. This is not the case; about half of the industrial enterprises in operation today are privately owned, some by Angolan private capital and some by foreign private capital. The same applies to the service sector. In fact, in a speech in December 1978, President Agostinho Neto categorically stated that the party and the state were not against private enterprise as such. However, what would not be tolerated is a situation where the involvement of private capital, whether Angolan or foreign, becomes so large or critically important as to exercise control over the economy. In other words, Angolan small and medium scale capital would be allowed to invest in enterprises, and large foreign capital welcomed as minority owners into joint-ventures with the state. The reasons why private capital has not responded to the invitation will be touched upon in the next section.

The catastrophic decline in industrial production is illustrated by the figures in Table 18. Only textiles, radio assembly and leather footwear have maintained or increased their 1973 levels. Among mass consumption goods, production of maize and wheat flour is half of what it was in 1973, while other products such as edible oils and fats, sugar, salt, soap, cloth-footwear and plastic-footwear, are down by factors of four to ten. There is virtually no production of luxury consumption goods, except the assembly of television sets. A handful of motorcars are assembled, but these cannot be considered as a luxury. Most cars go into essential state service; the few that end up in private hands constitute a 'necessity' because of the tremendous inadequacy in public transport facilities.

Fifty percent of working factories are in essential food processing, thirty percent in other essential mass consumption goods like textiles and footwear, and the remaining 20 percent in intermediate and capital goods that link into mass consumption. In terms of monetary value, essential food processing is half of non-food mass consumption goods, and the two groups together make up eighty percent (see Tables 16 and 17). These trends, however tentative, are a step in the direction of socialist industrialisation.

The volume of industrial production is so low that it can at best meet the needs of only a fraction of the urban population, which today stands at about 1.6 million (20 percent of a total population of about 7.6 million). To supply the rest, the state imports from the West, Eastern Europe, and North and South America.

In addition to the tremendous lack of skilled workers, mechanics, technicians, engineers, economists, accountants, administrators and managers, there are several reasons for the breakdown in industrial production. The first of these is the disruption in the supply of industrial raw materials, intermediate goods and spare parts. Although money is made available for importing a substantial part of these requirements, there are great delays in their arrival at the factory gates, caused by a lack of advanced planning and ordering, and frustrating delays in unloading and customs clearance at the ports. Secondly, there is an absence of a commitment to work. Absenteeism is rife at all levels and among all strata of workers and employees. The reason given is the need to queue up at the government shops to get essential food, at the government clinics to get medical treatment, etc. While there is some truth in this, there is also, in large measure, the use of these excuses to avoid turning up for work. A third factor is the absence of a tradition of industrial self-discipline, and an unwillingness (or inability) on the part of management to impose industrial discipline. Lack of skills in the workforce and of technical personnel, is, of course, another serious problem. Finally, there are stoppages in the supply of electricity and water, caused by a combination of factors, such as the breakdown in the now ancient Portuguese equipment, lack of maintenance and repair, and negligence of work procedures, tools and machinery, as well as sabotage.

State and urban dependence on oil and diamond revenues

From the preceding discussion, two central features that characterise Angola's present political economy stand out. Eighty percent of the population who live in the rural areas take care of themselves by growing their own food. They see no point in producing a surplus for the urban market, firstly because few traders come to buy and secondly where the traders do come, the money that the peasantry earns is largely useless. Socialised services, such as education and health care, have not yet reached the majority of the rural population. So at present, the peasantry gets almost nothing from the state and the urban economy; consequently, they can give nothing back. The rather tenuous rural-urban commercial link that had grown from the 1950s onwards has been broken.

The other key feature is the total dependence of the state and the urban population on the export income from oil and diamonds. Coffee used to be a third major source of export revenue, but production and exports have now fallen to ten percent of 1973 levels.

The urban population comprises employed and unemployed members of working-class households, the self-employed artisans, and the 'petty bourgeoisie' (all the salaried employees of the organs and institutions of the state and party). Characteristically, there are very few private traders, and the number of 'bourgeoisie' (owners of farms and real estate, commercial transport enterprises and construction firms) is rapidly diminishing.

While approximately half the total export revenue is expended on defence, the remaining half pays for the import of essential industrial consumption goods and the minimum food requirements of the urban population. That part of the urban population living in the *musseques* (shanty towns) can also obtain food by bartering artisanal goods and services with local peasants. This kind of petty commodity production and trade is still very limited, but it is an encouraging sign that productive skills exist and are being used to reduce dependence on state handouts.

Fortunately, oil and diamonds have been doing quite well on the world markets since independence. In fact, they are the only two sectors in the whole of the 'organised' economy that are performing satisfactorily.

The reasons are not difficult to find. Apart from the top priority given to them by the state, the Western multinationals which manage them make handsome profits. These sectors are really islands of Western enterprise and technology. The management, organisation, marketing, technology and the highly skilled personnel all belong to the multinationals; only the labour is Angolan. However, a petroleum school is training Angolans in middle level technical and management skills and its graduates are expected to enter the industry fairly soon.

Employees in the oil and diamond sectors have their own duty free shops which are even better stocked with all kinds of imported foods and consumer durables than the normal diplomatic ones. This is evidenced by the fact that the highest status symbols for foreigners in Angola are Volvo cars, sailing yachts—and cards for the 'oil' shops. One of the most delicious ironies of modern times is the fact that while the government of the United States is actively trying to overthrow the MPLA government, Cuban troops in Cabinda province are ensuring the security and safety of the installations and workers of an American company, Gulf Oil.

The best years so far for oil and diamond production were 1973 and 1974, when oil touched a peak of 65 million barrels a year and diamonds 2.3 million carats (see Table 9). Since independence, production has dropped, although in 1977 oil briefly touched the peak of 1973 (see Table 19). Diamond production seems to be recovering after the trough of 1977, when it had fallen to 0.35 million carats per year. However, substantial amounts are lost each year through theft and smuggling. In oil, the drop in production is linked to the fact that the old fields operated by Gulf in Cabinda are yielding less, while the new fields which have come on stream have yet to make up the difference.

In 1976, the Angolan state established its own oil company, Sonangol (*Sociedade Angolana de Combustives*). Under the Petroleum Law enacted in February 1978, Sonangol is the sole concessionary in Angola. However, it is empowered to enter into joint-ventures with foreign oil companies and to give them concessions on production-sharing terms. Production-sharing contracts require the foreign concessionaries to support the full cost of exploration for a minimum exploration period of five years. Exploration costs are to be recouped from the 'cost oil' component of production, while 'profit oil' is usually shared 70–30 percent, rising to 95–5 percent in line with cumulative production. An innovation in these contracts is the inclusion of a 'price cap' clause, which reserves for the state any extra profits due to crude oil price increases in excess of the rise in companies' costs.[21]

As of 1983, three foreign oil companies are in production. Gulf, which is the largest with over 70 percent of total oil production in Angola, operates the offshore fields in Cabinda. 'It negotiated a 49–51 percent participation contract with Sonangol, under which it pays a royalty of 16.7 percent and tax at 65.7 percent on the realised prices for its 49 percent share of production.'[22] Next comes Petrangol, accounting for about 26 percent of total production. It is owned jointly by Sonangol and Petrofina of Belgium, and operates on the on-shore fields in the Congo and Kwanza basins. Texaco, which works the Block 2 field off the mouth of the Congo river, comes last at 3 percent.

The entire continental shelf (excluding that off Cabinda) has been divided into 13 blocks for the purpose of offshore exploration. Of these, blocks 1 to 9 (excluding 5) have already been awarded, while negotiations are going on for blocks 5, and 10 to 13. In addition to Sonangol, the following foreign companies are involved in prospecting for oil in the blocks that have been awarded: Agip, Elf-Aquitane, Petrangol, Naftagas, INA Naftaplin, Texaco, Mobil, Petrobras, Petrofina, Total, Deminex, Union Texas, Cities Service, Kuwait Petroleum Corporation, AZL Resources, Volvo and Sulpetro, Hispano, Getty, Murphy, Overseas Drilling and Marathon.

Their prospects of finding new commercially viable oil fields are high. It is estimated that Angola has between 55 and 65 million tons of proved recoverable reserves of crude oil, about 400 million tons of total recoverable resources and about 2,500 million tons of overall prognostic resources.[23] One recent discovery, of substantial deposits in the Takula fields of Cabinda, came on stream in 1983. The National Bank of Angola and the Ministry of Petroleum estimate that the production of crude oil will rise to 77 million barrels a year by 1985, bringing in an export income of US $2,300 million (see Tables 20A and 20B).

Diamonds are mined in the north-eastern province of Lunda, bordering on Zaire, by Diamang (*Companhia de Diamantes de Angola*). It has a monopoly on all diamond mining. Its majority share ownership and control used to be in the hands of the South African multinational De Beers, which is controlled by Oppenheimer's Anglo American Corporation, but the Angolan State has taken over 77.2 percent of the shares, and most of the rest are held by the huge Belgian company *Société Generale*. The state share is held by a parastatal, the *Empresa Nacional de Diamantes de Angola* (ENDIAMA). However, the De Beers group still has a grip on the marketing of diamonds through its central selling organisation, the Diamond Corporation, in London. A foreign firm, Mining and Technical Services, advises Diamang on the technical management of the mines.

Until 1975–76, Angola was the fourth largest producer of diamonds in the world. In 1974 its production was 2.4 million carats, which declined sharply to 0.35 million carats in 1977, but has now climbed back up again to 1.4 million carats (see Tables 19 and 20A). Export income from diamonds fell to US $126 million in 1981, but the Banco Nacional de Angola is hopeful that it will reach US $140 million by 1985.

Diamond smuggling is a problem that the state has not yet managed to solve. Lunda province is large, remote, and sparsely populated, and is difficult to police. Apparently, vast fortunes in convertible foreign exchange are being made by the smugglers, who are both Angolan and non-Angolan. In mid-1983 there was a severe crackdown. Hundreds were arrested, including airline pilots, army officers and top officials of the party and the state. They were subsequently put on trial and sentenced to long terms of imprisonment.

Since 1978, Angola has been showing a deficit in its foreign exchange current account balance. The situation became particularly worrying in 1981, when this deficit reached US $615 million, having started from the modest deficit of only US $11 million in 1978 (see Table 22). In 1981, the goods and services trade balances showed deficits of US $243 and US $423 million, respectively, and the total foreign exchange reserves had dropped to US $116 million, equivalent to half a month's imports of goods. The fall in export revenue by 20 percent in 1981 compared to 1980, was due to the combination of a fall in oil production and a fall in oil prices, the latter as a result of the oil glut on the world market. It was reported that Angola had to sell its oil in 1981 at about US $27 per barrel, a fall of US $7 over the previous year. The government moved swiftly to counteract this trend. In 1982, it cut down imports of goods and services by 30 percent and 15 percent respectively, thereby reducing the current account deficit by 66 percent to the figure of US $200 million only.

As Table 22 shows, the government intends to stick to a policy of modest growth (in real terms) of imports. It hopes that, by 1985, as a result of increasing oil production and exports, the deficit in the current account balance can be reduced to a mere US $70 million, and that the total reserves will rise to US $619 million corresponding to two and a half month's imports. It was expected that by 1983 the liquidity crisis would have been overcome (see Table 22), but this has not been the case (see Postscript).

The government of Angola has been very cautious in taking loans from abroad. It has tried to resolve its balance of payments problem by cutting down imports to the absolute essentials. Its record of prompt repayment of loans and interests and a debt servicing ratio of between 10 and 18 percent has impressed foreign bankers, who have given Angola a high credit rating. They are keen to offer more (and larger) loans, but wisely the Angolan government is not rushing headlong into their embrace.

The negative side of the cutting down of imports is that it has hit the supply of essential raw materials, intermediate goods, spare parts, tools and equipment that industry desperately requires. These come mainly from Western Europe (see Table 21B). The proportional share of industrial inputs in the main commodities import bill was about 20 percent in 1979. (We have not included into this statistic the 'machinery' item shown in Table 21B, because it is likely to be made up in large part by passenger vehicles, heavy-duty freight vehicles and defence equipment). This was already small enough. But now that it has been cut back even further, the crisis within the manufacturing industry has deepened (if it is possible to imagine dropping below rock bottom!) This, to say the least, would seem to be a shortsighted policy.

Crisis measures

As the economic crisis deepened, the Central Committee met on the 18th and 19th February 1983 (in its 9th and 10th sessions) and adopted a 'crisis plan' (*Plano Global da Emergência*). This was approved by the Seventh Session of the People's Assembly (the national parliament) on 23rd February 1983. Presenting the crisis plan to the People's Assembly, President José Eduardo dos Santos outlined its contents.[24] He emphasized measures that would improve the living and working conditions of the middle and high level Angolan cadres in high positions in the socio-economic sectors. He said that this skilled elite was growing very discontented. It was leaving state jobs either to take up posts with foreign private companies operating in Angola, or to emigrate abroad. (It is estimated that in recent years between 5,000 and 10,000 skilled Angolans have left the country for Portugal and Brazil.) Their dissatisfaction arose from perennial shortages in essential foodstuffs and consumer goods, lack of adequate and decent accommodation, and lack of private transport.

The President openly admitted that the party had made a mistake by appointing to top positions party political cadres with no suitable qualifications, experience and competence. This led to incorrect decisions in the state organs and enterprises, and invoked the justified hostility and alienation of honest and committed technical cadres. He promised that this error would be corrected, and that qualified technical cadres would be appointed to managerial positions. He gave an assurance that the authorities would take urgent action to improve the supplies of essential commodities, provide good accommodation and private transport to the elite, and appealed to their patriotic sentiments to remain in the country and help in national reconstruction. He pointed out, however, that some were leaving because they rejected the socialist politics and ideology of the country.

Turning to other vital issues, the President indicated that, for the duration of the crisis plan, all resources would be concentrated on executing only the following tasks:

1. Increase the production of oil and diamonds, the principal source of export revenue.

2. Improve the supply of essential foods and other consumer commodities to the defence and security forces and to the rural and the urban populations.

3. Increase food production by the peasantry (in particular maize, sugar, rice, edible oil, eggs and poultry, fish) by offering them industrial consumer

goods in exchange in rural markets i.e. commercialisation of peasant agriculture.

4. Repair and maintain vehicles, and equipment for electricity generation and distribution, and other major industrial equipment.

5. Rehabilitate and improve long distance transport of goods and passengers.

6. Rehabilitate the production of construction materials.

7. Combat big endemic diseases.

8. Increase the production of salt and coffee. Other key tasks would be improvements in the system of determining the prices of commodities and controlling them, in the keeping of accounts by state organs and enterprises, and in the collection and keeping of statistics.

The priorities of the plan meant that other development projects and activities put forward in earlier plans would be held in abeyance. No new investment projects would be started except in the electricity sector. The investment in already ongoing development projects would be cut by 50 percent. In 1983 the budget deficit would be eliminated and the budget balanced by sharply reducing state expenditure (see Table 23). The strong restrictions on, and control of, imports imposed in 1982 would continue, but this would not affect the imports of basic foods and essential spare parts, which would continue at former levels.[25]

Besides the overall crisis plan, each ministry and state organ in the economic and social sectors has been given its own detailed crisis plan, where each task has been identified and targets set in detail. These sector plans are not available to the general public—they are totally confidential. It is likely that the officials of one ministry may never get to see the crisis plan of any other ministry, except at the level of the very top officials. The coordination of individual sector crisis plans takes place in the Ministry of Planning, which alone knows the whole picture.

ESTABLISHING THE CONDITIONS FOR SOCIALISM

Revolutionary change in political structures

The most important thing that has happened in Angola is that a revolution has been set in motion by thousands of MPLA militants dedicated to the task of establishing a socialist society. The dedication of those who are in the forefront of this revolutionary process is underpinned by a solid historical materialist understanding of Angola's colonial experience, and of the impediments placed in their path by imperialism and by internal social classes opposed to socialist change. While thus an essential precondition has been met for beginning the long march toward socialism—in itself a giant step, given the profound backwardness in which the Portuguese colonial regime had submerged Angola—it is by no means a sufficient condition for a successful outcome, as we know from several historical examples. Things can go wrong along the way. This section will be devoted to an analysis of the obstacles that lie in the path of building socialism in Angola.

Let us begin by reassessing the important political changes that have occurred since the founding of the People's Republic in November 1975. The First Congress of the MPLA was held in December 1977, after months of pre-paratory work among its members in various provinces. At this Congress, the MPLA, which until then was a broad-based movement incorporating different political trends and ideologies, decided to change itself into a Workers Party (Partido Trabalho) with an explicit Marxist–Leninist ideology, and a democratic centralist structure. The movement was re-constituted and renamed the MPLA-Partido Trabalho (MPLA-PT) on 10 December 1977. The programme of the party affirmed that the 'MPLA is the party of the working class, uniting workers, peasants, revolutionary intellectuals and other workers dedicated to the cause of the proletariat in a solid alliance'. It went on to assert that 'The workers, peasants and revolutionary intellectuals in close alliance will exert democratic revolutionary dictatorship against internal and external reaction, creating conditions for installing the dictatorship of the proletariat in the phase of building socialism. [During the transition there would be] tremendous class struggle.'[26]

Elections to the new Central Committee of the party were held. The criterion of eligibility that had been used for electing the old (pre-Congress) Central Committee was retained, i.e. that the candidate should have spent at least eight years working as a militant in the party. Although this would guarantee the inclusion of members from the peasant class, who had entered the militant structures early on and taken part in the armed struggle, it would exclude those clandestine members from the urban working class who were unable to join the militant structures until they emerged after the April 1974 coup in Lisbon ended the fascist regime in Portugal.

In order to keep places open for the members of the urban working class (until they became eligible at the next Congress) out of a total complement of 60 full and 15 alternate members, 15 full and four alternate places were left vacant. The remaining 45 full and ten alternate places were contested by a list of 22 candidates from the MPLA, 45 from the FAPLA (who were nearly all veteran guerrillas from the first war of liberation) and some from the floor, put forward by the provisional delegations.

Out of the MPLA list of 22, six were rejected, 13 elected as full members and three as alternatives, three were elected from the floor, and the rest came from the FAPLA list. The new Central Committee had three full women members. The political bureau of eleven full members and three alternates was elected by the new Central Committee from among its members. All the members of the old Central Committee were elected onto both the new Central Committee and the new Politbureau. The mass organisations for women (OMA), trade union members (UNTA), the youth (JMPLA) and children (Pioneers' OPA) had already been formed before the first Congress. Except for the JMPLA, which was turned into the youth wing of the party, the others were allowed to retain their non-party character.

The broadly based liberation movement MPLA had decided to transform itself into a vanguard Marxist–Leninist party of militants. Not all of the 110,000 (card-carrying) members of the old liberation movement could be admitted to the new party. Certain criteria and selection procedures were agreed upon. Obviously all those would be eligible who had a long history of participation in the armed struggle and/or in the militant structures, and whose experience would be of value to the new party.

As for candidates from the rest of the old membership and entirely new candidates from outside the liberation movement, the selection procedure would be as follows. At least two militants (i.e. full members) of MPLA-PT would have to propose the name of the candidate to a meeting of all the workers in the workplace of the candidate, or in the case of a peasant, to a meeting of all the villages. The assembled gathering would conduct an open debate on the candidate's merits as a good worker, as a loyal comrade who helped and supported other workers, as one with socially responsible behaviour and way of life, and of course, as someone without any hidden history of anti-MPLA activity. If this general assembly approved the candidature, it would be put up to the Central Committee which had the right of veto before final approval. In selecting candidates, those with a working class or peasant class background would be given preference.

This selection procedure, which was officially given the name of the 'Rectification Campaign', began on 4 February 1978, the seventeenth anniversary of the start of the armed struggle. Two kinds of membership were created: militants (i.e. full members) and aspiring militants. The latter would be on probation for one year, if they were industrial workers, and for two years if they were not. At the end of the probation period, during which opportunities would arise to assess the merits of the candidate, the aspirant would be either confirmed or rejected.

By the time of the First Extraordinary Congress held in December 1980, the rectification campaign had resulted in the selection of 31,098 members, of whom 15,294 were militants and 15,804 aspirants. About 9 percent were women and 51 percent were workers and peasants. The following pyramidal party structure was established, in which each body was elected by that directly below it:

Provincial Committee

Rural or Urban District Committees

Area or Village Committees

Sector Committees

Cells

A minority of the party membership were assigned to full time fully paid party work. The great majority, however, carried on with their usual work as peasants, industrial workers, office employees, etc. For this majority, party work was unpaid work that had to be done in addition to earning a livelihood. They received no privileges through party membership; rather they had to take on extra duties and responsibilities for the sake of their political commitment.

After 1977, President Agostinho Neto increasingly devoted his energies to the task of building the institutions and structures of people's power. Constitutionally, the party had supreme authority in the country, and the organs of the state were obliged to follow its guidelines and directives. But it was also imperative to create people's structures which would connect the people to organs of state power, so that they could exercise their influence to make sure that the state kept their interests in the forefront. The people's power structures envisaged were, at the base, the local assemblies at village and urban district council level elected directly by universal adult franchise. These local assemblies would in turn elect from among themselves the deputies to the provincial assemblies; which in turn would elect the People's Assembly (the national parliament). Tragically, before he could see these established, President Neto died on 10 September 1979. It fell to his successor, President José Eduardo dos Santos, to push ahead with this task.

In 1980, it was felt that elections to local assemblies could not precede elections to the provincial and people's assemblies. The security situation was grave in the central and southern provinces because of continued attacks by the South Africans and the UNITA bands; no census had been held since 1970 and up-to-date electoral rolls had not been compiled. It was therefore decided to defer the local assembly elections to a later date, but to go ahead with the election to the provincial assemblies and the People's Assembly in August 1980, through an electoral college elected by people at their workplaces, villages, military units, etc.

The candidates who stood for election had to go through the same process of exposure to a public enquiry and to debate by assemblies of workers and peasants in the same way as party members. Candidates had to be approved by these popular gatherings. But they did not have to be party members. The party, its youth wing and the mass organisations all put forward candidates for election; many elected deputies, however, are not party members. The constitution was amended in August 1980 to dissolve the Council of the Revolution, which until then had acted as the legislative body, to be replaced by the People's Assembly.

As Wolfers and Bergerol point out,

> The social [class] breakdown of the province assemblies was 40% workers, 30% peasants with 10% each for three other groups—combatants and security workers, workers in the state machinery, and intellectuals. The [People's] National Assembly is a rather different body: one third (31%) of its 203 deputies are political and administrative leaders [in a sense, the former Council of the Revolution] ; 29% are workers, 24% peasants, 10% defence and security workers, 3% intellectuals and 3% workers from the state machinery.[27]

The relationship between the party and the People's Assembly was clarified by Lucio Lara, a veteran leader of MPLA, at that time ranking next only to President José Eduardo dos Santos in the party. He stressed that there was no organic link between the People's Assembly and the party, and the latter was not under direct instructions from the former.

When not in session, the provincial assemblies and the People's Assembly deputies continue their usual work as peasants, workers, soldiers, etc. They are in constant touch with the realities and problems faced by the people in their daily lives. At the very first session, and in following sessions, these assemblies have strongly criticized the state organs for not doing enough to ease the severe material hardships faced by the people. The People's Assembly sessions are televised and broadcast live on radio. It is not a mere rubber stamping body, but has on occasion rejected or amended legislation proposed by the government. It meets twice a year. In the interim it delegates its work to a Permanent Commission composed of eleven deputies elected by the assembly, on the recommendation of the Central Committee of the party, and some deputies who are also members of the Politbureau.

The President of the party is, by virtue of his office, also the President of the People's Republic, President of People's Assembly, the Head of the Government, and the Commander-in-Chief of the armed forces. He appoints the ministers, the provincial commissioners and other officers, who then have to be approved by the People's Assembly. The government and the state organs are accountable to the People's Assembly, which, in principle, is elected every three years.

At the First Extraordinary Congress of MPLA–PT held in Luanda in December 1980, there were 463 delegates compared to the 300 who attended the First Congress in 1977. Among them there was a much greater proportion of young and recent entrants to the party—57 percent of the participants had been admitted to the party since 1974. This resulted in a much livelier debate and critique of the policies pursued by the party and the state since 1977. The positions in the Central Committee that had been held vacant to facilitate the entry of urban working class members were now filled, after amending the rule concerning a minimum period of eight years militancy to five years so that those who had joined the militant structures after 1975 would qualify.

The other major task undertaken by the Extraordinary Congress was to adopt a set of new scaled-down targets in the productive and other economic and social sectors, in the place of the ambitious ones of 1977, which had shown themselves to be unattainable in the intervening years.[28] The rectification campaign to elect more members into the party was to continue.

Changes in the relations of production

The Law of State Intervention enacted in February 1976 allowed for the nationalisation and confiscation of private property. In May 1979, a new mining law was passed which stated that all the minerals in Angola belong to the Angolan people. Between 1975 and 1980, the state completed the nationalisation of banks, insurance companies, internal and external trade, public transportation and freight distribution, education, health, and, in the productive sectors, some 6,000 plantations and farms abandoned by the Portuguese, as well as 5,000 similarly abandoned industrial enterprises, most of them small scale. In the absolutely vital sectors of oil and diamond mining, the state had acquired majority ownership. The nationalisation measures did not touch some fifty large manufacturing enterprises, owned by non-Portuguese capital from West Germany, Britain, South Africa and Belgium. They were left in the hands of their former owners, except for the minority shares held by the departed Portuguese, which were taken over by the state.

Thus, one of the central tenets of Marxist theory, that the major means of production and distribution should be socialised, has been formally accomplished. Why has this socialisation not been accompanied by any development of the productive forces? This is the question that we will now address.

Stagnation in the productive forces

As pointed out earlier, the state has not intervened in the subsistence peasant sector, and we analysed the reasons why the peasants' production and productivity has not increased. We turn now to former Portuguese settler farms and plantations taken over by the state, the reasons for their low productivity, and the wider forces behind Angola's economic failure.

After independence, contract labourers abandoned the farms on which they were working. The abolition of forced labour ended the practice of punishment for leaving the plantations. Many labourers went back to the more humane living that subsistence farming gave them. Others drifted into the towns in search of a better livelihood. The state had raised the wages of the agricultural workers substantially, but this increase in cash income proved pointless, as supplies of food and consumer goods ceased. On a great many farms, not a single experienced manager or technical person remained to guide the technically unqualified workers.

The military situation has curbed production severely. Work on the coffee plantations in the north, for example, was traditionally done by tens of thousands of migrant workers from the Central High Plateau of Benguela, Huambo and Bié. In the slack season, they would go back to spend a few months in their home villages to help in family agriculture. This migration was essential, both to their economies and their family and community lives. As the UNITA raids on the Central Plateau persisted, and the security situation worsened, the migrant workers no longer wished to risk their lives travelling back and forth between the northern and central provinces. They gave up their work in the coffee plantations and stayed in their home areas in the centre of the country. As a result, coffee production collapsed and the plantations went to physical ruin.

There was very little that the state could do to prevent this from happening. It concentrated its meagre resources of labour and technical and managerial staff on a couple of hundred state farms in order to produce essential foodstuffs. Help was provided by Bulgarian and Cuban technical personnel who had experience in running state farms in their own countries. Machinery and chemicals were introduced. However, to judge from the very low production figures (cited in the last section) these state farms have failed. Their value of output has been lower than the value of the inputs put into them. The amount of foreign exchange spent on machinery and chemicals and on paying foreign technical and managerial cadres has not been offset by corresponding savings in imports of food. The land and labour productivity of the state farms are a fraction of that of farms of comparable size in the West. The only argument that can be made in favour of these state farms is that they contribute to the training of Angolans in the skills required to run modern agriculture.

Another serious issue, especially in industry, is that of labour practices. Workers avoid work, and so do the managers. Workers and managers come to their workplaces in the morning, record their presence for the sake of their job security, wages and salaries, and disappear after a while. What do they do the rest of the workday? No systematic investigation has been undertaken; one has to go on impressions.

Workers do have to spend some time queuing for essential commodities, hunting around in different parts of the town to find government shops which may have something to sell. But this cannot be the case every day of the week, especially when their wives and relatives (who usually have no formal jobs) are also queuing up. As for the managers, the queuing excuse is not applicable, because there are no queues in their shops. It seems that the skilled workers spend their time away from the factories in providing services in exchange for other services and goods in the so-called informal sector. (This kind of activity is called *esquema* in popular parlance.) One has no clue as to what the managers do.

The lack of industrial 'self-discipline' is endemic in all workplaces. The process of industrialisation began only in the 1960s, and has been severely interrupted since 1975. It has not gone on long enough for an 'industrial culture' to become firmly established among workers, managers and others living in the urban areas. Work efficiency is very low because of the combined and cumulative effect of: the absence of systematic and planned execution of work; the impossibility and indeed the inadvisibility of relying upon someone to do a piece of work he has been given to do; lack of care of tools, implements, and machines; the persistence of anarchic individualism among all strata of employees, but in particular among the middle and top levels.

The government itself has contributed to the problem. Angola inherited and retained the incredibly inefficient and labyrinthine bureaucratic procedures that the Portuguese imposed upon the country. The Angolan state has added to this a system of centralisation of authority and decision-making. Then there is the universal bureaucratic phenomenon that each state organ, ministry, or department wants to build and extend its own little empire, guard its territory from encroachment by others, which inevitably leads to severe lack of communication and co-operation between different state organs. The result is virtual paralysis of the state machinery, and extra-ordinary delays in accomplishing simple tasks. It can take, for example, between three and six months to get a vehicle registered; six to eight weeks to get customs clearance for incoming landed air freight; half a dozen visits to the bank in as many days to complete a simple transaction that would take a few minutes in a developed industrialised country.

Even assuming an uninterrupted growth of industrialisation and industrial culture, the internalisation of industrial self-discipline by all sections of the urban population is bound to be a slow process. The urban and industrial workforce in Angola, in all categories from blue to white collar workers, has been given opportunities to voluntarily improve their commitment to work and performance at work through political education, political campaigns and the creation of workers' councils. The results have been dismal. The question arises whether the imposition of disciplinary measures from the outside would have been more successful. In any given workplace in Angola, the workforce is structured into an hierarchy of authority, involving many levels. In theory, a person at a subordinate level is obliged to carry out the orders of a person at a superior level. In practice, it is difficult to implement this. Subordinates ignore or evade orders, or delay executing them as long as possible. This applies equally to the behaviour of middle management. Non-chalance pervades. The situation can be summed up by saying that we have in Angola *a case of hierarchy without authority*.

Theft and corruption have begun to make inroads into moral values. The grave shortages in food and essential consumer goods that have persisted over the last few years have put a premium on these goods. They can be exchanged for other desirable goods, or sold for extremely high prices on the parallel open market (popularly called *kandonga*). This temptation has proved too strong for sections of the working class and the managerial strata. Goods are pilfered from the sea ports, airports, warehouses of the state organ for internal trade, in transport between warehouses and governmental shops etc. Dockworkers are notorious for liberally helping themselves to all kinds of goods from the cargo that the ships discharge at Luanda and Lobito ports. This is often done with the connivance of the security guards who get their share. On the other side of the social spectrum, it is strongly assumed that some top state officials and a couple of government ministers have been caught accumulating large sums of money in convertible currency abroad through 'shady' import deals, granting of supply contracts to foreign companies, and the smuggling of diamonds.

What is to be done?

The political structures and institutions that make it possible for Angola to move towards socialism have been established. Colonial relations of production have been swept away. Now the state owns and controls most, if not all, the means of production and distribution in the 'organised' sectors of the economy. But these achievements remain empty of content from a socialist point of view until the shortages of food and essential mass consumption goods are overcome. Of all the problems facing the People's Republic, this is the most explosive. Other fundamental conditions for establishing socialism, although amenable only to longer term strategies, also need to be initiated now. These are: the halting *and* reversing of the present rapid decline in the forces of production; the closing of the widening gulf between the masses and the vanguard party; and the transforming of the political apathy of the workers and peasants into political commitment.

The undeclared war by South Africa against Angola has been going on for almost a decade. There is little prospect of it ending in the near future. Even if the South Africans withdrew their troops, they would continue the war through their UNITA puppets. So, one way or another, war conditions will prevail for the next few years. The urban population has become tired, sullen and cynical at the shortages of essential commodities and the breakdown of essential services. The shortages have to be overcome in spite of the war. In fact, President José Eduardo dos Santos has publicly stated that one can no longer attribute the disastrous fall in production and the attendant shortages only to the war. The fault lies within the present system. It has to be attacked and rectified.

As we saw in the last section, peasants can be persuaded to produce enough surplus food for the urban population, only: if traders can be relied upon to visit them regularly in the heart of the countryside; if essential industrial and consumption goods are available for purchase in adequate quantities; and if these transactions take place at *real* prices (*vis à vis* industrial goods) which are not exploitative. The role of the private retail trader is absolutely crucial.

At a policy level, the Angolan government is keen that small private entrepreneurs should become active in the economic life of the country. This is a wise decision, in view of the disastrous experience made by Tanzania, Vietnam and Mozambique to abolish small private enterprise and replace it by government agencies and co-operatives. All three have now been forced to retrace their steps. However, policy statements will not provide a solution if they are not accompanied by measures that will make it reasonably worthwhile for the small entrepreneur to put in his or her effort.

The primary incentive would be the ability to buy consumer goods, some real estate, building materials and the inputs to keep his or her enterprise functioning smoothly. Thus both the peasant's and the private trader's logic lead directly to the key role of the availability of essential consumer commodities, essential services and building material. Since it is impossible for the state to import more consumer commodities than it is already doing, *the only solution lies in greatly expanded domestic production*. Even if the war were to end tomorrow, the export revenue released from the defence effort should not be spent on consumer imports, but should be invested in development projects, including the import of means of production.

So far, the state has manifestly failed to revive industrial production, despite increased wages and social benefits for the workers, increased salaries and privileges for the industrial managers and state officials, increasing and expensive employment of foreign technicians and skilled cadres, and continuing imports of industrial inputs, spare parts and machinery. The real reason for the failure lies in the unwillingness of the workers, managers and state officials to work productively for even the statutory minimum hours, to accept and execute their work responsibilities, and not least the inability of the work leaders, managers and state officials to work to a preconceived and collectively agreed plan, and their unwillingness to learn from foreign technicians, and *cooperants*. In this connection, one should point out that the whole planning exercise has become farcical at the level of both the central Ministry of Planning and the sectoral ministries of agriculture, industry, etc. They have become mere paper exercises with no grounding in reality (as is shown by a comparison of planned targets and actual results given in Tables 13 and 18. The actual results range from one half to one tenth of the planned targets).

This situation leaves the state with only two options in the realm of consumer goods industry, either run it as a 'military operation' with iron discipline and severe penalties for non-performance, or hand it over to private entrepreneurs, with the state determining only the list of products to be manufactured and the range of prices to be charged. The first option assumes the existence of thousands of technically competent Angolan cadres who are at the same time totally committed to socialism ('red and expert'), to take over the management of the enterprises. Not even a couple of hundred of such 'red and expert' Angolan cadres are available today, let alone thousands! Those who have the technical know-how, such as the higher petty-bourgeoisie, are hostile to socialism, with their hostility taking on the passive form of indifference and non-performance. It is often claimed by top officials of the party and the state that they cannot effectively deal with the shortcomings of industry, because they need all the technical cadres they can get to work in the defence forces and cannot spare any for the economic and social sectors. That being the case, the 'military' option cannot be realised. Sooner or later the second option of private enterprise has to be taken.

What would this return to private enterprise mean? All internal commerce (both wholesale and retail) would be privatised. As private shops opened, the government shops would close. The state farms would be closed down as well. State intervention in the market would be partial and exercised through import controls to ensure that the present nominal and token government prices would rise to realistic levels while private sector prices would not rise above government-recommended ones. This would put an end to the socially and socialistically unjustified present practice of massively subsidising (through imports based on export revenue) non-peasant, particularly urban, consumption.

In addition, the production of mass consumption goods would be handed over to small and medium capital. (It is in principle possible through state and working class intervention in the mechanisms for extraction and distribution of the surplus to prevent the concentration and centralisation of smaller capital into larger capital, thus making sure that the dominant socialist character of society is kept intact.) The state organs, as well as the private sector, would have the power to dismiss any employee, in whatever stratum, who consistently defaults on his duties and responsibilities. The Angolan state has willy-nilly fostered the illusion that the state-owned enterprises can eventually guarantee the satisfaction of all essential material needs of the population, in particular the non-peasant population. This has created the wholly unrealistic expectation that the state is a 'big daddy' or, 'Father Christmas' which can freely dispense goods and services. (This is of course the negative side of the oil and diamonds bonanza.) This illusion must be ended through an ideological campaign backed up with sanctions.

What kind of class struggle?

The number of workers employed in the 'organised' sectors (i.e. employed wage labour in agriculture, mining, construction, manufacturing and services) in Angola today is a very small fraction, less than two percent of the total labour force. The employed industrial proletariat, which in Marxist–Leninist theory is regarded as the leading revolutionary class, is even smaller, at about one percent. This working class is almost totally unskilled. Thus, both quantitatively and qualitatively, the Angolan wage-employed working class is very weak.

Since independence, this class has shown no vigorous outward signs of a revolutionary socialist consciousness, or of explicit class struggle against the higher strata of the petty bourgeoisie. When the party speaks of an ongoing class struggle between the working class and the upper petty bourgeoisie it presumably does not mean this in any direct sense, but in the dialectical-materialist sense of an 'objective' class struggle. (The peasantry stand outside of all this; isolated in the countryside, they are involved in a class struggle only in so far that their sons in the armed forces are so engaged.)

The working class does not automatically acquire a revolutionary consciousness. Lenin stressed that it was the task of revolutionaries (irrespective of their class background) to make the working class conscious of its revolutionary potential and transform it into the social force that will make the revolution. The same applies in the Angolan situation.

The current struggle, however, is not between social classes, but between the 'political radicals' and the 'defenders of privilege' in the state and in the party. Their power and influence seem to be evenly matched, resulting in a dynamic equilibrium as the pendulum swings back and forth. Agostinho Neto, who favoured the line advanced by the 'radicals', appointed a number of (admittedly technically unqualified) party political cadres to the very top positions in the state organs and enterprises to oversee the work of the top bureaucrats.

A few years later, in 1983, the 'privilegists' managed to reverse the situation, when José Eduardo dos Santos was compelled by the disastrous non-performance of the state enterprises to remove some of the political appointees and put 'technocrats' in their place. The 'privilegists' not only want to consolidate their present material privileges within the state and party, but to extend them by taking up entrepreneurial activity outside of the state sectors. They are privileged only in comparison with the masses in Angola; in comparison with the elite of the other African countries, their privileges shrink into nothing.

Given this relative non-affluence and absence of riches, it seems far-fetched to talk about a 'class struggle' between the two groups. But the struggle is not about the present possessions, but about the future. If the 'privilegists' succeed, their line will entrench a class society and divert Angola from the road to socialism. The 'radicals' have refrained from launching a real offensive against the 'privilegists' for fear that the latter may try to destabilise the state internally, which would be catastrophic given the current external destabilisation efforts of South Africa and the USA.

It is in this context that one must understand the concessions offered to the 'privilegists' by President José Eduardo dos Santos in February 1983. Until the South African aggression ends, the 'privilegists' must be kept happy. And when it does end, and the gears of the internal struggle really mesh, the outcome will depend critically on the leadership of the armed forces, FAPLA. Only then will it become clear how deep and effective the politicisation of FAPLA along Marxist–Leninist lines has been.

The party has thus far been unable to shake the masses out of their political apathy. The stringent criteria for party membership, the concentration and centralisation of information and authority at the very top of the party and the state, and the condition of ignorance in which the general public is kept with respect to the overall situation in the country (no explanations are offered even when important events occur, such as dismissals of ministers and Central Committee and Politbureau members), have resulted in a feeling of 'them' and 'us'. This gap is growing wider and holds dangers for the socialist revolution in Angola.

POSTSCRIPT, DECEMBER 1985

The war situation

In early December 1983, South Africa launched new attacks deep into the southern parts of Angola from Cunene province, which it had occupied during the earlier invasions (see appendix). This was the largest and most well-coordinated invasion since the big 'Operation Protea' of August 1981. According to Angolan sources, the invading force consisted of about 10,000 regular troops of the South African Defence Force (SADF), organised under three motorised infantry units and two paratroop battalions. To the great surprise of the SADF, this invasion was no 'walkover': it met fierce resistance from well-trained and well-armed FAPLA units, and the fighting was intense, especially in and around the towns of Cahama, Cuvelai, Cassinga, Mulondo and Caiundo. By mid-January 1984 this phase in South Africa's undeclared war against Angola came to a halt, by that time the SADF had occupied an additional 80,000 square kilometres of Angolan territory. The South Africans were by then deeply worried by the losses inflicted by FAPLA on the SADF and the high combat morale and fighting efficiency of the Angolan troops. The number of dead on the South African side were many more than the 27 officially admitted by the Pretoria regime. The Angolans say that their ground-to-air missiles brought down several enemy aircraft, a claim denied by the SADF.

Three major intentions can be discerned behind the South African operation: first, to disrupt the attempt by SWAPO freedom fighters to cross over into Namibia in large numbers under the cover afforded by the rainy season; second, to knock out, through bombing raids, the ground-to-air missile defence system set up by the Angolans in the southern region; and third, to stretch FAPLA's capacity to its limit so as to relieve pressure on the UNITA rebels. In October 1983, FAPLA mounted a big, concerted effort against UNITA in the areas where it had been staging well-publicised commando raids. This FAPLA offensive was successful in dealing severe blows to UNITA in several strategically important areas, such as the Mussende district in Kwanza Sul province which contains the road link between the provincial capitals Kuito and Malanje. Hundreds of UNITA guerrillas were killed, many more driven out from their operating areas and large quantities of arms seized.

Both the halting of the invasion by mid-January 1984, and the opening of talks with the Angolans to see if a ceasefire could be arranged, were closely linked to the fact that the government in Pretoria was unwilling to pay the internal political price for the much higher casualty figures to its troops that would necessarily result from a prolongation of the war in the face of FAPLA's unexpectedly strong capacity to fight back. The Soviet Union's public warning that it would not tolerate further advances by the SADF deeper into Angola also made a strong impact; as did the knowledge that no country in the West, including the USA, would actively take the South African side if the war became internationalised. The tripartite talks between the Angolans, the South Africans and high-ranking officials of the US State Department led to the signing of a ceasefire agreement in mid-February 1984 in Lusaka. A Joint Monitoring Committee (JMC) comprising 300 FAPLA troops, 300 SADF troops and some US officers was set up to monitor the implementation of the agreement, the full text of which has not been made public. According to reliable sources the agreement commits South Africa to the removal of all its troops from Angolan territory by 31 March 1984, and commits Angola to halting the movement of SWAPO guerrillas from Angola into Namibia. These sources say further that the agreement does *not* commit South Africa to stop its aid to the UNITA rebels.

It had become quite obvious that South Africa, by physically patrolling the long and sparsely populated border areas, was unable to stop the movement of SWAPO guerrillas into Namibia. It thought it had now found the solution to this problem through the ceasefire agreement by making Angola accept responsibility for confining SWAPO to its camps. South Africa could now blame Angola for any increase in SWAPO activity within Namibia; it could threaten reprisals for alleged Angolan slackness (as, on 2 July 1984, Pik Botha did during his meeting with Alexandre Rodrigues Kito in Lusaka); it deprived Angola of the 'SWAPO card', pushing it into a defensive posture of having to react to more and more South African demands without getting anything new in return.

It was not until as late as April 1985, i.e. 14 months after the signing of the agreement, that South Africa completely withdrew its troops. Although by July 1984, the bulk of its occupying forces had left, it had still maintained a couple of battalions—numbering about 1,000 soldiers—inside Angolan territory, halting the 'disengagement process' until April 1985. These delaying tactics served two purposes: first, to put pressure on the Angolan government to enter into talks with the UNITA rebels, while at the same time installing and strengthening the UNITA forces in the evacuated areas; second, to revive the issue of linking Namibian independence to the withdrawal of Cuban troops from Angola. This ploy has failed. The Angolan government has categorically and consistently rejected any dialogue with UNITA, repeatedly proclaiming its intention to eliminate UNITA militarily and politically. The latest such reaffirmation came in President José Eduardo dos Santos's opening speech at the Second Party Congress in Luanda on 2 December 1985. On the 'linkage issue' the Angolan government's response was to lay down three major conditions that South Africa would have to fulfil before the withdrawal of Cuban troops from the southern war zones could be contemplated:

1. Completely withdraw its armed forces from Namibia, and allow United Nations troops to be established in Namibia. The first step would be the

withdrawal of the South African air force and ground troops from the Angola-Namibia border, which would then come under the control of the United Nations troops.

2. Cessation of all support to the UNITA rebels, accompanied by a UN-supervised dismantling of UNITA bases in Namibia.
3. An undertaking to implement UN resolution 435/8, on Namibian independence.

These and other conditions—Angola's commitments in return for the fulfilment of these conditions, and the detailed timetable of the withdrawal of the Cuban troops to positions behind the 13th parallel over a period of three years, in phased response to South Africa keeping its side of the bargain—were made public in a letter, on 20 November 1984, from the Angolan government to the Secretary General of the United Nations. As expected, South Africa rejected these proposals.

Why did South Africa, having dragged its feet for 14 months, decide to vacate the Angolan territory it had occupied? It was part of a propaganda effort to counteract the international condemnation that followed South Africa's scuttling of the process of Namibian independence by installing the so-called 'Transitional Government of National Unity' in Windhoek in May 1985. This puppet regime, consisting of a coalition of a number of small and disparate political groups, including the interests of tribal chiefs, has been wracked by internal conflicts. It has now very little credibility within Namibia, not to speak of the world outside.

The Joint Military Commission was disbanded on 16 May 1985, following the complete withdrawal of South African troops this time round. Meanwhile, political contacts and high-level political meetings were going on between Angola, South Africa and the USA to reach an accord on Namibian independence, on the presence of Cuban troops and on preventing a renewal of the war. These discussions, some of which were publicised and some kept secret, were held in Lusaka, Sal (Cape Verde) and Maputo. Dr Chester Crocker, the US Under-Secretary for Foreign Affairs specialising in African matters, played a leading role in arranging and conducting these meetings. Two events put an abrupt stop to all this: on 21 May 1985 an Angolan patrol in Cabinda province bordering on Zaire and the Congo Republic hundreds of kilometers north of Luanda, intercepted a South African commando group of nine men preparing to blow up Gulf Oil Company's vital oil storage tanks in Malongo. In the battle that followed, two of the commandos were killed, six managed to escape, while the leader of the group, a white South African officer named Captain Wynand Petrus du Toit, was captured alive. On 23 May, when the news broke, the South African government tried to 'explain away' the presence of the commando group some 1,400 kilometers north of the Namibian border by saying that it was on an 'intelligence mission', 'gathering information about ANC and SWAPO bases, as well as Cuban involvement with them in the area south and north of Luanda'. Even South Africa had never previously claimed the presence of ANC and SWAPO in Cabinda, 1,400 kilometres north of the Namibian border! Of course, nobody, least of all the USA, South Africa's leading ally, believed this cock-and-bull story.

At the press conference, du Toit described in detail the nature of his mission and how it was mounted. The commando group had sailed on a South African naval destroyer from Saldahna Bay in the Cape and came ashore in Cabinda on inflatable dinghies. They planned to infiltrate the Malongo oil storage tank farm and blow up the six tanks with mines. They were to leave behind Cabinda Gulf uniforms and UNITA propaganda material, to create the impression that UNITA guerrillas had carried out the attack. If successful, the Malongo incident would have caused untold material, psychological, political and diplomatic damage to the Angolan government, because of the total dependence of the Angolan state on its oil revenues. Its credibility as a protector of the oil installations would have been shattered, with unforeseeable consequences for the future of the Angolan oil sector. The USA was furious with its South African ally for planning to destroy US-owned installations (Gulf Oil is based in the USA) and for endangering US lives. On 20 June, at the Security Council meeting that unanimously condemned South Africa for the 'flagrant violation of Angola's sovereignty and territorial integrity' the US delegate, Warren Clark, said that the USA had 'made [its] deep displeasure known both in public statements and directly to the government of South Africa' and that the USA had 'received no satisfactory explanation from the [South African] government for its conduct'. The Angolan government cancelled all planned contacts with South African officials and indefinitely suspended all future contacts.

The other incident was the repeal of the Clark Amendment by the US Senate and the US House of Representatives in June/July 1985. The Clark Amendment, passed in 1976, forbade the US government to give support, whether covert or overt, to the UNITA rebels. Following the repeal, the US government has allocated to UNITA up to US $50 million worth of military equipment and US $27 million so-called 'humanitarian' aid. As a result, Angola broke off its ongoing direct dialogue with US officials.

The dialogue was, however, resumed towards the end of November 1985 at a meeting in Lusaka between the Angolan Interior Minister, Alexander Rodrigues Kito, and the US Under-Secretary of State, Chester Crocker, at which a timetable for future meetings to discuss Angolan security and the future of Namibia was agreed. The Angolan Vice-Minister for Foreign Affairs, Venancio de Muna, also took part in this meeting.

The continuation of UNITA attacks

The raids by UNITA against civilian, economic and infrastructural targets continued during 1984 and 1985. While most of these have occurred in the central highland provinces of Benguela, Huambo and Bié, where UNITA claims ethnic support by the Ovimbundu, a few spectacular hit-and-run attacks have also been mounted as a far afield as the diamond-mining region in the north-east, and districts adjoining the capital city Luanda. The attacks on non-combatant civilians, as in Longonjo and Huambo province, and in Calombaloca, about 70 kilometers south-east of Luanda, where, respectively, about 140 and 30 civilians lost their lives, is both a sign of UNITA's desperation and an attempt to spread a sense of terror and insecurity among the population. Among the more important infrastructural targets attacked in 1985 were the electricity transmission lines from the Cambambe Dam to Luanda and N'dalatando, which took more than a week to repair. The Benguela railway, connecting the ports of Benguela and Lobito to the central highlands and reaching up to the Shaba province in Zaire, has been sabotaged many times. US, British and Filipino employees were captured as hostages, and then released in well-orchestrated publicity campaigns in attacks on the diamond-mining area of Luo, near Lucapa, in North Luanda province, which also put the Cuango diamond-mining division out of action.

Despite its spectacular hit-and-run attacks, well-publicised in the Western media, UNITA has been unable to occupy and control any even moderately-densely populated area for any reasonable period of time, even in its traditional operating areas among the Ovimbundu in the central highlands. It 'occupies' and 'controls' only an extremely sparsely populated region in the south-east corner of Angola, in Cuando-Cubango province adjoining the Caprivi Strip in Namibia and bordering on south-western Zambia. UNITA has built its base in the town of Jamba in this 'occupied' area. Western journalists and Western sympathisers of UNITA are taken to Jamba and wined, dined and lionised by Savimbi in luxury accommodation in order to give the impression that he effectively 'controls' a chunk of Angola. But it is now no longer a secret that the UNITA leadership is riven by internal strife, resulting in some executions and assassinations, and that thousands of UNITA fighters have surrendered to FAPLA, the Angolan armed forces.

To dislodge UNITA from Cuando-Cubango, and in particular from Jamba, FAPLA mounted an offensive from May to September 1985, using jet fighters, bombers and heavy artillery. FAPLA ground troops made rapid advances and were closing in on Jamba when, on 16 September 1985, the South African Defence Force (SADF) again invaded Angola in order to rescue its UNITA ally. There was an international outcry against the invasion, this time by even those Western nations such as the USA, Britain and West Germany, which on earlier occasions had either remained silent or expressed only mild disapproval. South Africa trotted out the usual excuse: that it had marched in to prevent 'SWAPO units from carrying out their plan of attacking targets within Namibia'. Even the Reagan administration, that staunch supporter of the apartheid regime, felt constrained to reject this 'explanation', pointing out that the border between Angola and Namibia had been quiet for months before the invasion and there was no evidence that SWAPO was preparing a major incursion.

During the invasion, SADF went into action against FAPLA with its

Mirage fighters and Canberra bombers; in particular in Mavinga not far from Jamba, where intense fighting was going on between FAPLA and UNITA troops. Exposed to SADF's own attack, FAPLA ground troops had to abandon their attempt to take Jamba. Three days after the invasion began, on 19 September 1985, the C-in-C of SADF, General Constand Viljoen, announced that 'South Africa was withdrawing the 500 soldiers who had entered Angola on 16 September, because the operation against SWAPO had been successfully completed'.

It seems very likely that when the rainy season ends, in March 1986, FAPLA will again attempt to take Jamba. If it decides to bring in its Mig-23s, Sukhoi 20/22 fighters, Soviet surface-to-air missiles, Swiss-made Pilatus reconnaissance aircraft, Spanish Aviocan C-212 counter-insurgency aircraft, French Gazelle and Dauphin helicopters, which are technically superior to the equipment available to the SADF, viz Impalas, Mirage F1s, obsolete Canberra bombers and Buccaneers, it may rout the SADF and drive UNITA out of Jamba. This technical superiority of FAPLA is beginning to cause serious problems for South Africa, and that is the reason for the statements from Pretoria in November 1985 accusing some frontline states of posing military threats to the security of South Africa. In anticipation of FAPLA's March 1986 offensive against UNITA, the US $50 million worth of military equipment donated by the USA to UNITA is likely to include radar systems and surface-to-air missiles.

In our earlier analysis we argued that even if the war between Angola and South Africa were to end, South African support to UNITA would continue. Events since February 1984, when the ceasefire agreement came into force, have confirmed that analysis. Further, there is little reason to doubt that, to a certain extent, UNITA has become independent of its South African paymasters. In all likelihood, UNITA has built up reserves of arms, ammunition and other war materials, sufficient to enable it to operate on its own initiative for a while should South Africa decide to discontinue its support; provided that it reverts from fixed-position defences, as at Jamba, to classical, roving guerrilla tactics. But one thing is certain: UNITA cannot seriously threaten the Angolan state built and controlled by MPLA. That state has successfully withstood ten years of constant attack and destabilisation by not only UNITA, but the far superior imperialist forces of South Africa, covertly assisted by the USA and some other Western powers. This, however, does not mean that UNITA will cease to be a thorn in the flesh for the Angolan government—it will persist with its sporadic destructive activity for many more years.

The internal situation in South Africa and its impact on Angola

The severe crisis in which the apartheid regime of South Africa now finds itself has been gathering momentum for many years. On 16 March 1984, at Nkomati, South Africa compelled the Frelimo government in Maputo to submit to signing an undertaking to expel the African National Congress (ANC) from its transit bases inside Mozambique. This undertaking—implemented post-haste—was in return for South Africa's promise to cease supporting the Renamo rebels (also known as the MNR) in Mozambique and to curb Renamo's destructive activity—a promise which was never fulfilled. The South African government was, however, enabled to briefly persuade both itself and the world at large that it had scored a triumph against both the ANC and the frontline states, and was in total control of the internal situation in South Africa. That illusion was shattered as the gathering crisis exploded late in 1984, with the black majority rebelling and revolting in the shanty towns across the country. The massacres of the unarmed, defenceless, peaceful black mourners and demonstrators at the hands of the South African police, paramilitary and military at Sebokeng (September–November 1984, 150 killed), at Crossroads (February 1985, 18 killed and 225 wounded), at Uitenhage-Langa (March 1985, 69 killed, 180 wounded) and at Mamelodi (November 1985, 12 killed, a still unconfirmed number wounded) are witness to the panic which has gripped the apartheid regime, which proclaimed a state of emergency in July 1985 and clamped down censorship on the media. Nearly 1,000 people have been killed (almost all unarmed blacks) and many more have been wounded since the rebellion began in late 1984. Armed attacks by ANC guerrillas have increased rather than decreased since Nkomati, the latest being rocket attacks on 28 November 1985 on the strategic SASOL plant in the Transvaal where oil is synthetically produced from coal—the rockets used had a range of 13 kilometers (eight miles)—indicating the growing power and sophistication of the arms available to the ANC. The economy is in dire straits with the rand falling dramatically against the dollar, foreign investment and loans drying up, foreign capital leaving the country and bankruptcies piling up. On 1 September 1985, the South African government unilaterally imposed a four-month suspension on repayments of its foreign debt of more than US $17,000 million (17 billion), because of the steep decline in its foreign exchange reserves and earnings. All the indications are that the unilateral moratorium on debt-repayment will be extended beyond January 1986, bringing in its wake further stops in loans to South Africa by international banks and financial institutions. Top white business, community and church leaders have met the ANC leadership in Zambia to discuss ANC's attitudes and plans. The authority of the apartheid state and its black representatives no longer applies in the areas where the black majority live. It has lost the initiative politically, economically and militarily. The white Afrikaner population is deeply divided and confused. The white English-speaking population as a whole wants the ANC and the black majority brought into the political process and power sharing. The SADF no longer takes its orders from the collective Cabinet, but from van der Westhuizen who effectively controls the state Security Council, and his protector and close friend, President P. W. Botha. P. W. Botha's position itself is in severe doubt as the power struggle for succession to replace him in 1986 gathers apace between the two most likely candidates: the conservative F. W. de Clerk (Minister of National Education and leader of the dominant Transvaal National Party caucus) and the reform-oriented Gerrit Viljoen (Minister of Cooperation and Development — Black Affairs).

The fluid situation and the many imponderables make any reliable guesses as to how the crisis will develop further impossible. The scenarios stretch from the ANC sharing effective political power to outright all-out war between the diehard white Afrikaners and the black majority and the front-line states. *But whatever the eventual outcome, it will deeply affect Angola and all other frontline states. Therefore, the analysis and prognosis made in this postscript and the later sections of this study should be regarded as tentative, for they assume that the apartheid state will continue to be viable and dominant over the next few years, which may not be the case at all. It is equally possible that the apartheid state will collapse within a short time, dramatically altering the political, economic and military configurations in the entire Southern African region, including Angola.*

The economy in 1984

The Minister of Planning, Lopo do Nascimento, presented the national plan for 1984 to the People's Assembly at its seventh session in January 1984.[29] He stressed that the economic crisis continued to be as grave as in the previous year, and the present plan was thus a 'crisis plan' as was the one in 1983. There had been no recovery in the extremely low figures for marketed domestic agricultural produce and industrial output. Road, rail and air transport continued to remain severely disrupted. The only bright spot was oil production, which was confidently expected to reach 71.8 million barrels, an increase of 15 percent over the 1983 figure (see Table 24). Correspondingly, the export revenue from oil was expected to go up to US $1,804 million, registering an increase of 17 percent over the 1983 figure of US $1,540 million (see Table 25). The increase in oil production was owing to new off-shore fields coming on stream, following large invest-ments over the last five years by both the Angolan state and private foreign oil companies. Investment in the oil sector would continue at a high level, going from US $558 million in 1982 to 540, 606 and US $650 million respectively in 1983, 1984 and 1985.

In contrast to oil, diamond production and export would see no increases. In fact, export revenue from diamonds was expected to decrease from US $106 million in 1983 to US $100 million.

The increase in oil revenue would be used, in part, to increase the imports of essential foods and basic consumer goods, on average by 18 to 20 percent. These imports were expected to cost US $820 million, i.e. 45 percent of the oil revenue. In distributing these, the requirements of the defence forces would have first priority, followed by the needs of the waged workers in industrial and agricultural enterprises and the general urban population.

The deficit in the foreign exchange current account balance and the accompanying foreign exchange liquidity crisis persisted through 1983, and is likely to remain so in 1984. This assessment is based on the fact that the character and magnitude of the dominant foreign exchange expenditures will remain unaltered, given the ongoing crises on the economic, political and defence fronts, viz about 50 percent of total export revenue to finance the defence effort, 30 percent for imports of essential foods and consumer goods, and 20 percent for debt servicing.

The expenditure on 'economic and social development' in the planned budget for 1984 (see Table 23) is 27,700 million kwanzas (approximately US $920 million). It is broadly divided into three parts, as follows:

Table 23

	Million Kwanzas	*Percentage*
Investments (Ministries only)	14,000	50.5
Expenditure on state-owned enterprises	11,000	39.7
Price subsidies	2,700	9.8
Total	*27,700*	*100*

As indicated, the investment item above refers exclusively to the ministries: it *excludes* all investment financed through bank loans and credits, development aid and commercial channels, such as the massive investments in the oil sector. Therefore, this item fails to reflect the true character and magnitude of the total investments being made in the economy, both for maintaining the present productive equipment in running condition and for importing new equipment. State-owned enterprises absorb nearly 40 percent of the vote for 'economic and social development', but a comparison of this expenditure of 11,000 million kwanzas with the revenue they produce of 14,600 million kwanzas reveals the very sorry state in which they are. The budget deficits for 1983 and 1984 are substantially less than the peak of 1982, both in absolute and relative terms (see Table 23) thanks to increasing oil revenue. The deficits are covered by printing more kwanzas, which helps to perpetuate the present purely mythical nature of the Angolan currency.

In presenting the 1984 plan to the People's Assembly, Lopo do Nascimento put particular stress on keeping the foreign debt at the present reasonable level. Angola's record in servicing its external debts is still very good. This performance, together with its oil wealth and its strict import regime, has given Angola a good credit rating with international lending institutions. Nevertheless, the Angolan state is very cautious, selective and restrictive in its borrowing.

The economy in 1985

Politically, the two most important events in 1985 were the Second Party *Conference* in January held as a preparation for the Second Party *Congress* in December. In a three-hour speech at the January Conference, José Eduardo dos Santos, who is President both of the MPLA-Workers Party and the Angolan State, gave a critical review of the situation in every major economic and social sector of the country. As on other occasions, the President pointed out that the severe economic crisis in Angola was due not only to the war conditions but also to the shortcomings among Angolan cadres and institutions. The new aspects in the approach to the economy that emerged from the President's speech and the work of the January Conference, were the intentions to increase decentralisation and small private entrepreneurial activity in agriculture, manufacturing, and construction industry. Concrete guidelines and targets for implementing these new policy directions were to be worked out for presenting to the December Second Party Congress.

As in 1983 and 1984, a one year 'crisis plan' was presented to and adopted by the People's Assembly, and was enacted into law by the President in April. The details of the contents of the 'crisis plan' have not been made public. It is, therefore, impossible for independent, outside analysts to assess the merits and the realism of the plan, both in respect of its targets and measures at implementation. The only concrete priorities made known are the same as in the last two years, and very general, viz highest priority for the adequate supply of food and other essential consumption goods for the armed forces and the urban population, followed by rehabilitation and renewal of industrial and infrastructural plant (rather than investments in new projects) expansion of investment and production in the oil sector, and expansion in education and technical training.

With the exception of the oil sector, all other productive, distributive and infrastructural sectors of the economy are in the same deep crisis as in earlier years. The total dependence of the state and the urban population on imports of food and essential consumption goods, financed by oil revenue, has remained unchanged. The rural population has very little access to imported or domestically produced industrial consumption goods. The grave shortages continue. The measures to promote 'commercialisation of agriculture', through exchanging industrial goods for peasant agricultural produce, have remained at the experimental stage of occasional campaigns in a few places: the government has not yet put together implementable and practical measures and institutions that would lead to 'commercialisation of agriculture' on a self-sustaining basis.

The Second Party Congress in December 1985 produced a lot of documentation ('*Projecto Tese*') containing proposals, targets and measures for each sector and branch of the economy and society. These have been arrived at in a mechanical way, making a fetish of figures. In the absence of objective forces and conditions in the political, economic, social and cultural spheres that can successfully motivate the population on a self-sustaining basis to implement the plans, the '*Projecto Tese*' will remain solely exercises on paper.

The oil sector is booming. Angola is now the second largest producer and exporter of oil in sub-Saharan Africa, after Nigeria. The production in 1984 was 74.5 million barrels, an increase of 17 percent on the 1983 figure. This is expected to increase to 85 million barrels in 1985 (15 percent higher than 1984). If this rate of growth is sustained, the 1990 production would reach 200 million barrels. The increases in production have come from new oil wells in Cabinda (Gulf Oil) and in Block Three off Soyo (Elf Aquitaine). At an average price of US $25 per barrel, and exports of crude oil at about 181,000 barrels per day, earnings from export of crude oil in 1984 are estimated to be US $1,650 million (1.65 billion) as compared with US $1,490 million (1.49 billion) in 1983.

With the increase in oil revenue, the deficits in the current account of the balance of payments recorded in 1981 ($648 million), 1983 ($34 million) and 1984 ($57 million) may have been overcome in 1985.

Diamond production and export have continued their downward trend from the peak reached in 1980. There are several reasons for this: UNITA attacks on the diamond-mining region, which led to the closure of the Cuango mining division with a ten percent fall in overall production; large-scale theft and smuggling; and great difficulties in maintaining and keeping open transport and communication lines between the remote interior Lunda province in the north-east bordering on Zaire, where diamonds are mined, and the port and capital city Luanda on the west coast. In 1984, diamond production was 0.902 million carats as compared to 1.034 million carats in 1983 (1.226 in 1982, 1.4 in 1981 and 1.485 in 1980). The average selling price on the markets in London and Amsterdam fell from US $91 per carat in 1983 to $64.2 per carat in 1984, a decrease of about 30 percent! Angola's diamond export earnings fell by 38 percent from US $94 million in 1983 to US $58 million in 1984.

The breakdown of *export earnings* for 1983 and 1984 are as follows, in *millions* of US *dollars*:

	1983	*1984*
Crude oil	1,495	1,650[a]
Refined petroleum	82	85[a]
Coffee	71	80
Natural gas	32	65[a]
Diamonds	94	58
Total, incl. others	*1,859*	*2,020[a]*

a = Estimates. Source: Economist Intelligence Unit, *Quarterly Economic Review of Angola*, No. 3, 1985.

Angola continues its policy of diversification in trading partners and in sources of aid, credits and loans. It now has trade, aid, credit and loan arrangements with Western and Eastern European countries, the EEC and the COMECON, the USA, USSR, Brazil and China. It is also an active member of the Non-Alignment Movement, hosting a NAM meeting in Luanda in October 1985. It plays the leading role in the association that brings together the five Lusophone countries of Africa.

Angola exports a substantial part of its oil and diamonds to the USA, UK, and other Western countries, which also supply the bulk of its imports of foodstuffs, consumer goods, industrial raw materials and intermediate goods, machinery, equipment, vehicles and spare parts. The value of this two-way trade has been growing strongly as the following examples show:

US Trade with Angola ($ mn)	*1982*	*1983*	*1984*
Imports from Angola	697.3	911.4	1,010.0
Exports to Angola	158.5	91.0	103.0

UK Trade with Angola (£ mn)	*1983*	*1984*
Imports from Angola	45.7	158.6
Exports to Angola	22.8	35.6

French Trade with Angola (Fr mn)	*1983*	*1984*
Imports from Angola	7	12
Exports to Angola	640	872

Source: Economist Intelligence Unit, *Quarterly Economic Review of Angola*, No. 3, 1985.

Angola is the USA's fifth largest export market and third main source of imports *in Sub-Saharan Africa*.

Angola's medium and long-term external debt is still modest compared to its export income. It amounted to US $2,279 million ($2.279 billion), an increase of about 8 percent over the 1983 figure. Debt-service in 1984 was 15.5 percent of total current account receipts, as compared to 16.9 percent in 1983.

The Central Bank of Angola (*Banco Nacional de Angola*) has now adopted the -international standard accounting procedure, wherein the different categories of income from oil are classed approximately under the international-conventional headings. Using this new procedure, it has issued a Balance of Payments account (see Table 26) which differs substantially from that given in Table 22.

APPENDIX

War damages

In a White Book[30] entitled *The Acts of Aggression by the Racist Regime of South Africa against the People's Republic of Angola* the Angolan authorities have presented in detail, among other things, their estimates of the costs of the direct and indirect damages caused by the undeclared war by South Africa on Angola. We give below a summary of those estimates:

In US $ millions
For the periods

Sector	Mar 1976-June 1979	July 1979-Dec 1980	Jan 1981-Dec 1981	Total for the period Mar 1976 to Dec 1981
Agriculture & livestock	142.5	141.14	144.96	428.6
Industry		12.25	15.06	27.31
Construction	21.65	33.8	33.8	89.25
Means of transport and miscellaneous equipment	52.8	21.04	28.13	101.97
Fishery	17.75	5.0	Included in industry above	22.75
Commerce	14.28	12.64	15.89	42.81
Administration, housing and miscellaneous social services	44.32		115.84	160.16
Health		3.8		3.8
Education		1.32		1.32
Petroleum refinery & export of refined petroleum			36.55	36.55
Total for all sectors	293.3	230.99	390.23	914.52

Thus the estimated damage for the period 1976–81 totals about US $914 million. If we add to this the damages caused by the South Africans during 1975–76, which the Angolan government estimates to be about US $6,700 million, the total rises to US $7,614 million. This is more than twice the GDP for 1980 which at 1980 prices was US $3,600 million. The most extensive damages have occurred in agriculture and livestock, means of transport and general machinery, communications and electricity infrastructure, public buildings and private dwellings, and social services infrastructure.

A United Nations multi-agency fact finding mission[31] which visited Angola in 1981 estimates that up to the middle of 1981 about 712,000 people had been displaced by the war. A large part of them are now in relief camps. Although international agencies contribute to their emergency relief, the care of displaced persons continues to be a heavy burden on the Angolan state.

Notes

1. For a detailed account of the second war of liberation see M. Wolfers and J. Bergerol, *Angola in the Front Line* (Zed Press, London, 1983). They present conclusive evidence of the collusion between the USA, South Africa, Zaire and France to destroy the MPLA and install their client groups, FNLA and UNITA, in power in Luanda. The intimate collaboration between Portugal and UNITA is unmasked with the help of official Portuguese documents. The deep involvement of the CIA, as well as that of Zaire, South Africa and France, was first brought to the attention of the world by the disclosures of the ex-CIA agent John Stockwell in his book *In Search of Enemies: A CIA Story* (Futura Publications, London, 1979). The tribal, ethnic and racial ideologies of FNLA and UNITA, as well as their pro-imperialist stand, are discussed in detail by Wolfers and Bergerol.

2. G.J. Bender, *Angola under the Portuguese: The Myth and the Reality* (Heinemann, London, 1978) pp. 228 and 236; Tables 1 and 8.

3. G.J. Bender, ibid., and C. Rocha Dilolwa, *Contribução à História Económica de Angola* (Imprensa Nacional de Angola, Luanda, 1978) p. 209.

4. For an account of these atrocities and massacres, see B. Davidson, *In the Eye of the Storm – Angola's People* (Penguin, London, 1972) and M. Wolfers and J. Bergerol, *Angola in the Front Line*.

5. The former fascist regime in Lisbon and the colonial administrations in the Portuguese colonies assiduously tried to cultivate the myth that the Portuguese were not racist and did not practice racial discrimination and racial violence in the colonies. This myth has been thoroughly exposed by G. Bender, who shows the extent and depth of the racist thinking and practice of the Portuguese rulers in Angola in his scholarly work. Whilst it is quite proper to debunk and demystify the claims by the Portuguese rulers that they were 'non-racial' and 'racially tolerant', and to put the record straight, this should not be regarded as an attempt to denigrate the majority of Portuguese immigrants. To quote Davidson: 'Most of the Portuguese [who came to live in Angola] have been poor people of small pretensions and even smaller education, whose ideas about wealth, comfort or their own careers have not been greatly different from many of the Africans they have lived among. . .This tended to a certain easygoing tolerance "at the base", if seldom to anything approaching friendship. Does this argue for the Portuguese regime's ever-repeated claim to operate a non-racist, a non-

discriminatory system? Unhappily, not in the least. The Portuguese claim to "non-racism" is empty of truth in any systematic sense, just as is the myth of "five centuries of presence".' B. Davidson, *In the Eye of the Storm*, pp. 57–58.

6. C. Rocha Dilolwa, *Contribução à História ·Económica de Angola*.

7. G.J. Bender, *Angola under the Portuguese*, pp. 229–230.

8. To quote Bender, 'Lusotropicologists and many foreign writers have extolled the virtues of the poor, uneducated Portuguese peasant, praising him as the bulwark of white settlement in Angola. Their argument, in short, was that the closer Europeans and Africans were to each other's cultural level (usually interpreted by class), the more amicable would be relations between the races. This belief not only appeared in the fantasies of Gilberto Freyre, Salazar and Caetano, but in the works of respected scholars such as Jorge Dias and Ralph Delgado—who considered these rustic peasants the *fina flor* of Portuguese colonization.' ibid., pp. 224–225.

9. Ibid., p. 231; Table 21.

10. As Basil Davidson points out, the Portuguese are 'a much abused people. More than most others, they have suffered from the greed and irresponsibility of rulers, especially over the last fifty years or so. Their conduct in Angola has often reflected these miseries at home. Yet the Africans are well aware of this: they too have suffered from bad rulers, whether their own or the Portuguese, and this too has made for a certain tolerance and sympathy in mutual woes.' B. Davidson, *In the Eye of the Storm*, p. 59.

11. J. Duffy, *Portuguese Africa* (Harvard University Press, 1959) p. 154.

12. United Nations, *Report of the Sub-Committee on the Situation in Angola (A/4978)*, 1962, p. 32.

13. G.J. Bender, *Angola under the Portuguese*, pp. 143/144. The references made here by Bender to Caetano and Galvão are: M. Caetano, *Relações das colónias de Angola e Mozambique com os territórios estrangeiros vizinhos* (Imprensa Nacional, Lisbon, 1946); H. Galvão, *Santa Maria: My Crusade for Portugal*, Trans. W. Longfellow (World Publishing Co., Cleveland, 1961).

14. Ibid., p. 126.

15. M.R. Bhagavan, *Angola: Prospects for Socialist Industrialisation* (Scandinavian Institute of African Studies, Uppsala, 1980) p. 38; Table 6.

16. The facts and figures quoted in this section on industrial production are taken from M.R. Bhagavan, ibid., where the original primary sources of information are stated.

17. To give some examples: phosphates, uranium, titanium, copper, gold, manganese, bauxite, mica, nickel, cobalt, chrome, vanadium, beryllium, wolfram, tin, lead, limestone, asphalt rock, rare earths and radioactive elements.

18. Mass and luxury consumption goods are defined with respect to the purchasing power of the social classes in Angola in the decade before independence and the prices prevalent then. For details, see M.R. Bhagavan, *Angola: Prospects for Socialist Industrialisation*.

19. For details, see M. Wolfers and J. Bergerol, *Angola in the Front Line*.

20. For the sources of 1973 figures see M.R. Bhagavan, *Angola*. The 1981 figures are from the Ministry of Industry in Luanda.

21. Economist Intelligence Unit, *Quarterly Economic Review of Angola*, Annual Supplement, 1982, p. 12.

22. Ibid.

23. For more details and analysis of the oil economy in Angola, see M.R. Bhagavan, 'Angola', in P. O'Keefe and B. Munslow (eds), *Energy and Development in Southern Africa: SADCC Country Case Studies*, Part 1 (Scandinavian Institute of African Studies, Uppsala, 1984).

24. See the Angolan monthly *Novembro*, No. 63, February 1983, pp. 8-16.

25. In an interview he gave to *Africa Economic Digest*, No. 8, March 1983, the Angolan Minister for External Trade, Ismael Martins, said that imports of maize in 1983 would stay, as in 1982, at about 90,000 tons, and consumer commodities would be imported from France, Brazil and Argentina under export-financing agreements.

26. Cited in M. Wolfers and J. Bergerol, *Angola in the Front Line*, p. 165.

27. Ibid., p. 188.

28. These were published in *Orientações Fundamentais Paro O Desen-volvimento. Económico-Social: Periodo de 1981-1985* (Luanda, 1980).

29. *The National Plan for 1984:* Speech delivered by Lopo do Nascimento, Minister of Planning, during the 7th meeting of the People's Assembly, in January 1984, when the National Plan for 1984 was presented and adopted. *Angola Information Bulletin*, No. 71, 30 April 1984.

30. *Livro Branco das Agressóres do Regime Racista de Africa do Sul Contra a República Popular de Angola: 1975-1982* (Ministry of Foreign Affairs and the MPLA-Workers' Party, Luanda, 1983).

31. *Report of the United Nations Multiagency Fact Finding Mission to Angola* (29 August-13 September 1981); UNDRO, New York, 1982.

Table 1
Number of pupils and students registered in educational establishments in 1973

Type of School	Number of Establishments	Number of registered pupils and students
Primary	5,210	517,421
Middle	108	40,024
Secondary	69	18,324
Technical	60	13,467
Commerce	4	1,493
Agriculture	8	482
Secretarial and Office	27	2,212
University	1	3,094
Teachers' Training	5	386
Public Services	7	362
Nursing	4	557

Source: C. Rocha Dilolwa, *Contribução à História Económica de Angola* (Imprensa Nacional de Angola, Luanda, 1978) p. 337.

Table 2
Angola's population structure
Total area: 1,246,700 sq. kilometres

	1970[a]		1973[b]		1983[c]	
	Number	% of population	Number	% of population	Number	% of population
Total population	5,620,000		6,034,000		7,649,000	
Rural population	4,767,000	85	5,046,000	84	6,040,000	79
Urban population	853,000	15	988,000	16	1,609,000	21

a) These figures are based on the 1970 census and the interpretation by Carlos Rocha Dilolwa, pp. 217-219. No comprehensive national census has been held since 1970. In 1983, a census of the capital city Luanda was taken, but the results of this have not yet been published.

b) Estimated on the basis of a 2.4 percent per annum growth rate for the total population, 5 percent for the urban population and 2 percent for the rural population, with respect to the 1970 figure.

c) Estimated as in (b), but with respect to 1973 figures.

N.B. The figures for 1973 and 1983 should be taken as very rough indications. Being 'guesstimates' their validity is limited. But they are useful for obtaining an approximate idea of the structures and the numbers involved. In particular, it should be borne in mind that since 1980, the populations of the urban areas of the Central Highlands have been swelled by several hundred thousand peasants fleeing the terror and starvation conditions caused by the UNITA bands in the neighbouring countryside. This is particularly so in the cities of Huambo, Kuito and Benguela. It is a moot point whether these peasant refugees from the countryside now constitute a part of the urban population. In the figures given in Tables 2 and 3, they have *not* been counted in, as it is likely that these refugees will return to their villages once UNITA has been defeated.

Table 3
Structure of the Labour Force

	1970		1973		1983	
	Number	*% of labour force*	*Number*	*% of labour force*	*Number*	*% of labour force*
Total labour force	3,000,000		3,236,000		4,203,000	
Rural labour force	2,453,000	81.8	2,603,000	80.4	3,173,000	75.5
Urban labour force (including mining)	547,000	18.2	633,000	19.6	1,030,000	24.5
Subsistence peasants (including pastor-alists)	2,209,000	73.6	2,344,000	72.4		
Wage labour in agriculture (including fisheries, livestock, and forestry)	244,000	8.1	259,000	8.0		
Wage labour in industry (including mining and construction)	158,000	5.3	183,000	5.7		
Wage labour in services	214,000	7.1	248,000	7.7		
Salaried employees in all sectors	100,000	3.4	116,000	3.6		
Private entrepreneurs	75,000	2.5	86,000	2.6		

Source: C. Rocha Dilolwa, *Contribução à História Económica de Angola* (Imprensa Nacional de Angola, Luanda, 1978). The figures have been computed as in Table 2, using the same growth rates, but applied to the labour force rather than the populations.

Table 4
Average monthly salaries and daily wages in Luanda, 1960–70 (in escudos)[c]

Monthly salaries/wages

Portuguese Top Managers	50,000	(excluding all fringe benefits)[a]
Portuguese Middle Managers	25,000 to 30,000	(excluding all fringe benefits)
Portuguese Skilled Worker	12,000	
African Unskilled Worker	–	
African Domestic Servant	600	(excluding board and shelter)

Average daily wages 1960–70

African Casual Worker	20
African Agricultural Worker	20[b]

Sources: Author's interviews with people resident in Angola during the 1960s and early 1970s.

a) One of the interviewees, a highly placed official, estimated that fringe benefits amounted to 60,000 escudos per month.

b) Also see G. Bender, *Angola Under the Portuguese: The Myth and the Reality* (Heinemann, London, 1978) p. 226.

c) From 1949 to 1971, US $1 = Angolan Escudos 28.75. From 1971 to 1973, US $1 = Angolan Escudos 27.25.

Table 5
Price of foodstuffs in Luanda, early 1970s

| | | | *Price in escudos* | |
Commodity	Measure	*1971*	*1972*	*1973*
Maize flour	1 kg	7.79*	7.58*	n.a.
Rice (2nd grade)	1 kg	8.00	7.80	9.00
Fresh fish	1 kg	10.30	14.40	15.00
Sesame seed oil	1 kg	n.a.	n.a.	22.50
Palm oil	1 kg	n.a.	n.a.	10.00
White sugar	1 kg	4.70	4.80	4.77
Lard	1 kg	15.40	12.40	22.37
Milk (fresh)	1 litre	6.00	6.40	6.00
Butter	1 kg	55.20	56.40	54.00
Cheese	1 kg	52.50	53.90	54.60
Eggs	1 dozen	18.20	17.80	18.33
Chicken	1 kg	27.40	25.00	30.00
Mutton	1 kg	33.00	36.00	36.00
Pork	1 kg	33.10	40.00	40.00
Beef	1 kg	36.00	36.00	36.00
Beer	0.75 litre	9.10	9.70	9.00

Source: Instituto Nacional de Estatística, *Anuário Estatística*, Vol. II, Provincias Ultramar; *Boletim Mensual de Estatística*, Dec. 1973.

*Our estimates are based on the assumption that the price of maize flour will have risen by at least the same degree as that of rice over the period 1964–72; the price in 1964 is available, and it is 5.34 escudos for one kilogram of maize flour.

Table 6
Average daily wages in manufacturing[a] (in escudos)

| | Skilled Workers | Unskilled Workers | Annual increase in wages (%) | |
			Skilled Workers	Unskilled Workers
1969	124.1	25.6	–	–
1970	138.0	27.6	11.2	7.8
1971	154.9	27.7	12.2	0.3

Sources: *Anuário Estatístico* Vol. II, Provincias Ultramar. Published by the Instituto Nacional de Estatística. For mining wages, M. de Andrade and M. Ollivier *The War in Angola: A Socio-economic study*, Tanzania Publishing House, Dar es Salaam, 1975.

a) In the mining sector, the average daily wage of an unskilled worker was 16 escudos, if we go by the figures of the biggest mining employer, Diamang.

Table 7
Consumer price index in Luanda

	1965	1969	1970	1971	1972	1973	1974
	100	125	134	141	152	172	205
Annual percentage increase			7.2	5.2	7.8	13.1	19.2

Source: Banco de Angola, *Boletim Trimestral*.

Table 8
Marketed Agricultural Produce in 1973
(units in metric tons)

Produce	Metric Tons
Wheat	11,210
Rice	42,820
Maize	333,780
Beans	33,500
Potatoes	68,500
Dried cassava (mandioca)	61,800
Sweet potatoes	n.a.
All vegetables	n.a.
Groundnuts	12,970
Sunflower seeds	21,000
Sugar	81,900
Cotton	79,280
Tobacco	4,500
Coffee	210,000
Palm oil	17,780
Citrus fruits	15,600
Bananas	95,480
Pineapple	34,800
Cocoa	440
Sisal	78,900
Beef	23,890
Pork	3,560
Goat and mutton	6,920
Chicken	n.a.
Eggs (in 1000s)	36,130 (in thousands)
Milk (1000 litres)	554,960 (in thousand litres)
Logs of wood (m^3)	n.a.
Sawn wood (m^3)	n.a.

Source: Ministry of Agriculture, Luanda.

Table 9
Major mineral production before independence

Product	Year	Quantity
Oil (petroleum)	1974	8.9 million metric tons
Diamonds	1973	2.3 million carats
Iron ore (exported)	1973	6.1 million metric tons

Sources: Economist Intelligence Unit, *Quarterly Economic Review of Angola*, various issues.

Table 10
Structure of manufacturing production in 1965 and 1973

	% of total manufacturing production	
	1965	*1973*
Mass consumption goods		
Food processing (including oils and fats from vegetables and animals)	28.5	19.5
Textiles and other products	12.3	11.7
Miscellaneous products[a]	2.6	2.1
Luxury consumption goods		
Food processing	7.7	15.0
Textiles and their products	0.2	0.9
Beverages (alcoholic and non-alcoholic)	14.0	11.5
Tobacco products	7.6	5.7
Miscellaneous products[a]	0.3	3.9
Intermediate goods		
Wood and wood products	0.3	0.6
Pulp, paper and paper products	3.6	3.0
Chemical products	2.5	4.2
Petroleum refinery products (including derivatives of petroleum and coal)	9.7	4.0
Rubber and plastic products	0.3	1.1
Ceramic and glass products	0.5	0.8
Non-metallic mineral products	7.0	4.8
Capital goods		
Iron and steel products ⎫		2.5
Metal products ⎭	2.4	3.9
Non-electrical machinery	none	0.8
Electrical machinery and gadgets (excluding consumer durables)	0.5	1.9
Transport equipment (excluding passenger motor vehicles, motorcycles and bicycles)	none	2.1
Professional equipment	none	negligible
Total value (in million escudos)	*2,998*	*13,724*

Sources: *Anuário Estatístico* 1960 to 1972; *Boletim Mensal de Estatística* (Instituto Nacionale de Estatística, Delegação de Angola, 1973).

Note a) 'Miscellaneous' covers everything after food processing, textiles, beverages and tobacco products have been taken out of the list of goods given under mass and luxury consumption.

Table 11
Structure of imports in 1965 and 1973
(excluding armaments)

	% of total imports	
	1965	*1973*
Consumer goods		
Food processing (including vegetable and animal oils and fats), beverages, tobacco products	19.3	13.3
Textiles and their products	17.5	10.5
Articles of clothing, various garments (including footwear), costume jewellery, etc.	2.1	0.9
Leather and fur goods	0.5	0.2
Miscellaneous	0.5	0.7
Intermediate goods		
Mineral products	2.4	5.4
Chemical products	8.2	11.1
Plastics, rubber, resins and their products	3.5	4.1
Wood and its products	0.4	0.2
Paper and its products	2.4	2.2
Ceramic and glass products	1.9	1.6
Capital goods		
Basic metals and their products	10.0	11.6
Machinery and gadgets (including consumer durables)	14.8	22.9
Transport equipment	14.3	13.6
Professional equipment	1.5	1.6
Total value (in million of escudos)	*5.59*	*13.2*

Sources: *Comércio Externo*, Vol. 1, 1960 to 1972; *Boletim Mensal de Estatística*, December 1983.

Table 12
Principal exports in 1974

Product	Metric Tons	Million Escudos	% of principal exports by value
Oil	7,400,000	14,980	55.4
Coffee	217,500	6,270	23.2
Diamonds (in carats)	2,100,000	2,460	9.1
Sisal	66,720	1,270	4.7
Iron ore	5,240,000	1,210	4.5
Raw cotton	12,960	500	1.9
Bananas	65,700	290	1.1
Sugar	9,680	40	0.1

Source: *Africa South of the Sahara*, 1982-83, Europa Publications (Section on the Angolan economy by R. Pélissier).

Table 13
Marketed domestic agricultural produce.[a, b] (*units in metric tons*)

Product	1977 Planned Target	1977 Actual Production	1978 Planned Target	1978 Actual Production	1979 Planned Target	1979 Actual Production
Wheat	5,600	3,450	6,840	627	11,590	1,261
Rice	3,640	3,410	16,010	1,438	14,360	2,075
Maize	50,500	36,788	143,780	2,740	161,660	19,692
Beans	6,700	1,002	18,470	679	17,140	868
Potatoes	23,000	1,703	37,190	2,739	50,440	3,087
Dried cassava (mandioca)	120,000	1,141	57,700	6,011	51,900	7,502
Sweet potatoes	t.n.s.	n.a.	t.n.s.	1,246	t.n.s.	3,282
All vegetables	t.n.s.	3,352	19,000	13,061	54,200	10,023
Groundnuts	2,800	1,171	4,350	357	2,070	399
Sunflower seeds	950	1,533	13,880	449	19,440	747
Sugar	n.a.	n.a.	n.a.	39,000	n.a.	60,000
Cotton	6,000	1,423	20,500	179	21,320	1,633
Tobacco	950	245	920	926	1,740	622
Coffee	80,000	68,350	75,000	25,172	30,000	18,704
Palm Oil	2,700	n.a.	7,230	n.a.	4,730	2,259
Citrus Fruits	11,900	3,027	9,000	1,047	7,700	3,478
Bananas	12,000	2,050	15,900	2,212	14,890	2,937
Pineapple	8,600	386	4,900	519	3,000	1,803
Cocoa	t.n.s.	n.a.	t.n.s.	160	t.n.s.	50
Sisal	t.n.s.	3,070	t.n.s.	6,987	t.n.s.	7,043
Beef	19,070	3,409	18,560	6,036	17,500	6,213
Pork	7,770	2,486	5,930	1,071	5,390	1,004
Mutton & goat meat	1,540	135	1,880	193	1,070	358
Chicken	7,290	3,550	5,630	1,317	4,820	1,223
Eggs (in 1000s)	34,000	8,750	43,400	16,590	30,100	6,706
Milk (1000 lit.)	t.n.s.	n.a.	5,170	n.a.	2,530	699
Logs of wood (m^3)	t.n.s.	n.a.	72,700	41,382	94,530	23,569
Sawn wood (m^3)	t.n.s.	n.a.	30,450	5,962	26,690	6,668

Source: Ministry of Agriculture ('t.n.s.' means 'target not set').

a) This is purely domestic produce sold through government channels and government shops. It does *not* include imported products.

b) This does *not* include products that are sold in the private, parallel market (at extremely high prices). These figures are to that extent underestimates.

c) Source for 1982 targets is *Orientações Fundamentais Para O Desenvolvimento Economico-Social: Periodo de 1981–1985* (Luanda, 1980) pp. 38 and 61.

1980		1981		Targets set in 1980 for *1982,* at the First Extraordinary Congress of MPLA–PT in December 1980[c]
Planned Target	*Actual Production*	*Planned Target*	*Actual Production*	
5,160	524	t.n.s.	210	
15,390	3,205	9,783	1,242	14,000
149,580	30,840	92,078	23,649	85,000
8,320	693	4,419	1,069	5,000
59,500	8,793	50,609	9,104	37,000
23,790	8,452	35,706	19,027	30,000
13,140	4,611	t.n.s.	4,497	t.n.s.
86,590	17,494	51,553	27,703	t.n.s.
2,060	282	1,700	714	4,000
12,080	896	7,157	705	10,500
n.a.	80,000	n.a.	n.a.	45,000
16,080	1,453	10,470	1,046	20,000
1,790	251	953	1,393	700
30,670	36,576	63,807	23,877	35,000
8,800	3,406	6,419	3,613	5,000
15,210	3,432	7,340	3,558	4,000
28,270	10,695	39,022	10,801	35,000
18,230	2,212	16,638	647	18,000
t.n.s.	n.a.	t.n.s.	n.a.	t.n.s.
t.n.s.	n.a.	t.n.s.	241	t.n.s.
12,670	4,593	12,169	3,409	13,000
2,520	740	3,637	759	5,000
710	241	t.n.s.	301	t.n.s.
4,330	2,226	9,818	427	8,000
44,370	8,716	52,661	4,251	60,000
4,240	n.a.	1,628	969	5,000
75,740	45,359	132,156	31,496	150,000
29,480	7,133	24,410	7,399	50,000

Table 14
Prices of basic commodities in Luanda, 1983

		Price in Kwanzas (approximate)	
Commodity	*Quantity*	*Government Shops*	*Open, parallel market*
Cassava flour (mandioca)	1 kg		1000
Fish	1 kg	100	500
Meat	1 kg	130	
Chicken	1 kg	120	
Maize flour	1 kg	25	1000
Beans	1 kg		1250
Rice	1 kg		
Edible oil			
Sugar	1 kg	44	
Onions	5 medium sized	Vegetables and	1000
Tomatoes	5 medium sized	fruits are almost	500
Bananas	10 medium sized	never available in	500
Cabbage	1 medium sized	government shops, in	200
Carrots	7 medium sized	particular 'people's	500
Charcoal	1 kg	shops (lojo do povo)'. Charcoal is never on sale in government shops.	600–800
Adults' Clothes			
Shirt	1	Clothes also are	1500
T-Shirt	1	almost never avail-	1000
Skirt	1	able in government shops.	2000
Children's Clothes			
Underwear	1		500
Shorts	1		800
Frock	1		1500
Mirror	1 small sized		500–800

Source: Author's field research. In 1983, *official* exchange rate was 1 US Dollar = 30 kwanzas, the *unofficial* exchange rate was 1 US Dollar = 1,000 kwz.

Table 15
Average urban monthly income (in kwanzas)

Category[a, b]	Monthly salary in kwanzas (approx)
Top civil servant	35,000
Top manager	35,000
Top engineer	32,000
Top technical cadre	32,000
Middle civil servant	16-18,000
Middle managerial cadre	16-18,000
Middle level technical cadre	22-27,000
Middle level office workers	13-16,000
Middle level secretarial staff	10-13,000
Skilled factory worker	10-15,000
Unskilled manual worker	5-7,000

Source: Author's field research.

Notes: a) Officially, the salary levels span a scale of 1 to 19, the lowest being 1 at 5000 kw/month, the highest being 19 at 35,000 kw/month. b) The bulk of cash income earners lie in two broad categories: 10,000-15,000 kw/month, and 15,000-25,000 kw/month. The top end (35,000/month) and the bottom end (5000/month) are thinly populated. Thus the dominant income differential is 1 to 3.

Table 16
Distribution of factories by sector and ownership, 1983

Sector	Number	State owned	Privately owned	State and private joint venture
Food processing	72	60	10	2
Light industry	46	19	24	3
Heavy industry	30	18	10	2

Source: Ministry of Industry, Government of Angola.

Table 17
1981 percentage distribution by monetary value of industrial output

Sector	Branch		% of total
Food processing		29	
	Beverages		14.5
	Sugar		2.6
	Flours		6.4
	Oils and fats		2.6
	Conserves		1.5
	Others		1.4
Light industry		53	
	Textiles		32.9
	Hides and other textile substitutes		1.6
	Tobacco products		5.8
	Wood products		0.5
	Light chemicals		12.2
Heavy industry		18	
	Basic chemicals		3.4
	Heavy metal fabrication		3.6
	Light metal fabrication		5.2
	Metallurgy		2.5
	Radio and television assembly		3.3

Source: Ministry of Industry, Government of Angola.

Notes: Total absolute value of manufacturing output was 12,814 million kwz. 30 kwz = 1 US Dollar (approximately).

Table 18
Output in manufacturing industry

	1973 Actual	1980 Actual	1981 Plan Target	1981 Actual	Targets for 1982
Consumer Goods					
Maize flour (Tons)	62,000	57,308	46,500	47,066	110,000
Wheat flour (Tons)	87,000	46,936	51,200	36,757	85,000
Vegetable oils and fats ('000 litres)	16,750	4,847	4,500	3,327	12,700
Sugar (Tons)	82,000	25,217	24,350	19,905	45,000
Salt (Tons)	96,717	23,844	24,000	20,040	t.n.s.
Beer ('000 litres)	130,000	71,376	73,000	67,091	230–260,000
Soft drinks and aerated water ('000 litres)	56,000	24,282	24,312	27,649	45,000
Margarine (Tons)	3,400	1,519	1,300	898	3,500
Table wine ('000 litres)	13,620	n.a.	10,000	6,705	t.n.s.
Meat conserves (Tons)	6,100	331	n.a.	305	t.n.s.
Fruit and veg. conserves (Tons)	9,300	2,232	2,190	1,675	t.n.s.
Roasted coffee (Tons)	n.a.	1,305	1,510	1,268	t.n.s.
Instant coffee (Tons)	n.a.	4	12	15	t.n.s.
Tobacco products (Tons)	8,483	1,821	2,298	2,311	t.n.s.
Textiles (cloth) ('000 sq. metres)	17,600	18,546	17,000	18,619	25,000
Soap (Tons)	18,400	8,372	6,000	7,277	24,000
Leather footwear ('000 prs.)	300	303	366	388	1,000
Cloth footwear ('000 prs.)	1,100	207	262	159	500
Plastic footwear ('000 prs.)	2,000	227	100	107	1,000
Matches ('000 boxes)	68,400	22,938	55,782	44,876	80,000
Plastic bottles ('000)	13,326	1,054	1,280	1,201	t.n.s.
Cutlery ('000)	2,661	1,304	t.n.s.	900	t.n.s.
Assembly of bicycles	36,518	6,919	3,500	4,840	t.n.s.
Assembly of radios	25,821	82,744	95,000	90,055	220,000
Assembly of televisions	n.a.	8,682	21,800	15,219	50,000
Assembly of motorcycles	5,288	6,308	6,500	7,605	7,200
Assembly of motor cars	n.a.	384	590	351	1,200
Foam mattresses	58,194	65,977	69,000	51,075	130,000
Blankets	972,000	238,517	162,000	148,628	800,000
Intermediate Goods					
Plywood (Cubic metres)	13,517	2,861	3,000	2,429	20,000
Paper (Tons)	10,948	4,016	t.n.s.	4,067	t.n.s.
Paper pulp (Tons)	32,438	1,757	t.n.s.	1,793	26,000
Paint (Tons)	8,449	4,072	5,105	4,483	t.n.s.
Glass (Tons)	n.a.	1,296	11,270	6,539	t.n.s.
Vehicle tyres	359,000	87,086	100,000	72,570	140,000
Tubes for vehicle tyres	318,000	53,577	50,000	45,512	t.n.s.
Small dry batteries ('000)	4,329	3,153	4,000	2,931	t.n.s.
Wet heavy batteries	62,598	50,127	50,000	33,778	95,000
Metal containers (packing materials made of metal e.g. gas cylinders, etc.) ` (1000 units) (Tons)	29,540	892	7,000	6,777	t.n.s.

Table 18 (continued)

	1973 Actual	1980 Actual	1981 Plan Target	1981 Actual	Targets for 1982
Capital Goods					
Assembly of buses	n.a.	116	250	173	400
Electric wires and cables (Tons)	n.a.	447	570	546	t.n.s.
Zinc sheets (Tons)	12,009	3,970	4,000	3,817	t.n.s.
Construction iron and steel (Tons)	27,000	3,595	2,500	2,654	20–24,000

Sources: For 1973 figures: *Boletim Mensal de Estatística,* 1973–74 (Inst. Nacional de Estatística, Delegação de Angola). For 1980–81 figures: Ministry of Industry, Government of Angola, Luanda. For 1982 targets: *Orientações Fundamentais para O Desenvolvimento Económico-Social, Periodo de 1981-85* (Central Committee Secretariat of MPLA–PT, Luanda, 1981).

Table 19
Production of oil, diamonds and coffee

Product	Units	1977	1978	1979	1980	1981	1982
Crude oil	Million barrels[a]	63.0	49.5	52.1	49.7	47.3	47.4
Diamonds	Million Carats	0.353	0.4	0.841	1.48	1.4	1.225
Coffee	Thousand Tons	68.35	25.17	18.7	36.57	23.87	17.4

Sources: Ministries of Petroleum, Industry and Agriculture.

a) To convert to metric tons use the formula 1 metric ton = 7.33 barrels of crude oil.

Table 20A
Physical volume of exports

Product	Unit	1981 *a*	1982 *b*	1983 *b*	1984 *b*	1984 *b*
Crude oil	Million barrels *c*	37.9	43.8	43.4	54.7	77
Refined petroleum products	Thousand tons	511	510	500	500	500
Liquefied petrol- eum gas (LPG)	Million barrels	None	None	2.1	2.3	2.3
Diamonds	Million carats	1.4	1.2	1.3	1.4	1.4
Coffee	Thousand tons	44.64 *d*	37.2 *d*	45	45	47

Source: Banco Nacional, de Angola, and Ministry of Petroleum.

a) These are actual export figures; b) These are estimates and projections by the bank; c) To convert to metric tons use the formula 1 metric ton = 7.33 barrels of crude oil; d) Export figures for coffee are nearly twice the production figures for the years 1981 and 1982, because a large part of the exported coffee comes from *old* stocks. To convert to bags, use the formula 1 bag = 60 kg.

Table 20B
Monetary value of goods exports (in US $ millions) *a*

Product	1981 *b*	1982 *b*	1983 *c*	1984 *c*	1985 *c*
Crude oil and refined petroleum products	991	780	1,380 *d*	1,680 *d*	2,300 *d*
Diamonds	160	126	130	140	140
Coffee	108	85	90	90	90
Liquefied petroleum gas (LPG)	–	–	40	50	50
Others	12	9	3	10	10
Total	*1,271*	*1,000*	*1,643*	*1,970*	*2,590*

Source: Banco Nacional de Angola.

a) The official exchange rate in 1983 was approximately 1 US Dollar = 30 kwz; b) Estimates by the bank; c) Projections by the bank; d) Based on the following estimated prices for one barrel: 1983: US$ 32; 1984: US$ 31; 1985: US$ 30.

Table 21A
Main commodities traded (in million kwanzas)[a]

Exports	1978	1979	Imports	1978	1979
Crude oil	16,507	26,746	Foodstuffs	5,383	7,326
Oil by-products	1,103	2,498	Textiles, and		
Coffee	6,732	6,700	footwear	1,447	2,341
Diamonds	2,997	4,219	Machinery	3,940	11,016
Cement	90	59	Consumer goods	2,209	1,293
Sisal	82	165	Chemicals	563	801
Fishmeal	60	40	Raw materials	4,099	3,051
			Tools	478	1,191
			Medical goods	1,040	716

Source: *Angola Hoje e Sempre* (Angola Today and Forever), Government of Angola.

a) 30 Angolan kwanzas = 1 US $ (approximately).

Table 21B
Direction of trade (% of total)

Imports from:	1979	1980	Exports to:	1979	1980
Western Europe	56.4	51.6	North America	21.4	31.8
Comecon (CMEA)	15.7	16.9	Latin America	35.1	28.9
Latin America	9.8	10.8	Western Europe	28.5	22.2
North America	5.6	7.1	Comecon (CMEA)	6.9	6.3
Africa	3.0	2.2	Africa	3.4	4.1
Others	9.5	11.4	Others	4.7	6.7

Sources: Banco Nacional de Angola; Africa Index.

Table 21C
Origin of major imports in 1982

Country	Million US $
U.S.A.	158.4
France	118.8
Portugal	85.2
Italy	61.2
West Germany	58.8
Japan	51.6
U.K.	45.6
Belgium and Luxemburg	30.0
Netherlands	30.0
Spain	14.4
Total	*654*

Source: Ministry of Foreign Trade, Luanda.

Table 22
Balance of payments (in million kwanzas)[a]

	1978	1979	1980	1981	1982[b]	1983[c]	1984[c]	1985[c]
Goods exports	29,940	35,460	48,699	38,126	30,000	39,000	49,300	61,800
Goods imports	26,640	36,840	44,503	45,417	31,000	40,300	51,000	61,000
Goods trade balance	3,300	-1,380	4,196	-7,291	-1,000	-1,300	-1,700	800
Services exports	1,844	9,000	10,620	6,206	10,000	13,000	18,400	24,000
Services imports	5,564	13,350	16,354	18,899	16,000	17,800	20,500	26,500
Unilateral transfers from abroad	90	300	508	1,505	800	1,500	1,500	1,500
Services trade balance	-3,720	-4,350	-5,734	-12,683	-6,000	-4,800	-2,100	-2,500
Current account balance	-330	-5,430	-1,030	-18,469	-6,200	-4,600	-2,300	-200
Long and medium term:								
New debts			12,490	14,828	10,200	16,100	19,800	20,300
Reimbursements			-5,474	-7,718	-7,000	-9,800	-13,500	-16,100
Balance of capital	1,950	1,950	7,016	7,110	3,200	6,300	6,300	4,200
Short term:								
New debts			5,646	14,720	12,200	9,600	14,500	16,200
Reimbursements			-8,417	-8,350	-9,000	-8,000	-12,600	-14,500
Balance of capital	2,040	4,290	-2,771	6,370	3,200	1,600	1,900	1,700
Overall balance	3,660	810	3,215	-4,989	200	3,300	5,900	5,700
Errors and omissions	-960	-360	-599	-804				

Table 22 (continued)

	1978	1979	1980	1981	1982b	1983c	1984c	1985c
Change in reserves	2,700	450	2,616	−5,793	200	3,300	5,900	5,700
Total reserves	10,920	11,370	9,260 d	3,467	3,667	6,967	12,867	18,567
Months of imports that can be covered	4.1	2.7	1.8	0.5	0.9	1.4	2.2	2.5
Debt servicing (percentage ratio of debts to exports)			9.5	17.4	17.5	18.8	20	18.9

Source: Banco Nacional de Angola, 1983 Memo.

Notes: a) 30 kwanzas = 1 US $ (approximately); b) preliminary figures; c) projected figures; d) This figure does not tally with the figures that follow it along the same row.

Table 23
State budgets 1981–1984 (in million kwanzas)

Revenue

Sector	1981 (kwz mn.)	1981 %	1982 (kwz mn.)	1982 %	1983[a] (kwz mn.)	1983 %	1984[a] (kwz mn.)	1984 %
State-owned enterprises	11,000	12.1	11,100	15.4	18,000	21.5	14,600	15.5
Joint venture enterprises (between state and private capital)	700	0.8	–	–	1,000	1.2	500	0.5
Taxes (mainly from oil revenues)	53,300	58.2	32,300	44.8	38,100	45.4	58,500	62.0
Other income	8,500	9.3	7,200	10.0	11,700	13.9	9,000	9.5
Loans	17,900	19.6	21,500	29.8	15,100	18.0	11,800	12.5
Total	91,500	100	72,100	100	83,900	100	94,400	100

Expenditure

Sector	1981 (kwz mn.)	1981 %	1982 (kwz mn.)	1982 %	1983[a] (kwz mn.)	1983 %	1984[a] (kwz mn.)	1984 %
Economic and social development	43,400	47.3	26,300	36.6	25,500	30.4	27,700	28.6
Social services and cultural activities	13,800	15.1	15,000	20.8	16,700	20.0	19,500	20.6
Defence	15,000	16.3	15,000	20.8	21,500	25.6	28,000	29.7
Administrative organs	11,800	12.9	13,700	19.0	11,200	13.3	9,600	10.2
Other	7,700	8.4	2,000	2.8	9,000	10.7	10,300	10.9
Total expenditure	91,700	100	72,000	100	83,900	100	94,400	100

Source: Ministry of Finance.

a) Projections.

Table 24
Estimates and projections of oil production (thousand barrels per day)

	1983	1984	1985	1986
	[a]177	220	272	341
	[b]173	178	235	250

Source: [a] Ministry of Energy and Petroleum, Luanda, February 1984; [b] *Oil and Gas Journal*.

Table 25
Estimate of export incomes*

	1983		1984	
	Million US $	% of total	Million US $	% of total
Crude oil and Refined oil products	1,540	88.5	1,804	90.2
Diamonds	106	6.1	100	5.0
Coffee	90	5.2	92	4.6
Others	4	0.2	4	0.2
Total	*1,740 *		*2,000**	

Source: Memo, Ministry of Planning, 1984.

*These figures do not tally with those given in Table 22, where the source is the National Bank of Angola.

Index

African National Congress (ANC): activity in Mozambique 183-4; development of 63; and Nkomati Accord 182-3

agriculture: in Angola, barter trade in 156; in Angola, cash crop farming 148; coffee in 149, 152, 170, 208; cooperatives in 79, 80, 81, 91; Ethiopian 19; failure of 2; planning in 20-22; production in Angola 147-9, 198, 202, 203; subsistence cultivation in 148, 149; technology in 19; transformation of 37n62; and women 78-82; in Zimbabwe 18, 23; *see also*: Cape Verde; food; labour; Mozambique; peasantry; state farms

Ake, Claude 60

Albright, D.E. 57, 70n3

Algeria: Communist Party in 62; revolution in 47-8; and socialism 26; *see also*: Fanon

Amin, Samir 59

Angola: balance of payments in 212-13; budgets in 214; communications in 144; corruption in 172; debt in 188; diamonds in 151, 160-4, 184, 187, 208; distribution of factories in 205; distribution of industrial output 206; economy in 142, 145, 149, 151, 184; education in 143, 144, 160, 170, 192; elections in 166-9; exports in 201, 209; finance in 156, 157, 163, 165, 185, 187; First Extraordinary Congress in 167, 169; foreign capital in 142, 169-70; foreign exchange in 163-5, 185; imports in 155, 157, 161, 184, 200, 211; industry in 142, 147, 149, 150, 151, 152, 158, 159, 160, 163-4, 170-72, 206, 207-8; labour force in 194-5; manufacturing production in 199, 207-8; minerals in 149, 191n17, 198; nationalisation in 169-70; oil in 150, 151, 160, 161, 162, 163, 164, 179, 180, 184, 186, 187, 188, 208, 215; parallel (black) market in 156-7, 172; population in 193; prices in 196, 204; Rectification Campaign 167; Second Party Conference and Congress 186; socialism in 140-215; trade in 17, 188, 210; and women 83-6; *see also*: agriculture; Cabinda raid; class; destabilisation; Jose Eduardo Dos Santos; FAPLA; FNLA; food; labour; MPLA; Neto; party; peasantry; People's Assemblies; private enterprise; Portugal; state farms; UNITA.

Arusha Declaration *see* Tanzania

Babu, M. 60

Barrett, Michèle 73-4

Beneria, Lourdes 74, 75

Biafra 46

Boserup, Ester 75

bourgeoisie *see* class

Cabral, Amilcar: class analysis of 50-51, 58-9; and decentralisation 96-100; and declassé elements 51; and *Directives* of 1965 96, 98; disagreement with Fanon 52; and economic transformation 99; and elections of 1972 98; and ideology 50; leadership of 9; and neocolonialism 49; and peasantry 13; and Portugal 52; thinking of 49-51

Cabinda raid 179-80

Cameroon: Marxist struggles in 67; Union of Peoples of Cameroon 70

Cape Verde Republic: agriculture in 111; aid, foreign to 110-11; land reform 109-10; militias 110; PAIGC (African Party for the Independence of Guinea and Cape Verde) 9, 25, 96, 97, 98, 99,

NEW FROM ZED

CARLOS LOPES

GUINEA BISSAU: FROM LIBERATION STRUGGLE TO INDEPENDENT STATEHOOD

This up-to-date and comprehensive account of Guinea Bissau's difficult transition from the anti-Portuguese struggle for national liberation to the very different challenges of independence and economic construction is the first to be written by a Guinea Bissaun. Drawing on documentary sources and the testimony of participants not usually available, Carlos Lopes's book considers the country's national question and PAIGC's attempts to handle it; the extent Amilcar Cabral's influence really penetrated; and the failure of the post-independence regime to use the principles of the liberation struggle in order to handle the pressures of statehood or to recognise the existence of ongoing class struggles — thereby precipitating the coup that overthrew President Luis Cabral.

This book's scholarly investigation of enduring class divisions and ethnic sensitivities deepens our understanding of the processes hindering the growth of new, popularly controlled state structures.

"A well-documented study . . . an illuminating work on the historical transformation from national liberation movement to state independence." Dr Lars Rudebeck

Carlos Lopes was born in Canchungo, Guinea Bissau. He studied at the International Institute of Development Studies in Geneva, and at the University of Paris I.

304pp Tables Charts Bibliography Index
Translated from Portuguese by Michael Wolfers
Hb 0 86232 288 X   £20.95 $32.95
Pb 0 86232 289 8   £7.95 $12.95

Africa ● Current Affairs ● History
August

RACHID TLEMCANI

STATE AND REVOLUTION IN ALGERIA

This wide-ranging account of Algeria since Independence shows how the FLN has pursued a succession of significant policies — a rapid build-up of heavy industry, militant pressure to push up oil prices, and a vigorous foreign policy based on non-alignment.

The author argues that internal class relations, and not merely the domination of external forces, have fundamentally shaped the Algerian state since Ottoman times. He examines the class that has come to control the FLN. He shows how workers' self-management has been displaced by a new clientilist alliance between the private sector and a dominant bureaucratic bourgeoisie. Its economic strategy is comprehensively criticised and the opposition of workers, Kabyle nationalists and Islamic fundamentalists surveyed.

This book is an important contribution to our understanding of post-revolutionary societies in the Third World.

"An incisive analysis of the formation of the modern Algerian state, offering a critical view of its economic and political development." Roger Hardy, Editor, *Middle East*.

Dr Rachid Tlemcani is a political economist who trained at the University of Boston. He now teaches at the University of Algiers.

256pp Tables Bibliography Index
Hb 0 86232 431 9   £18.95 $29.95
Pb 0 86232 432 7   £6.95 $10.95

The Maghreb ● Political Economy
July

MAINA WA KINYATTI (EDITOR)
KENYA'S FREEDOM STRUGGLE
THE DEDAN KIMATHI PAPERS
PREFACE BY NGUGI WA THIONG'O

The British captured extensive archives belonging to the Mau Mau, which to this day have not been made public. Here for the first time, as a result of years of village-level research, historian Maina wa Kinyatti has recovered some of the movement's — and its leader, Dedan Kimathi's — most important papers. Translated into English, they make startlingly clear the movement's own perspectives on their struggle and its difficulties, the relatively advanced nature of their goals as a national liberation movement, and their radical vision of a liberated Kenyan society.

By recovering this material, Maina wa Kinyatti has done Kenyan history a signal service. His Introduction, moreover, does not refrain from a trenchant critique of the limitations Mau Mau's particular brand of patriotic nationalism imposed on its struggle.

This book is a contribution to African history and an illuminating addition to the literature on revolutionary struggles in the Third World generally.

Maina wa Kinyatti is a prominent Kenyan historian who taught at Kenyatta University College until his imprisonment on political charges in 1982. Amnesty International have since adopted him as a Prisoner of Conscience. He is the author of *Thunder from the Mountains: Mau Mau Patriotic Songs* (1980).

160pp Translated from Kikuyu
Hb 0 86232 506 4   £16.95 $26.95
Pb 0 86232 507 2   £6.95 $10.95
Not for sale in East Africa

Africa ● History
July

TOYIN FALOLA (EDITOR)
BRITAIN AND NIGERIA: EXPLOITATION OR DEVELOPMENT?

Some of Nigeria's most prominent progressive historians have combined to write this tightly integrated account of the economic relationship foisted on Nigeria during British colonial rule. Contrary to conventional accounts, they argue that British rule was not an agent of development, but of exploitation and destruction.

How the European powers exploited Nigerian society before the age of colonialism is outlined, and the economic interests that subsequently prompted Britain to take the country over. The colonial economy is then examined: the new infrastructure to facilitate exploitation; the new system of agricultural and extractive production in the interests of the metropole; the unequal exchange inherent in British-Nigerian colonial trading relations; and the merely token industrialization that took place.

The authors stress the wider consequences of the destruction of indigenous institutions, the illusion of economic development that was created, and the relationship of the colonial era to the country's present-day economic distortions and political instability.

The Editor, **Dr Toyin Falola**, teaches History at the University of Ife and edits *ODU: A Journal of West African Studies*. His most recent book (co-authored) is *The Rise and Fall of Nigeria's Second Republic, 1979-1984*. Among the other well-known contributors are S.O. Osoba, S.A. Olanrewaju, A.G. Adebayo, and J. Ihonvbere.

272pp Index
Hb 0 86232 303 7   £18.95 $29.95
Pb 0 86232 304 5   £6.95 $10.95

Africa ● History
August

CIMADE, INODEP, MINK
AFRICA'S REFUGEE CRISIS
WHAT'S TO BE DONE?

Renewed famine in Ethiopia and the Sahel, as well as the Continent's ongoing wars and political repression, have created the world's biggest refugee problem. This up-to-date, factual picture of the situation in Africa highlights three regions — the Horn, where war and drought have joined in a deadly combination; Southern Africa where apartheid has forcibly relocated some three million people; and Central/East Africa.

What are the underlying causes of this tragedy? The authors argue that natural calamities are only part of the answer. The roots of the refugee crisis lie in the endemic weaknesses so many African states inherited from the colonial period — which render them vulnerable to the self-interested interventions of outside powers: the USA and the USSR; France and Britain. A concluding chapter appraises the proposals of the Second International Conference on Refugees in Africa.

'The authors have lifted the veil behind which this tragedy lies hidden and done research into the root causes of an evil which affects five million human beings.' Daniel Mayer, former President of the International Federation of Human Rights.

The authors come from Cimade, an organization founded during World War II to help displaced persons; Inodep, an NGO working in development education; and Mink, the International N'krumahist Movement.

224pp
Translated from French by Michael John
Hb 0 86232 469 6   £16.95 $26.95
Pb 0 86232 470 X   £6.95 $10.95

Africa ● Current Affairs
April

VUKANI MAKHOSIKAZI COLLECTIVE
SOUTH AFRICAN WOMEN ON THE MOVE

This remarkable book reflects the lives of African working-class women under apartheid. Women in suffering and in struggle. Women living in the cities of South Africa and in the bantustans; working in the factories and on white farms; and many surviving without jobs. The lives of all these women controlled by the pass and other apartheid laws and institutions, but above all, controlled by the fact of being women, African and working class.

The book talks for and about these women in their struggle to make ends meet in the face of rising rents and the soaring cost of food. It tells of their fight for adequate housing, for child care facilities, through church groups, through township women's organizations — struggling for a free and just society, free not only from class exploitation and racial oppression, but also free from sexual oppression.

The authors are a Johannesburg-based women's collective who worked on the writing of this book over a period of three years. It is the product of many, many interviews conducted with women keen to tell the stories of their lives.

272pp Illustrated Maps Charts
Hb 0 86232 620 6   £14.95 $24.95
Pb 0 86232 621 4   £5.95 $9.95
Copublished with the Catholic Institute of International Relations
Not for sale in Australia, Canada, South Africa or the United States

Africa ● Women
Already published

CHIBUZO NWOKE

THIRD WORLD MINERALS AND GLOBAL PRICING: A NEW THEORY

This study examines the distribution of the enormous wealth inherent in the Third World's mineral resources. Dr Nwoke criticises the bargaining model usually used to explain relations between global corporations and Third World governments. Instead he develops the Marxist theory of ground rent to argue that today's mineral crisis lies in the struggle between Western mining companies and the Third World over which side can appropriate most 'rent' from international mining. Only if the Third World can realize the full surplus profit available, can it maximize its producer power. Supported by evidence from all over the world, Dr Nwoke's book constitutes a major theoretical advance, as well as having significant political implications.

"Nwoke's extension of Marx's rent theory to the sphere of mining is original, enlightening and explicated with clarity. It helps make sense of OPEC and similar phenomena, and thereby speaks directly to the political options that are open to us." Immanuel Wallerstein

Dr Nwoke is a Research Fellow with the Nigerian Institute of International Affairs. He holds a doctorate from the University of Denver. His articles have appeared in *Monthly Review, Africa Today,* and *Review: A Journal of the Fernand Braudel Center.*

272pp Tables Bibliography Index
Hb 0 86232 441 6   £18.95 $29.95
Pb 0 86232 442 4   £6.95 $10.95

Political Economy ● Development Studies
September

ANN SEIDMAN

MONEY, BANKING AND PUBLIC FINANCE IN AFRICA

This textbook is designed for economics students and those already working in banks, public financial institutions and planning. Its comprehensive treatment assembles information from all parts of the Continent, while concentrating on the very diverse experiences of Nigeria, Tanzania and Zimbabwe.

Monetary and fiscal questions are dealt with in the context of the practical development problems caused Africa by the impact of the world capitalist system. These questions include control of the banking system, appropriate tax policies, how to raise capital, debt management, and relations with the transnational commercial banks as well as the IMF and World Bank.

Professor Seidman supplements conventional economic analysis with a radical approach critical of its assumptions and perspectives. She also analyses the planning, budgetary and banking experiences of socialist countries in Eastern Europe and Asia so that the advantages and pitfalls inherent in their attempts to chart an independent economic course may become better known.

Professor Ann Seidman is a distinguished economist who has taught in many different African countries, including Ghana, Tanzania and Zimbabwe, as well as holding appointments at various U.S. universities. She is the author of eleven books on development strategy, planning and multinational corporations in Africa.

384pp Tables Charts Bibliography Index
Hb 0 86232 429 7   £22.95 $35.95
Pb 0 86232 430 0   £8.95 $13.95

Political Economy
July

RONALDO MUNCK
THE DIFFICULT DIALOGUE
MARXISM AND NATIONALISM

Marxist thinkers have long had to confront the stubborn fact of nationalism. This book surveys their attempts to grapple with the enduring power of this manifestation of non-class consciousness.

Starting with the early attempts by Marx and Engels, Dr Munck traces the twists and turns of Marxist debate on the National Question through the European thinkers at the turn of the century — Kautsky, Bauer, Borochov, Luxemburg, Lenin and Stalin. He highlights the subsequent perspectives of Third World Marxists — Sultan Galiev from Central Asia, Roy in India, Mariategui of Peru, Mao, Che Guevara and Cabral. He also discusses the practical problems of national rivalries between socialist states (notably in Indo-China) and within them (the cases of Yugoslavia and the USSR itself). The reader gets a lucid picture of the dynamics of the debate, its diversity, and the defects that persist in Marxism's troubled relationship with nationalism.

Recommended as a student text for courses in Political Science, Third World politics, and Marxism.

Dr Ronaldo Munck, an Argentinian sociologist, teaches at the University of Ulster. He has written extensively on Third World politics, including *Politics and Dependency in the Third World* and *Revolutionary Trends in Latin America.*

192pp Bibliography Index
Hb 0 86232 493 9   £18.95 $29.95
Pb 0 86232 494 7   £6.95 $10.95

Political Science
May

PARTHA CHATTERJEE
NATIONALIST THOUGHT AND THE COLONIAL WORLD
A DERIVATIVE DISCOURSE?

PUBLISHED FOR THE UNITED-NATIONS UNIVERSITY

A leading Indian political philosopher criticises Western theories of Third World nationalism — both liberal and Marxist. He also provides in this highly original essay a profound exploration of its central contradiction: setting out to assert its freedom from European domination, it yet remained a prisoner of European post-Enlightenment rationalist discourse.

Using the case of India, he shows how nationalist thinking never escaped a Eurocentric framework whose representational structure corresponded to the very structure of power it sought to repudiate. And so the historical outcome has been the transformation of Third World nationalism by ruling classes into a state ideology legitimising their own rule.

This profound exercise in political philosophy questions the legitimacy of the currently predominant formulations of nationalist ideology in the Third World. It anticipates a new generation of popular struggles that will redefine the content of Afro-Asian nationalism, and the kinds of society that people wish to build.

Professor Chatterjee has taught at many universities in India and North America, as well as holding visiting appointments at St Antony's College, Oxford, and the Australian National University. Among his already published works are *Arms, Alliances and Stability* (1975). He is an editor of *Subaltern Studies: Writings on South Asian History and Society.*

208pp Bibliography Index
Hb 0 86232 552 8   £16.95 $26.95
Pb 0 86232 553 6   £6.95 $10.95
Not for sale in India

Asia ● History ● Political Science
April

Hanlon, Joseph
MOZAMBIQUE
The Revolution Under Fire

'This book should be read by everyone who wants to understand the true measure of the problems of post-colonial reconstruction in the world we have now.'
New Statesman

'This book's scope is as broad as Hanlon's knowledge of contemporary Mozambique.'
African Business

Machel, Samora
SAMORA MACHEL: AN AFRICAN REVOLUTIONARY
Selected Speeches and Writings

'Now for the first time in English . . . one of Africa's outstanding leaders is made accessible, even to those with no prior knowledge of Mozambique.'
Morning Star

'A well-organized and translated collection . . . These speeches must be indispensable reading for everyone who wants to understand the nature of the Mozambican struggle, and, beyond that, the wider character of the whole African struggle against the legacy of the past and against the neo-colonial or merely subversions of today.'
Basil Davidson, *Liberation*

Davies, Robert H., *et al*
THE STRUGGLE FOR SOUTH AFRICA
A Reference Guide to Movements, Organisations and Institutions (2 volumes)

'. . . an indispensable Guide.'
Village Voice (USA)

INDEPENDENT KENYA

'*Independent Kenya* has a definite unparalleled historical significance.'
Journal of African Marxists

Babu, Mohammed
AFRICAN SOCIALISM OR SOCIALIST AFRICA?

'I have no doubt that this important contribution to our understanding of contemporary Africa will endure for a long time and stimulate further thought and action.'
Race and Class

De Bragança, Aquino and Wallerstein, Immanuel (editors)
THE AFRICAN LIBERATION READER
Documents of the National Liberation Movements (3 volumes)
Vol 1: The Anatomy of Colonialism
Vol 2: The National Liberation Movements
Vol 3: The Strategy of Liberation

A comprehensive, three-volume project which brings together the key documents of the history of Southern Africa during the crucial years 1960-1975.

Wolfers, Michael, and Bergerol, Jane
ANGOLA IN THE FRONTLINE

'The wealth of information this book contains . . . makes it essential reading.'
Anti-Apartheid News

Astrow, Andre
ZIMBABWE: A REVOLUTION THAT LOST ITS WAY?

'A very serious and carefully argued book . . . which forces us to ask ourselves just the questions we should be asking . . . namely how to go forward from the national democratic revolution into socialism, and how to limit and even redress the gains of the petite bourgeoisie . . . This well-produced book ought to enjoy a wide readership.'
Moto

Cutrufelli, Maria R.
WOMEN OF AFRICA
Roots of Oppression

'Cutrufelli . . . makes an important contribution to the literature of women in Africa. Suitable for undergraduate and graduate reading on women in general, and development in particular. Also useful for studies on cultural change.'
Choice

'Uses Marxist methods of analysis and creatively applies them to the concrete African condition. This book should be read by all our women.'
Zimbabwe Herald

Obbo, Christine
AFRICAN WOMEN
Their Struggle for Economic Independence

'The women in her study, encountering particularly harsh urban conditions, emerge as resourceful and courageous.'
Choice

Palmberg, Mai (editor)
THE STRUGGLE FOR AFRICA

An excellent introduction to the history of contemporary Africa; ideal for students and young people. A clear and easily understood text with hundreds of photographs and illustrations, brings to life the social and political aims of liberation movements throughout Africa.

Lefort, René
ETHIOPIA: AN HERETICAL REVOLUTION?

'The best history so far of those dark and terrible years between 1974 and 1979.'
Richard Trench, *The Middle East*

'The only serious treatment of the most fascinating chapter in contemporary African history.'
Le Monde

'The most complete account of Africa's most complex revolution — detailed and objective.'
Jeune Afrique